Prais

If the Buddh

WITHDRAWN

"Heartfelt and practical approaches to helping your child find his/her inner voice and personal path in life. More important, Kasl focuses her discussion on the most important aspect of successfully raising children—self knowledge. I believe that parents of every age can benefit from this book. I did."
—Toni A. Rehbein

"What a beautiful, rich, and wise book on parenting. Charlotte's interpretations and applications of the Buddha's teachings give deep relevance and power to parenting. I plan to read and reread it, hoping that it is not too late to reparent myself. Then I shall send copies to my grown children and all involved in formulating public policy."
—Cynthia B. Aten, MD, former associate clinical professor of pediatrics and of nursing, Yale University

"I have been working on a haiku book, called *Tattoos on the Buddha*, that has an introduction titled "What Happened to Those Kids the Buddha Gave Piggyback Rides?" Well, I think you found one—Charlotte Kasl. So cash in. Draw from her deep, beautiful, caring well—and love more, hoot louder from joy; help a heart dance—then another & another & another."
—Daniel Ladinsky, bestselling Penguin author of poetry and translator of Hafiz

"Simple but profound. This is a book that encourages parents to care about all children, not just their own. It provides a model of parenting that could transform the world. I wish I could give a copy to every new parent on the planet."
—Jean Kilbourne, filmmaker, media critic, author of *So Sexy So Soon*

"A kind, practical, and wise guide for parents helping their children become confident, loving, and productive members of the human community. Her philosophy of child-rearing is right-on—love and responsibility!"

—Dorothy Hinshaw Patent, author of more than 100 nonfiction books for children

"An insightful guide to peaceful parenting, covering everything from a child's relationship to food, technology, and money to helping a child feel understood. It is the one book every parent should read!"

—Linda S. Baechle, president, YWCA, North Central Indiana

"Dr. Kasl provides a wonderful blend of Buddhist wisdom, practical suggestions, psychological research, and her own rich perspective of being a mother. Parents will find this book very helpful in their efforts in promoting healthy brain development."

—John Arden, PhD, author of *Rewire Your Brain*

"I wish I had read this before I had my kids, because Kasl's wisdom would have saved many a situation. The many examples from her own motherhood and examples from her interviews would have greatly simplified my parenting. From the heart of a mother to the hearts of all concerned about peace."

—Starshine, mother of four, middle school teacher for twenty-five years, Quaker, astronomer

"Books on child-rearing abound, but this one is different.... A unique, practical, and philosophical guide that parents will find inspiring, useful, and full of opportunities for opening new paths of relationship with their children. This is parenting through a different lens—a hopeful and powerful lens that includes changing policy at all levels to create peace, for both the individual and our society."

—Augusta Souza Kappner, president emeritus, Bank Street College of Education

"Charlotte Kasl has given the world a great gift in this book. One sees the connection between how we raise all of our children and how we create a world of peace, justice, and true sustainability. She includes easy-to-follow advice on child-rearing, including a tender glimpse at her own life. But she also includes many opportunities for all of us to search our own souls and grow through exercises and inspiring stories of real people trying, failing, forgiving, and courageously growing in wisdom."

—Betsy Mulligan-Dague, executive director,
Jeannette Rankin Peace Center

"Charlotte's new book is a bright light reminding us that parenting, like all paths in life, is a spiritual journey. This is a must-read, even if you don't have children and just need a guide on parenting yourself!"
—Angela Shelton, author, performer

"This is NOT at all the average parenting book. . . . The result of embracing this wisdom is a growing bond of trust and caring between parent and child, plus the child's awareness of how love overrides a desire for more than we need, and even how the food habits they learn can either nourish or do damage to their brains. Such philosophy pervades this excellent book and makes us wish we could have been that wise much sooner!"

—Joan Mathews-Larson, PhD, author of
Seven Weeks to Sobriety; *Overcoming Depression Naturally*,
founder of Health Recovery Associates Treatment Program

"This book serves as a meditation and journaling guide, a manual for opening up dialogue among kids and adults, a source book on the best and latest research on adult/child dynamics, and a review of the theories and frameworks that undergird effective peacemaking. It's a book you will mark up and use over and over again."

—Carol Kuhre, founding director, Rural Action, Ohio

"Inspired, inventive, and heartwarming. I've thought for years that there is one clear way to fix the world: by doing a better job at raising our children. *If the Buddha Had Kids* rings true on every page, not just for making a household peaceful, lively, and fair but for making the whole world that way. Setting out on the adventure of parenting, you couldn't take a better volume along than Charlotte Kasl's *If the Buddha Had Kids*."

—John Thorndike, author, *The Last of His Mind: A Year in The Shadow of Alzheimer's*

"In this fine book, Charlotte Kasl traces the crucial roles of clear values and healthy family relationships in nurturing strong, empathic, and competent children. I recommend it to all parents who hold hope that their children will be part of a more peaceful world."

—Jean D. Harlan, PhD, retired clinical psychologist

"The world needs this book! Parents will benefit from Charlotte's well-informed and down-to-earth guidance in raising children who are safe, secure, peaceful, loving, and bonded to the well-being of others as well as to their own."

—Peggy McIntosh, associate director, Wellesley Centers for Women

"What an insightful experience to read this book! Rich with imagery and brimming with ideas, every chapter provides guidance on raising children in the twenty-first century with love and peace."

—Rhea A. Ashmore, EdD

"Charlotte takes parents beyond good intentions by giving them the skillful means to bring out the best in themselves and, in turn, help their children express the best in themselves. . . . For everyone who wants to feel more compassion."

—Georgia Milan, MD, medical director, Women's Care Center, St. Patrick Hospital

PENGUIN BOOKS

If the Buddha Had Kids

CHARLOTTE SOPHIA KASL, PH.D., a practicing psychotherapist and workshop leader for more than thirty years and a best-selling author, has had longtime connections to feminism, Buddhism, Quaker practice, and Reiki healing. She is an internationally recognized expert on trauma and addiction and created a sixteen-step empowerment model as an alternative to Alcoholics Anonymous, which is being used extensively in the United States and Canada. She has written numerous books and articles on relationships, joy, sexuality, healing, and addiction, weaving together many aspects of spirituality and psychology to bring a holistic empowering approach to all her work. She has led parenting groups and is a founding member of Attach—The Association for Treatment and Training in the Attachment of Children. Her books include *If the Buddha Dated*; *If the Buddha Married*; *If the Buddha Got Stuck*; *Many Roads, One Journey*; *Women, Sex, and Addiction*; *A Home for the Heart*; and *Yes, You Can! Healing from Trauma and Addiction with Love, Strength, and Power*. Formerly of Minneapolis, Minnesota, Kasl now lives in an octagonal house near Missoula, Montana, where she writes, hikes, plays the piano, and has her psychotherapy practice.

If the Buddha Had Kids

Raising Children to Create
a More Peaceful World

CHARLOTTE SOPHIA KASL, PH.D.

PENGUIN BOOKS

PENGUIN BOOKS

Published by the Penguin Group
Penguin Group (USA) Inc.,
375 Hudson Street, New York, New York 10014, U.S.A.
Penguin Group (Canada), 90 Eglinton Avenue East, Suite 700, Toronto, Ontario, Canada M4P
2Y3 (a division of Pearson Penguin Canada Inc.) • Penguin Books Ltd, 80 Strand, London WC2R
0RL, England • Penguin Ireland, 25 St Stephen's Green, Dublin 2, Ireland (a division of Penguin
Books Ltd) • Penguin Group (Australia), 250 Camberwell Road, Camberwell, Victoria 3124, Australia (a division of Pearson Australia Group Pty Ltd) • Penguin Books India Pvt Ltd, 11 Community Centre, Panchsheel Park, New Delhi – 110 017, India • Penguin Group (NZ), 67 Apollo Drive,
Rosedale, Auckland 0632, New Zealand (a division of Pearson New Zealand Ltd) • Penguin
Books (South Africa) (Pty) Ltd, 24 Sturdee Avenue, Rosebank, Johannesburg 2196, South Africa

Penguin Books Ltd, Registered Offices: 80 Strand, London WC2R 0RL, England

First published in Penguin Books 2012

1 3 5 7 9 10 8 6 4 2

ISBN 978-0-14-311631-8

Printed in the United States of America
Set in Albertina MT   •   Designed by Elke Sigal

ALWAYS LEARNING   PEARSON

0316 0677

In memory of Ginelle

To Dylan, Kelsey and Maria

～

To parents everywhere:
I wish you
Peace, patience, wonder and humor
For bringing up children to keep their joy, natural acceptance
of diversity, and capacity for wonder. May we instill in their hearts
the desire to see all people as their brothers and sisters, to develop
a consciousness of being part of one earth and one people, and
to promote justice, goodwill, and understanding

Your children are not your children.
They are the sons and daughters of Life's longing for itself.
They come through you but not from you,
And though they are with you yet they belong not to you.

You may give them your love but not your thoughts,
    For they have their own thoughts.
You may house their bodies but not their souls,
    For their souls dwell in the house of tomorrow,
    which you cannot visit, not even in your dreams.
You may strive to be like them, but seek not to make
    them like you.
For life goes not backward nor tarries with yesterday. . . .

—KHALIL GIBRAN, on children, from *The Prophet*

Contents

Prologue

Good-bye, Ginelle

May 2006
Fleming, Ohio

I can feel the heat and humidity already bearing down on me at eight in the morning as I walk through the Appalachian hills. The walk down this familiar winding road has been my morning ritual for many years on visits to my daughter, Ginelle, her partner, Jed, and their six-year-old son, Billy. But this visit is sadly different from all the rest. Ginelle is in a nursing home in the final stages of pancreatic cancer, and her son is facing the loss of his mother.

I want to be present for Billy—not lost in my own grief, yet not too stoic either. I'm nearing the end of a thirty-three-year chapter of my life in which I parented a child who had been born to a traumatized fourteen-year-old, had suffered numerous sudden separations, and was attached to me by a thread so thin it barely held at times.

Ginelle walked into my life on the sixteenth of August 1973. She was just over three years old when her social worker, Mrs. G., picked her up from the foster home on two hours' notice and brought her to me. I was standing on the porch at the home of my social worker, Margaret Bridgewater, when Ginelle got out of the car looking well scrubbed in a pink dotted swiss dress, her blond hair pulled back into a ponytail, tears shining in her huge blue eyes. A well worn snoopy dog was tucked under her arm. "Oh, Charlotte," Margaret exclaimed, "she's beautiful. She could be yours." I thought, *She's too beautiful to be mine.*

Mrs. G. walked with her into the living room where I was sitting on the floor with assorted toys, including an autoharp. She knelt down, put her arm around her, and said, "Ginelle, this is your new mommy." Ginelle looked at me sadly and asked, "Do you have a little girl?" I said, "I think you're going to be my little girl." Then, as if a switch flipped inside her, she started to play with the Russian nesting doll, the word for which—*matryoshka*—eventually morphed into *ma rooster.*

As I walk down this winding road in the Appalachian hills I realize it may be only two or three more days that I will be able to feel the grip of Ginelle's strong hand, or hear her voice, or watch her chatting and smoking with her sister on the front porch of the nursing home. Only two days earlier I had met Ginelle's biological mother. "Oh, Mom," Ginelle had said casually, "this is Darnelle." This significant moment was noted with a "hi" from Darnelle and my response, "I'm really glad to meet you." Over the next few days I loved talking with Darnelle, watching her gestures, and hearing her straightforward way of speaking, so much like Ginelle's.

I take Billy for a walk so the others can have time with Ginelle and he can get outside. He is a lovable, energetic, and affectionate boy. When we pass a cemetery, he wants to walk around the gravestones. He asks me what happens when people die and get buried— a scary subject for a six-year-old. He has not been told that Ginelle is near death, but, of course, at some level he knows it full well.

I am comforted by my daily walks in the early morning—uphill, downhill, past grazing fields, streams, and deep forests. I love the red barns, rolling hills, the Christmas tree farm, and the frame houses with drooping or highly decorated porches. This heart of rural Appalachia is familiar to me from having lived nearby in Athens,

Ohio, many years ago when I taught piano at Ohio University and Ginelle was a little girl.

I'm staying in the trailer with Ginelle's partner, Jed, and Billy. The boy has lately been watching TV and playing video games nonstop. I worry that these things are all that is holding him together. He falls out of bed in the morning and parks himself in the big easy chair in the middle of the living room facing the TV, and it begins. When he gets home from school, it's more of the same, though he does accept all invitations to play with me outside. He tells me that he was told not to let me see the video games that involve killing and blood. Violent videos and action movies have been steady fare since he was very young.

Billy had barely been accepted into kindergarten because of his lack of skills. (I didn't know this was possible.) Most of the toys I had sent to him—blocks, Legos, and games—ended up strewn around the house or swept into the trash. From early on, I had been concerned when I saw Ginelle leaving him alone with a bottle or feeding him without looking him in the eyes, but I understood it; she couldn't do for him what no one had done for her. As Billy grew older, I remained concerned about the lack of songs, reading, games, and exercise provided to him, and the fact that his diet largely consisted of french fries, cookies, Chicken McNuggets, and Mountain Dew.

On a recent trip, I'd brought a card table and chairs and was happy when we all sat down together to play Rummikub. It soon became the family game table. Billy and I played checkers and concentration together every time I visited.

Jed is a warmhearted, hardworking father who loves family life. He is adamant that Billy will go to college so he won't end up making a low salary in an overheated factory like he and his dad have done. Ginelle has always said she's not worried about saving for college. "He'll probably get a full scholarship to Harvard," she'd say. I let her words pass with an inward sigh.

When I had asked her if she would like a book or a magazine on parenting, she had responded, "It would be okay," in her usual noncommittal way. Ginelle had mastered the art of the vague response, and I had long ago concluded that anything but "yes" meant "no."

But didn't they know, I often wondered, that college prep starts at birth, that patty-cake, songs, games, stories, rhymes, drawing, and playing with blocks are about learning, just as surely as the ABCs? Didn't they know that always having the TV on, playing violent video games, and drinking huge quantities of caffeinated soda were part of why Billy was so jumpy, so easily frustrated, and had such a short attention span?

Like many grandmas, I had familiar questions going through my head. Should I say something? Should I send them articles about early learning, or the importance of helping a kid brush his teeth? Should I send them a subscription to *Parents* magazine? Would they resent it or would it help? Would I be interfering? Should I go to Jed and try to enlist his help when my daughter politely let my words go in one ear and out the other?

During my more recent visits, I took great pleasure in seeing Billy up and ready for school in the morning. I loved watching him charge out to meet the yellow bus as it came over the hill, lights glowing in the early morning fog. He was always the first one on the bus, ready for the hour-long ride to school that he easily accepted.

Billy loved learning. At the end of his kindergarten year his teacher said he had made the most progress of any student, and had edged up considerably to somewhere around average work. He was a sponge for knowledge. Ginelle blamed his preschool for his early troubles, but Jed said he thought he and Ginelle had also played a part.

Billy's difficulties with learning had nothing to do with his parents' good intentions. Jed regularly took Billy to visit his grandfather, aunts, cousin, and friends. Ginelle and Jed didn't believe in hitting him, and neither parent used alcohol or other drugs. They wanted the best for him but didn't seem aware of how crucial the early years of childhood are for learning at all levels, or that a series of windows for developing different skills open for a while, then slowly close.

Watching people's insensitivity to children as little people with feelings was heightened in my early days with Ginelle. She was four when I brought her back to Athens, Ohio, after being away for a year. I was amazed at how often people talked about her as if she weren't there. They'd see her riding in the grocery cart and remark, "Oh, she's so cute—such big blue eyes, where did you get her?" If Ginelle would cringe or pull away, someone might say, "Oh, she's so shy."

As she got older I was faced with many awkward, naïve comments when people heard about her time in group homes and her behavioral problems. There would be a pause in the conversation before the inevitable question was asked: "How *old* was she when you adopted her?"

"Three years, four months," I would answer. My chest tightened during the inevitable pause before the next comment.

"You really think her troubles go back that far? You'd think she wouldn't remember much about that time." After a while I stopped telling people about attachment security, or the traumas of Ginelle's early separations from at least seven crucial people, or about the eighteen months of life-threatening violence in her original home.

Other people couldn't help but mention my profession: "Do you really think such a *short* time could make *that* much difference . . . and with you being a psychologist and all?" I tried not to be defensive about these thoughtless, ill-informed remarks.

I felt immensely relieved years later that Deb, Ginelle's counselor at a group home in Minneapolis, understood the impact of her early experiences and tried to get Ginelle to understand that they were related to her lack of trust, her habit of shoplifting, and her wanting to run away when she felt close to people. Deb treated me with kindness instead of taking the usual stance of blaming the mother. I also felt great satisfaction when Foster Cline, an expert on children with attachment disorders, said at a workshop, "If you haven't lived with one of these kids, you don't have a clue."

The day before Ginelle died, Jed's family and I went to Billy's graduation from kindergarten. Ginelle was too sick to go, but, bless her heart, she held on until the next day. Billy got to have his special moment. I smiled as a procession of children entered the gymnasium, walking single file on a painted line and stepped up onto the tiered bleachers to sing, recite poems, and show what they had learned. They received their diplomas, one by one, with a formal handshake.

Another reprieve from my grief came as a visit from the muses. During one of my morning walks, thoughts of a book on parenting entered my mind—a book that would be easy to read and understand, a book for caregivers and parents, like Ginelle and Jed, or maybe for Billy one day. I planned to say all the things I never felt able to say to them about attachment, the importance of a smile, about holding, reading, playing, about having lots of new adventures, and about not flooding a young child's mind with violent images.

I wanted it to be a book for parents who wanted to bring compassion, empathy, and nonviolence to their child rearing, parents who wished to help their children develop confidence and a clear sense of who they are. I wanted it to address the growing incidence of depression among children. I also wanted the book to be inclusive of different races, cultures, and economic levels.

Ultimately, it became this book, which explores what it takes to raise children who feel good about themselves, who are resilient, courageous, creative, and have a capacity for awe and wonder and the ability to form close relationships—a book that forms the roots of developing a global consciousness and a sense of fairness, justice, and goodness toward all people.

Introduction

Parenting for a Peaceful World

Creating peace in the world starts with parenting,
families, and community.

This book is about raising children to become resourceful, fulfilled human beings who contribute to peace and justice in the world by feeling steady within themselves, by having authentic relationships with their family, friends, and community, and by experiencing themselves as part of humanity.

Peace in parenting starts with creating a sense of safety in our children by expressing warmth, tenderness, responsiveness, and delight. It includes being genuine, natural, and clear with our children. We are the adults, the ones who will guide our children. And when our actions, behavior, tone of voice, and words are in harmony, we create safety. If they are dissonant and unnatural, our children will feel that something is off or wrong. If we are not sincere with them, if we wear masks and present façades to our children, they can sense it in their bodies even though they may not realize it consciously.

When we are authentic—that is, when we don't assume roles that are defined by ego, agendas, impossible ideals, and expectations—we are able to engage with our children on a deep level. Being present and attuned in this way supersedes the need to operate out of fear, which is usually expressed through control.

It is also necessary to set clear limits and relate to our children in a way that is appropriate for their age. Parents often don't understand that children are crying or resisting them because too much is being expected of them at their stage of brain development or they are caught in a power struggle. At the same time, we need to encourage young children to develop their vast capabilities, which are with them from birth.

> *Truth is but another name for God.*
> —GANDHI

Along with principles of Buddhism, Zen, and my psychotherapy practice, I draw on teachings from the Society of Friends (Quakers) and other peace churches, as well as from all teachings that support nonviolence. Quakers have embraced and written about nonviolence in parenting for many years. I have been associated with this community for thirty years and have watched many Quaker children grow into competent, socially conscious adults.

Quakers use no sacred texts to the exclusion of others. We are encouraged to learn from all sources and find what feels true for ourselves. Listening for our deepest truths—hearing and honoring that "still small voice within" and having the courage to live by it is at the core of Quaker teaching. The teachings of the Society of Friends and of Buddhism share the values of simplicity, service, meditation, kindness, and the many aspects of nonviolence. They also both emphasize the importance of being strong and courageous—traits that help us stay true to our values, even in the face of opposing beliefs.

The first day programs (the Quaker equivalent of Sunday school) and private yet inclusive schools that Quaker children attend are rich in experiential learning, noncompetitive games, and projects that require cooperation and communication. A broad understanding of all cultures is fostered. Children also expand their social awareness by taking part in service projects.

....

There is no way to peace. Peace is the way.

....

A huge banner with those words hangs over the entrance to the Quaker meeting house in Missoula, Montana. In many ways, this message embodies the intersection of Quaker and Buddhist teachings. In both traditions, the focus is on how we live moment to moment, how we show sensitivity for others and awareness of the deep interconnectedness of all sentient life in our actions and thoughts.

"Peace is the way" is an underlying teaching of this book, a guide to return to whenever we are facing a difficult situation.

A PRACTICAL APPROACH COMBINING MANY TRADITIONS

When we are training in the art of peace, we are not given any promises that, because of our noble intentions, everything will be okay.
—PEMA CHÖDRÖN, *WHEN THINGS FALL APART*

This is not a book about an idyllic and unrealistic vision of child rearing. It is meant to be practical. It includes ways to soothe yourself and stay centered when you are tired or aggravated or find yourself in the midst of a power struggle, or when your child is crying inconsolably and you can't figure out what to do. It suggests many ways to handle the times when you feel anger rising in your chest, when your jaw clenches and harsh words form in your mind—words you might have heard as a child and swore you would never say to your own children.

It will also help you to relax and enjoy your child—to share the delight and wonder of the first smile, the first step, the first words. One woman told me, "When I was pregnant, people talked about how hard parenting was, but few talked about the wonder of it all. My kids are now in their teens and it's been a rich and amazing experience . . . not that we don't have our moments."

From the Buddhist and Quaker perspectives, children learn through experience and by example. We don't teach abstract concepts to children, but instead we impart values of kindness, compassion, and awareness through our daily behavior with everyone we encounter. Going one step deeper, we bring our presence, truth, humor, and fallibility to our parenting rather than hiding behind a pretense of knowing everything or being perfect. This helps children learn to accept mistakes, make apologies, and accept their humanness.

Our love for our children is also reflected in the ways we help them discover their talents, hone their skills, and build confidence. Thus our behavior toward our children is grounded in the questions: Who are you? What do you need? What is your truth? How can I help you become your best self?

In addition to Buddhist and Quaker principles, I also draw on the Sufi poetry of Hafiz and Rumi, which illustrate beautifully the principles of joy, passion, love, beauty, and oneness. In addition, I have interviewed parents and children from many cultural backgrounds and religions—Jewish, Protestant, Quaker, Buddhist, Catholic, Mormon, Muslim, agnostic—and from different races and economic backgrounds. I sought out teens and young adults to interview who genuinely like their parents. This was typified by Angela, who said happily, "My parents rock," which subsequently became the name of a chapter. The pulse of this book is grounded in the many voices and stories that came to me from these people and from the clients I have worked with over the past thirty-five years. I have learned much from all of them.

THEMES OF THIS BOOK

Imagine the following themes as part of a mandala—all parts interconnected and important to each other. For example, helping children form good relationships is related to helping them feel secure, confident, and at ease with differences. These themes will also help develop resilience in children and prevent depression.

1. **Secure bonding.** Parents will learn how to create safety and security with an infant through smiling, making eye contact and being engaged, responsive, and attuned to the child's cues and needs.

2. **Child development.** It is important to be aware of different stages of development—physical, psychological, and emotional—in order to have realistic expectations for children as they grow.

3. **Mastery and self-esteem.** We can help children develop confidence and self-esteem by inspiring them to take on challenges, persevere, and solve problems creatively. Mastery also means helping children be at ease with their feelings—able to name them, voice them, and, over time, manage them so they are accessible but not overwhelming. *Self-esteem is not something we give a child through praise and judgment. Instead we help them develop their strengths, talents, and ability to form positive relationships so that they're able to live with confidence in the world.*

4. **"Us" thinking.** The heart of "us" thinking comes through empathy and comfort with diversity. It starts with children being free to be different from their parents. Eventually, we help children develop a consciousness of the connections between people, creatures, the environment, and the earth so that they are mindful of their choices and the possible consequences.

5. **Fascination and curiosity.** Parents can help children meet the world with an attitude of interest, fascination, and curiosity instead of fear or indifference. We contribute to their development when we encourage them to develop their sensory capacities for sound, smell, color, taste and touch.

6. **Critical, complex thinking.** Through our example, children learn to see situations from different perspectives and to bring an observant, questioning mind to everything from commercials to textbooks. Where do ideas come from? Who made them up? Who benefits from them? Who gets left out?

7. **Questioning.** We can help children feel safe to question, disagree, and come to their own conclusions, which may be quite different from their parents' views. Parents and children can have respectful dialogue that is interactive rather than authoritarian or more like a contest. This approach helps children learn to disagree respectfully and not feel threatened by differences. It also helps them learn that they have a right to say "no" to those who might seek to exploit them.

8. **Becoming one's best self.** Parents can help children explore and develop their abilities, pleasures, talents, and strengths by providing resources and experiences, and modeling perseverance and taking pleasure in doing well.

This book will help parents to raise a child who feels at peace within, which is the starting place for creating peace in the world. When a person accepts and feels at home in his own life, he is more likely to feel empathy and care for others. Going one step further, he is also more likely to be active in helping create a more just and peaceful world.

I The Heart of Buddhism for Parents

*T*eachings on Buddhism can seem complex and intimidating. Yet, at their core they come down to living deeply in our experiences, developing our awareness, seeing all life as interconnected, and understanding that it is our conditioned minds and expectations, not actual events, that create our suffering in life. Buddhism is about feeling at peace within, so we can attune, listen, understand, and feel empathy and compassion for others.

A starting place to understanding Buddhism is the Four Noble Truths.

1. The first noble truth is that life includes suffering, uneasiness, sadness, loss, illness, pain, and frustration. Babies cry; kids say, "no, I won't"; we feel hurt when our partner is withdrawing or when our teenagers would rather spend time with their friends than be with us; and we are often frazzled, afraid, and alone.

2. The second noble truth is that the cause of our suffering is within ourselves. Rather than looking outward for the things that cause us pain, we need to examine our own demands, desires, thirsts, cravings, and expectations. Our agitation results from the litany of "shoulds" in our mind, which create upset and worry: The baby shouldn't cry. I shouldn't be so impatient. My partner should help

out more. My son should do what I say. My daughter should call me more often. Essentially, we feel pain when we resist the *what is* of life.

3. The third noble truth is that there is a way out of our suffering if we accept what is and stop demanding that people and situations be different than they are. We learn to accept that events don't create our agitation; rather it's how we respond to them. For example, if the baby throws food on the floor, the reality is that there's food on the floor. It's when we say, *The baby shouldn't throw food, I can't stand it, I hate a messy floor* that we get upset. This is not to say that we don't address troublesome situations and look for creative solutions. But when we bring a calm acceptance to difficult situations, we are more relaxed, and thus able to be clear-headed and effective.

4. The fourth noble truth outlines an eightfold path of awakening and conscious living that offers a guide for bringing integrity, kindness, and understanding into our relationships, work, sexuality, indeed into all that we do. It's about achieving an awareness of our impact on each other and on the earth, which we show through our daily actions. It's about living a life that springs from the knowledge that we all come from the same Creator or Energy, that we are all life itself, and that to harm another is to harm ourselves. This doesn't mean we will never experience conflict or difficulties, or that children won't fight or struggle or have problems.

When we take a Buddhist or Zen perspective on life, we learn to recognize how our "attachments"—our scripts for others and images of how they should be—create a great deal of the discord between parents and children. When we pressure, criticize, cajole, or bribe children to get them to achieve the goals we set for them, they tend to dig in their heels, rebel, or form a false persona that masks their true selves. This creates fear and plants the roots of anxiety, depression, addictions, and superficial relationships, along with a chronic feeling of emptiness.

....

When we step back from our expectations and engage honestly with our children, take pleasure in their company, guide rather than demand, inspire rather than pressure, model rather than preach, we bring a peacefulness to our parenting that becomes internalized in our children.

....

Putting these principles into practice means helping children equate power, happiness, and success with stretching themselves, finding their passion, caring for others, being resourceful, and working in community with others. It's the antithesis of imposing rules, scripts, and values in a dogmatic way; rather, it's about teaching by example and helping children think for themselves. The deep sense of safety and compassion this instills becomes a barrier against the use of violence and aggression as ways to solve conflict.

THE PARAMITAS: "GOING TO THE OTHER SHORE"

The *paramitas* are described by Pema Chödrön as the six activities of the servants of peace. She lists the actions as generosity, discipline, patience, exertion, and meditation, all of which are attached to the sixth, which is Prajna, "the immense suffering that comes from seeking to protect our own territory."

Paramita means "going to the other shore," or "that which has crossed over." In life, we get on our little raft of teachings and practices and head across the river, but the raft starts to come apart and suddenly there is nothing solid to grab hold of. At that point we need to be able to swim, think for ourselves, and find our own way.

In terms of parenting, the *paramitas* speak to the generosity of spirit it takes to be a devoted parent. This includes the strengths and problem-solving abilities we hope to impart to our children. In Chödrön's words, "The idea of one right way sort of dissolves into the mist."

Buddhist teachings should not be used to be hard on yourself or to go against what feels right for you. Transformation starts with acceptance, not fighting with yourself. You do your best to be kind, honest, and open, but you also accept all feelings that arise. You can't transform what you're not aware of.

IMPERMANENCE:

> *"Where is the little girl I carried?"*
> —TEVYE, *FIDDLER ON THE ROOF*

Accepting impermanence is another Buddhist principle that applies to parenting. Everything is always changing—from the cells in our bodies to our passions, the seasons, our health, and definitely our children. One day they cry with frustration trying to use scissors for the first time, and a week later they do it with ease. Your seven-year-old is strong and independent in the afternoon, but wants to snuggle up like a little baby in the evening. We need to alter our responses and expectations constantly as we attune to the needs and abilities of our maturing children.

We learn to hold our children close when they need us while allowing them the freedom to create and spend time with a growing circle of friends, interests, and passions. Ultimately, we give them our blessing to leave home and form their own lives.

Although our children are intertwined in our lives, our own happiness is our responsibility. When we love with an open heart, we don't burden our children by using guilt or other covert tactics to make them feel responsible for our well-being. We accept that sometimes they need us and want us to be close and at other times they want independence. It's a dance of closeness and separateness that is like watching the rings expand when we drop a pebble in water. Our blessing means we accept whatever path they choose and realize that it is *their* sacred journey, and *our* job is to let go and bring meaning to our own lives.

LOVING-KINDNESS FOR YOUR CHILDREN

Loving-kindness is the beginning of peace.
—THE BUDDHA

Loving-kindness can be thought of as friendliness, goodwill, empathy, showing interest in others, warmth, and love. In other words, it's the path of peace. *Mettā* and *maitrī* are the Sanskrit words for loving-kindness.

Buddha's purpose in teaching loving-kindness meditations was to help soften or neutralize our judgments, anger, and sense of separation. Loving-kindness needs to emanate from within us and not be a pretense or mask that has us display a feeling that isn't really there.

Loving-kindness does not mean being "sweetness and light" all the time—that would be phony. It's about seeing from your heart into the hearts of others, and realizing that we are all fragile, strong, precious, and connected to each other. In terms of parenting, it's about taking delight in the wonder of this growing little person. It's also about a stance of guiding, teaching, and setting limits without being harsh, punitive, or overcontrolling.

LOVING-KINDNESS FOR YOURSELF: FROM CRITICISM TO REFLECTION

As a parent, offering mercy and kindness to yourself is the first step toward bringing kindness to your child. Instead of thinking, *What's wrong with me, I did that again?*, you learn to say to yourself, *Wow, I really feel angry and hurt about what she did. What's that about? How old do I feel?*

This helps interrupt the rote cycle of acting, reacting, judging, feeling remorse, and doing it over again—a cycle that is known in Buddhism as samsara, or the wheel of suffering.

....

You develop loving-kindness as you remember that we are all shaped by millions of fleeting experiences, luck, genes, and we are doing the only thing we know how to do in any given moment. This is true for your children, and it's true for you. In other words, What is, is. The first step is to step back and observe yourself.

....

LOVING-KINDNESS EASES SHAME

Buddhism does not recognize concepts such as sin, heaven, or hell. Instead, it teaches that we are insensitive or unkind because we are unconscious, asleep, or lacking awareness. The more we are awake and aware, the more we naturally feel kind toward one another. When you practice loving-kindness toward yourself and others, you are less likely to get lost in shame, that awful feeling of being damaged or inherently bad.

Letting go of shame is crucial to parenting because it helps you let go of rigidity, defensiveness, and the need to be right in order to cover up feeling so wrong inside. This allows you to own up to your mistakes with your children, to apologize when appropriate, and to lighten up and laugh at your foibles. As a result, you move from being a defensive authoritarian parent to a human being who is a role model for self-acceptance.

Our capacity for loving-kindness evolves as we learn to look beneath the surface of others' actions. We can see that the bully is afraid, the girl who gobbles down food is hungry for a friend, the angry parent needs to be lovingly held. Then we can ask ourselves,

"What's driving my own behavior?" You can then look beyond the surface when dealing with your child. *I see that you're angry. Is there something you need? You seem frustrated. What's going on?* You don't have to like what your child is doing, but you don't need to withdraw your care or love. Similarly, when you make a mistake or do something insensitive, you don't throw yourself out of your own heart. Treating ourselves and our children with loving-kindness and respect strengthens a web of peaceful coexistence that extends to the planet.

Every act of kindness, patience, and understanding creates an energy that, like the butterfly effect, reverberates around the world. Instead of creating separation, we make connection; instead of seeing people we don't understand as "the other," we see them as mirrors of ourselves.

This bring us to a version of the Buddhist blessing:

> *May all beings be well.*
> *May all beings be happy.*
> *May all people know they are loved.*
> *This is our daily contribution to peace.*

Beyond the Moment: The One Energy That Unites Us All

Energy can neither be created nor destroyed, it can only be transformed.

—ALBERT EINSTEIN

Beyond all concepts of right doing and wrong doing, there is a field. I'll meet you there.

—RUMI

Buddhism teaches us to drop out of the story of our lives and into a place without words or concepts. From that place you can step back and observe the unfolding drama, possibly with a sense of humor. You are in it, but not of it.

Peace comes when we realize that beyond our conditioned mind we are simply life itself—unchanging, enduring and one with spirit or our Buddha nature.

At another level, Buddhism teaches us to recognize the momentary rise and fall of our emotions—happy, sad, glad, mad. They're kind of like the continuous movement of rain, clouds, and sunshine.

It helps to remember the nature of these shifting emotions when you find that you've used the last diaper and it's late Friday night, or your child is throwing a fit in the supermarket, you're tired, or your teen is suddenly sulky. It's not better or worse than when you're smiling with delight as you watch your six-year-old play a frog in a school production, your teen comes up with an original science project, or your son walks into the kitchen and asks, "Is there anything I can do to help?"

These events are the current scene in the great big passing show of life, and our children are doing the same thing millions of other children are doing.

As you learn to relax into the moment your mind is free to accept the current drama or event, and you inevitably open your heart.

When you are less caught up in keeping track of your ego's calendar of expectations you become attuned to when your children truly need some special attention, help, or guidance. You become present without hovering and aware without intruding. Good parenting becomes a journey, not a goal.

2 I Didn't Know What I Was Getting Into

Parenting as a Spiritual Journey

> I do not want to touch any object in this world
> Without my eyes testifying to the truth
> That Everything is
> My Beloved
> Something has happened
> To my understanding of existence
> That now makes my heart always full of wonder
> And Kindness.
>
> —HAFIZ, "TODAY," THE GIFT

You are the "Beloved" and so is your child. Remembering this doesn't always make parenting easy, but it can help. If you approach parenting from the stance of *I'm willing to learn about myself* as opposed to wanting to create the child of your dreams, you can learn a lot about yourself—and you'll be a more skillful parent.

Children are little masters at triggering parts of us we'd rather not see. We are sometimes shocked to hear the voice of our own critical mother or angry father bursting out of us. We didn't know we could get so mad or feel so helpless. On the other hand, children show us we are capable of experiencing more tenderness, joy, and wonder than we knew was possible.

As we act and react in the human dance, we observe our conditioning in action. We're pleased, we're upset, we're angry, we're afraid. We approve, we disapprove. From this point of view, you may become able to have a skillful response rather than a reactive one.

....

If you are willing to meet all that arises within you—your disappointments and frustrations, your need to control, your impatience and fears—parenting will be a journey of great awakening. Make a vow: I am willing to know whatever arises in me.

....

If your patterns of behavior continue to be troublesome, it can be invaluable to take a parenting class or get counseling to help ease the old trigger points that seem to go off on their own and create pain and separation in your relationship with your child or partner.

Remember, a Child Doesn't Make You Upset

Frustration with your child comes from your reaction to your child's behavior. The spiritual journey means that you do not blame your child, or anyone else when you get upset or have an impulse to coerce, yell, punish, hit or shame your child. You ask yourself, *What was triggered within me? What am I resisting, disliking, wanting to be different than it is?* Notice your body's sensations, your tone of voice. What situations are easy for you? What brings an automatic reaction? Just notice, then talk with someone about it.

You can also learn to accept strong feelings. For example, if a young child is crying, most people's instinct is to feel uneasy until the child stops crying. But what if you could relax as you hold the crying child and be soothing without being agitated inside? Ask yourself, *What am I saying to myself that makes me so worried or agitated?*

That the baby will cry forever, or that I did something wrong? What am I protecting, defending, or struggling with? This reflection moves you toward a love that doesn't click on and off, but flows like a river through the thickets, meadows, and brambles of parenting.

Accept Your Child's Timetable

There is a wide range of what's considered "normal" development when it comes to crawling, walking, talking, and learning.

The less we attach to thoughts such as, *My child should be walking, talking, making puzzles by now,* the more we move away from conditional love. Conditional love means: *I like you when you do things my way, on my time line.* This often leads to pressuring a child, using bribes, or making statements that impart guilt or shame. The message we need to convey to our child is quite different: *You are always in my heart, even when we disagree, you are mad at me, or I'm frustrated with you. My love is stable, enduring, and not dependent on you being a certain way or giving me what I want when I want it.* This is unconditional love.

WHAT LENSES ARE YOU WEARING?

Another part of the parenting journey is learning to trust your observations about what works best for you and your child. Think of yourself as becoming a "parenting scientist": observe and take note of what works and doesn't work. You can read books, take classes, talk with friends, and draw from their wisdom, but your own experience is a valuable guide. This requires experimenting and noticing what elicits cooperation, and feelings of closeness and ease.

We all see the world through the "lenses" of our conditioning. They are partly genetic and largely a result of our childhood experience. People see through lenses of fear, worry, paranoia, rigidity, hopelessness, guilt, shame, or resentment. You might have a lens that says you'll be accepted if you always wear a happy face and do what others want, or that you should hide your mistakes in order to gain approval.

People also see through lenses of beliefs that people are essentially good, that effort helps you succeed, and that kindness and empathy help raise happy children. The lens you wear affects how you experience your children, and in turn, how they experience the world. For example, if a parent conveys the belief that their kid is a lot of trouble, the child is likely to see herself as unlovable, or think, *I'm not wanted*. Seeing your child through a lens of negativity will be absorbed into the child's sense of who they are. This often takes root and guides their impulses and choices. In fact, people who have developed addictions almost always have a painful, pervasive core of negative beliefs about themselves.

Fortunately, positive lenses have the opposite effect. The parents I interviewed who generally had positive experiences bringing up kids all said things like, *They're great kids. We're lucky. We really enjoy them. We have our moments, but we always know that we love them.* Imagine the energy from those thoughts and beliefs being transmitted to a child's heart and body through the days, months, and years of growing up! *My parents really like me, they feel lucky to have me in their lives. They enjoy knowing me.* The more you see your children in this light, the more likely they are to reflect your beliefs.

If you repeatedly use an anxious tone when you say, *Be careful! You can't do that! Call me if there's any trouble*, you may have a worry lens, which is likely to make its way into your child's inner emotional state and affect how he lives in the world. People often argue about this and claim that it's natural to worry. It would be truer to say something such as, "It's natural *for me* to worry because I *have* a worry lens." Someone else might not worry at all about the same things.

LEARN TO SEE CLEARLY IN REALITY

Can you name the lenses that color your view of your child? How do these lenses affect your perception of them or the way you relate to them? One tenet of Buddhism is seeing clearly in reality. Once you identify your lens, or the kinds of lenses you tend to see through, you can ask yourself, what is the evidence for this belief? If you're a worrier, for example, you might ask, *What is the real likelihood of danger? How many children are actually abducted while walking to school, riding a bus, or going to the movie with a friend at age eleven? How many children really drown at a swimming lesson?*

Since it's a common trait of humans to worry about things that are unlikely to happen and yet to ignore what might actually need their attention, you might next turn your thoughts to some truly important concerns. What are the effects of a child being ignored, shamed, or overcontrolled on a daily basis? What is a heavy diet of sugar and caffeine doing to your child? Are the antibiotics and hormones in the chicken or meat affecting her? What about violent videos? Or young girls being portrayed as vacuous sex objects in ads? Even more useful than worrying about theoretical dangers is to act on the positive effects of taking children to the library, museums, and parks, and making sure they get exercise on a daily basis.

Better yet, help your children learn skills so they feel competent crossing the street or walking to a friend's house or riding the bus.

A GLOBAL VIEW OF ALL THE CHILDREN

Imagine children being born all around the world. Parenting can narrow our vision so that we focus exclusively on our own child or children. But from a Buddhist perspective, we move from thoughts of *my* child to thoughts of *all* children. We are all parents of the next generation. Creating a more peaceful world means being able to hold all children in your heart and see through the differences among us to the commonalities. You can ask yourself, "What can I do for other children in my neighborhood, community, and around the world?" (This is an example of "us" thinking that we'll talk about more below, especially in Chapter 20.)

TAKE BREAKS FOR GRATITUDE AND BLESSINGS

While it's important to take a few minutes to have a good whine, acknowledge being tired or needing a rest, try *gratitude* as a way to revitalize your energy. When your child is upset, or you are tired, take a deep breath and take a moment to sit down. Then think to yourself, *I'm grateful* . . . and let the thoughts flow. Give thanks. *I'm grateful* . . . to have food, a bed, friends, talents and strengths. *I'm grateful* . . . to be able to wiggle my fingers or read this book. Then think of your child: the smiles, the landmarks of growing up, the wonderful times you've had, without allowing any negative interference to enter your mind.

Then breathe again, exhale deeply, let your mind travel around the world, and say a blessing for all children.

> *May all children be well,*
> *May all children have comfort,*
> *May all children have food,*
> *May all children have safety.*

....

The human circle includes all children as part of life itself. Remember that at a spiritual level the well-being of your child is linked to the well-being of every child on the planet.

....

3 The Twinkling in Your Eye

Before the Seed Is Planted

The time to start parenting is before you become a parent.

When a child is nothing more than a twinkling in your eye—a hope, a thought, a wish—it's time to examine the blueprint of your lives. Raising children who feel strong and confident in the world means starting with secure parents who have the emotional resources to devote to a child.

If you are part of a couple, how is your relationship with your partner? If you are a potential single parent, do you have good friends, a support group, living space?

Are you prepared for whatever it requires, even though you don't know for sure what that will be? The following questions are intended for heterosexual couples, same-sex couples, or individuals. When I refer to the mother, I could also say the mothering one.

SOME QUESTIONS TO ASK

1. How are your relationships with your partner, family, friends, or, possibly, religious/spiritual group?
2. Does the mother have someone who will be supportive? This is crucial, especially during the first year of the child's life. The

mother needs to be deeply cared for so she can give her attention to her child and not get depleted.

3. How are your finances? Can you manage having a child without getting unduly stressed? Will you have enough to eat, pay for doctor visits, and buy necessities?

4. If you are a single parent or a two-working-parent family, is there good child care available and can you afford it? Is there a family member who will help out?

5. Do you have time and energy to devote to a child? Will someone be able to take leave from work, or is there flexibility in the work schedule?

6. Are you willing to relinquish some (or many) of your activities so you can devote ample time and attention to your child?

7. If the mother smokes, will she give it up before trying to get pregnant or adopt a child? Are you both committed to living in a smoke-free home?

8. For the mother, are you eating well and getting enough sleep so you will be healthy during your pregnancy?

....

The deepest preparation is readying yourself to welcome a child into your life and into your heart, and to devote the time and energy required to help a child feel secure and loved.

....

PLANNING FOR BIRTH: LEARN ABOUT
THE DIFFERENT OPTIONS

The goal is to have a birth that is good for your baby and good for you. And that means that you need to have a voice in the process and be informed about all the possibilities.

I urge you to learn about birthing centers and about home birth. Some people have a negative reaction to these options, but to empower yourself as a mother, get as much information as you can.

I urge every woman who is pregnant or planning to have a baby to read *Pushed: The Painful Truth About Childbirth and Modern Maternity Care* by Jennifer Block. If you are informed about the many practices commonly used, you will be able to talk with your doctor or midwife about their approach and ask informed questions.

I am not advocating home birth, birthing centers, or hospital births. I am, however, urging women to have a voice in their birthing and to understand that, increasingly, birth is treated as a surgical procedure or put on a time line, often for the convenience of the hospital staff rather than the mother or baby.

I spoke with Jeanne Hebl, a nurse midwife, who helped create a birthing center in Missoula. Her center and affiliated home births have consistently had a two to three percent cesarean rate, compared to a rate greater than thirty percent in traditional hospitals.

They also provide for the birthing mother a doula—a woman support person who, research has shown, can have many positive influences during childbirth, both for mother and child.

In Jeanne's words, "Our philosophy is to go with the rhythm of the woman giving birth. There are no rules about how fast one is supposed to dilate, how long one should be in labor, or how long it should take for the baby to be born. We avoid all unnecessary procedures and tune into the needs and wants of the woman."

HOW WE TREAT THE BABY WILL BE REFLECTED IN HOW THE BABY TREATS THE WORLD

Living at peace in the world starts with bringing children into the world as peacefully as possible—for both mother and child. I attended a conference at which Joseph Chilton Pearce, author of *Magical Child*, a classic on children and natural development, spoke of the profound level of bonding that takes place when a newborn is immediately placed over the mother's heart and they start their relationship with their hearts beating together in a peaceful environment.

4 The Milk and Honey of a Secure Bond

Healthy Attachments

$\mathcal{A}$ loving, secure bond is the most fundamental and precious gift we can ever give a child—like planting a seed in fertile ground and giving it enough water and sunlight. Early experiences of parental tenderness and care echo throughout a child's life and give a deep, wordless sense of safety, security, and love.

To the baby, the mother epitomizes the themes from love songs: "You are the sunshine of my life," "It's paradise to be near you like this," "You're my summer, winter, fall, my everything." Lyrics like these intertwine love, joy, and the natural world. They evoke the essence of the first year of life and are similar to the feelings that later arise when we fall in love.

Again, I use the word "mother" in this chapter when talking about infant bonding, although I could also say "the mothering one" or "the nurturing one." Many men, both heterosexual and gay, have been wonderful primary caregivers for infants and young children. Because babies have traditionally been breast-fed and tended for by the mother, however, I use this term as the primary attachment figure. I have interviewed numerous men who were stay-at-home dads and whose eyes lit up when they described the deep bond they felt with their children. I encourage all fathers to be nurturing attachment figures with their children.

The Sweetness of Your Smile: The Power of Caring and Attachment

Think of a time when someone you cared about greeted you with a smile and warm eyes as they reached out to embrace you. Notice the feelings or sensations that arise within you as you recall that experience.

Now think of a time when someone you cared about was indifferent, cool, unresponsive, or seemed to ignore you. What happens inside you as you recall that time? Do you feel hurt, dull, or anxious? Do you start having thoughts such as, *Did I do something wrong? Is she mad at me for some reason?*

Multiply these thoughts and feelings a thousand times, and you start to understand the needs of an infant for warmth and tenderness in the form of smiles, holding, cooing, and delight in a parent's eyes.

There are many things parents can do to help create a secure bond with their child. You start by making eye contact, giving the baby your full attention, mirroring her sounds and facial expressions, and learning the cues that signify the need for holding, rocking, attention, play, food, or changing diapers. Most of all it's important to be present, and feel amazement and delight at this growing child. It also helps to remember that the child is usually trying to express a need— she's not out to upset you or make you feel badly.

It's important to remember that you mean the world to your child, more than you can ever imagine. From conception onward, your child attunes to your heartbeat, your voice, and your smell. She is affected by your level of relaxation or anxiety, by what you eat or drink, and by your sleep patterns and general health. From birth onward, your touches, smiles, kind eyes, and sounds merge into your child's sense of self.

If making eye contact or staying present to your child feels difficult, it can be part of your spiritual journey to notice what arises for you. If it's hard to make eye contact, ask yourself, "What am I feeling? What's that about?" Listen for your own unmet needs, resentments, and hurts and find a way to share them with another person, get counseling, be in a parenting group, or take action in your life to feel more at home with your body and feelings.

BABIES AND GROWING CHILDREN ARE
NATURALLY DIFFERENT

Parents I interviewed often spoke with amazement of the immense differences between their children. One child wants holding much of the time, while another is content simply being nearby for long periods of time. Your child responds differently to sounds, music, singing, rhymes, voices, shapes, soft fuzzy things, and colors. As children grow, they develop favorite stories; they find their way to different sports, instruments, and subjects in school; and they have different abilities. This is why such a huge part of attachment centers around the ability of parents to attune and respond to their ever-changing, developing, evolving children—to accept the differences and keep focused on helping the child become his or her true self rather than to fit an image of what the parents had hoped for. There is no guidebook for parenting that replaces a responsive caregiver who is attuned to the moment.

MEMORY WITHOUT WORDS

As I mentioned in the prologue, it amazed me how many people were surprised that my daughter had problems in life, since she had been adopted when she was "only" three. "You really think she can remember all that?" was the most frequent remark, as though conscious memory were the only kind!

Just as animals learn to recognize sounds, smells, and sights of danger or safety, so do infants. It's called procedural or implicit memory. A baby remembers the face of the mothering one—the smells, the tone of her voice, the way she moves when she changes a diaper or dresses the baby. Tiny children begin to coordinate their actions with their mother's when she dresses them.

Babies and toddlers quickly attune to people who are safe, as opposed to those who are frightening. They register warmth, and they also register the repeated distress of waiting a long time for someone to come when they cry, or the discomfort and tension of being held by a distracted or depressed caregiver. Infants register parents fighting, hitting, slamming doors. They are attuned to the energy field in the household. These are the undercurrents of memories without words.

While children don't have words for early neglect or traumatic experiences, they are often expressed in nightmares, dreams, fearful behavior, or lack of trust. They may also show developmental delays in crawling, walking, toilet training, and language.

According to Bonnie Badenoch, author of *Being a Brain-Wise Therapist: A Practical Guide to Interpersonal Neurobiology*, the foundation for resilience is set during this early time of life. The baby feels a need and cries or becomes fussy; the distress is met in a timely way with a positive response. As a result, the baby learns nonverbally that when you are upset, things can get better.

A parent's response to her child gradually becomes wired in the child's brain. *You care for me; I learn to care for myself. You value me; I learn to value myself. You are responsive to me; I learn to be responsive to myself and others.*

Procedural memories lay the groundwork for the way we feel in the world. In therapy, when a client says things like, "I've always felt unsafe, I've always felt anxious, or I've always felt worried that people will let me down," I start asking questions: What do you know about your birth? What was it like when your mother was pregnant and when you were born? What was the state of your parents' relationship? What was the birth itself like? (Often the client won't know, but if she can find the answers to some of these questions, much can be understood.)

I might also ask: If you imagine yourself as a baby crying in your crib, what comes to mind? Does someone come right away, or do you have to wait a long time? Imagine being your mother. What happens when you hear your baby cry? Are you irritated and impatient, or happy to respond? How does she feel holding you? What's her reaction when you spit up on her shoulder? Clients often have extremely visceral reactions to these questions.

Often when a person has an underlying anxiety that feels as if it's been there forever, that anxiety response stems from preverbal times: from a mother or caregiver who was distant, afraid, depressed, absent, or stressed. It could also stem from emotional or physical violence in the household.

OUR LITTLE VILLAGE: ATTACHMENT EXTENDS TO FAMILY, FRIENDS, AND COMMUNITY

When we have a family that circles around a child with adoration and joy, we deepen the child's sense of belonging and happiness. It creates many layers of safety. Mom is tired, so a neighbor comes over for a little while. The parents want a break so grandmother helps out or pays for child care. Children experience themselves as part of a little village: Uncle Larry takes me fishing, Aunt Sue takes me to a parade, Grandma Sophia buys me sand and takes me to find toys for my sandbox. I get to spend the weekend with Aunt Barb and my cousin. As the child grows, ideally he sees the grown-ups getting along and enjoying each other, which models an image of caring relationships and brings deep pleasure to the child.

When my daughter was little I owned a duplex and rented the upstairs apartment to people who delighted in having a child around. I would smile as she'd knock on their door and they would invite her up for a visit. Ginelle also had "Grandma next door," our dear friend Millie Bean, who was open to frequent visits. Sometimes when I'd come to get Ginelle, she'd be sitting quietly on Millie's lap or they'd be talking. It was a godsend to have other caring people in our lives. A single parent or even two parents just can't be available all the time. Besides, it's a rich experience for any child to have different people in their lives.

The other parts of the village that are good for both parents and children are community services and child-centered organizations. Many communities provide numerous activities for children—making masks or face painting for a parade, readings at the library, family nights at churches, and parks and recreation programs at a nominal fee.

All these people and activities create a circle around a child that enriches his life. Historically, children were brought up as part of a tribe, a clan, or an extended family, but today we often need to create that sense of community.

The night after my daughter died, I came back to the trailer exhausted. My first sight was of Billy nestled up sound asleep in the arms of his beloved Aunt Pam, who was sitting in the big easy chair—a solid presence, a warmhearted shelter for this little boy who had just lost his mother. As I watched him sleeping peacefully curled up in her arms, the big pink fuzzy slippers Ginelle had worn her last few days hanging from his feet, it was as if my heart turned over as a sweet tear came to my eye. Pam had been there as a steadfast auntie since his birth: she was unfailingly happy to see him, visited often, and she was central to his life. They were entwined in each other.

These loving family members become essential attachment figures in our lives: they are the ones who make us feel special, the ones a child can call on for their unique knowledge or talk to when things are tough at home or a parent is sick. Having people like this in a child's life is like having many trees in the forest, many flowers in the garden, and many fish in the sea.

Even though it's common for families to have rifts and difficulties, a parent should never take their child away from loving connections with grandparents, aunts, uncles, and good friends. In a civilized divorce, parents can still arrange visits, refrain from making negative remarks about others in the family, and simply say, "We're not getting along, but I'm happy for you to see them." To rip a child from these attachments is to leave him alone to manage a deep loss that can have a negative effect on her feelings of safety and future relationships.

....

The warmth and satisfaction of being deeply connected and treasured by a circle of close people naturally extends to others. The concept of "stranger" fades as children come to feel a kinship with lots of people. This sense of "all of us" is the mind-set needed to create a more peaceful world.

....

SIGNS OF HEALTHY ATTACHMENT IN AN INFANT

These are some of the signs that your child is feeling secure, having bonded well with parents and others in "our little village." As always, there will be variations with different children at different stages of development. The following can be seen as general indicators, not absolutes.

1. The baby or child readily makes eye contact, smiles and laughs reciprocally with the parents, and responds in a positive way to being held, touched, or joined in play.

2. The child is happy to see the parent after they have been apart.

3. The parent's presence is soothing and lowers distress . . . at least much of the time. A child may go through periods of crying seemingly inconsolably, but overall the child is comforted by the parent's care.

4. The infant begins to mirror the parent. If, for example, the parent sticks out his tongue, after a few times the baby does the same thing. Imitation is a sign of the child's deep feeling of connection.

5. The child develops an ability to handle increasing separations from the parent, from being in another room to being out of the home. This also depends on the warmth and skill of the caregiver in the absence of the parent. Children with secure connections to their parents are less likely to show chronic distress when left with others and are often happy to be going to a child care situation.

6. Well-attached children generally cry less, especially by the second half of the first year. One caveat is the child who is attachment-disordered. She may be seen as a "good" baby because she doesn't exhibit needs, but in reality she does not show emotion because she has given up trying to get a response from a parent. This is in contrast to a baby who is generally happy, easily soothed, and cries less because she feels secure.

THE POWER OF A HELPING HAND

While early attachment deficits are deeply felt, they are not always a life sentence. If one or more people enter a growing child's life in a meaningful way—a relative, neighbor, friend, teacher, or stepparent who shows deep care for and faith in the child—the plasticity of the brain allows the child to register this new information. Good schools where students are valued and bullying is not tolerated can also make a meaningful difference.

Yet while these healing relationships can have a huge impact, we would be well served as a society to provide early support to parents, children, and communities to make the lives of children safe and welcoming. It would be both humane and the best investment we could make in our society.

WHAT IS THIS ACHE THAT WON'T GO AWAY?

The long-term effects of a fragile or severed attachment can vary from person to person in severity and in specific symptoms. Most of the people who come for psychotherapy bear the scars of some form of anxious, dismissive or avoidant attachment. They may go through life with chronic feelings of loneliness, emptiness, or an undercurrent of despair or anxiety that people will leave them if they don't "do it right." It might be experienced as a dull ache that sits at the core of their being along with pervasive debilitating thoughts of being deficient, unlovable, or not able to count on anyone. No one symptom necessarily indicates a deficit in attachment security; rather, it is a constellation of symptoms that suggest attachment deficits.

1. There may be a tendency toward addictions, overachieving, intense anger, emotional volatility, physical illness, and sometimes suicide. The child has difficulty with follow-through, planning ahead, making a choice and taking steps to implement it.
2. The person may be compulsive and may become extremely competent in certain areas of life in reaction to feeling badly about herself. She may work relentlessly for acceptance, recognition, fame, or status, instead of starting from a centered place where she enjoys what she does.
3. There is difficulty forming close or secure relationships. The person may long for closeness and have a pervasive fear of being left or, by contrast, feel terror at the prospect of being swallowed up or harmed.

4. In extreme cases, there is a profound lack of empathy and a lack of conscience. This contributes to narcissistic, sociopathic, and criminal behavior. *The greater the lack of early attachment, the greater the likelihood of harmful behavior toward others. Our prisons are full of people who lacked secure attachments and safety during childhood.*

....

The prevailing trait of adults who have pervasive, insecure attachments is an inability to feel empathy and compassion. This lack allows them to exploit, use, profit from, or harm others without feeling remorse or guilt. This also plants the seeds of violence and war. By contrast, a secure attachment plants the seeds of peace.

....

A CONTENTED CHILD

I'll close this chapter with an image of childhood attachment as it happens.

My office assistant Leslie brings her fourteen-month-old daughter, Kera, to work for a few hours once a week. Most of Kera's time is spent in a carrier on her mother's back. She gazes around the room, smiles, and we sometimes play hide and seek as her mother moves around the office. Kera seems wonderfully content for long periods of time, often the prelude to dozing off in her little carrier. Her waking is as peaceful as her going to sleep.

Other times she wants to get out and run around the office for a while, which sometimes ends up with her crying or getting frustrated. This is followed by an image I savor. Leslie reaches out to her, picks her up, and puts her back in the carrier. Then Kera nestles into her mother's body resting her cheek against her back as a serene smile comes to her face and her body and breathing visibly relax. She is once again in her safe harbor and all is well. This is the normal cycle of attaching and being free to explore due to a secure bond.

Watching this gentle scene brings to mind images of people with addictions when, after a period of anticipation, they get that first drink, smoke, drug, candy—whatever brings relief. There's a sigh, visible feeling of relief, bodily relaxation, instant calming, just like Kera has when she snuggles up to her mother after being separated. My experience doing deep therapy with people struggling with addictions is that, at the core, they are longing for the safety of a mother's arms. Like Kera, they want someone to reach out, understand their need, draw them close and wrap them in the arms of their love. They want connection.

5 Attachment, Community, and Social Policy

Rx for the Culture

To parent for a more peaceful world, it is vital that we reach out to protect and care for all children. We need to weave a web around parents and their children if we want a healthy and vibrant next generation to work toward peace as well as a sustainable physical world.

According to L. Alan Sroufe, researcher and author of *The Development of the Person*, the rate of securely attached children has dropped from fifty-five percent to forty-five percent in the past generation. The rest fall into various categories, including avoidant, anxious, insecure, and reactive attachment disordered.

> If we as a society understood the power of early attachment, we would treasure it like clean air, sunshine, water, and fertile ground. The way we care for the most vulnerable among us mirrors our spiritual development and intelligence.

We need social policies that reflect the fact that children grow up to be adults, and that the care they receive as children has a direct relationship to their ability to be contributing adult members of society.

Our current policies with regard to children are like planting crops but not watering them, or building bridges without enough support to hold them up. They are shortsighted, ignorant, and unconscionable . . . and cost us enormously in the long run.

As part of the bonding process, a new mom needs time with her baby along with the security of enough money for food and rent. An anxious, worried mom often conveys these feelings to her baby. The United States ranks below 128 other countries when it comes to providing paid, job-protected maternity leave for mothers and parental leave for the father. *All but the United States guarantee health care for the mother and the baby.* Many also provide quality child care for a nominal fee. I believe this is directly related to the incredible incarceration rates within the United States that are far higher than any other country in the world.

The family value that truly shows respect and care for life is providing job-protected, paid maternity and parental leave and guaranteed health care for parents and their children.

Rx for the Culture

To raise children who make peace in the world, we need to improve the situation of all children, starting in our own communities. Support systems for parents and children are the greatest crime-prevention and addiction-prevention programs we could create—and prevention is far less costly than treatment programs, high school dropouts, incarceration, and the accompanying social problems.

Here are my suggested prescriptions. What might you add to the list?

1. Prevention, prevention, prevention. Let's start with teen pregnancies. Teen childbearing in the United States costs taxpayers (federal, state, and local) at least $9.1 billion according to a 2006 report by Saul Hoffman, Ph.D., and published by the National Campaign to Prevent Teen Pregnancy. Most of the costs of teen childbearing are associated with negative consequences for the children of teen mothers, including increased costs for health care, foster care, and incarceration.

   We know what helps prevent teenage pregnancies: access to birth control and encouraging girls to play sports and to take part in music, theater, and other activities. We need to encourage girls to think about a future career and provide access to good schools and vocational or college education. We also need sex education and relationship education in schools, instruction that focuses on responsibility in relationships and not bringing a child into the world that one is not prepared to parent.

2. Universal health care for all pregnant women and their children, before and after birth.
3. Paid maternity leave with job security mandated for all mothers for at least four months, preferably six, with options for partial pay beyond that time.
4. Parental leave or reduction in work hours for the partner or the primary parent that allows more participation in caring for the child, as well as giving support to the primary caregiver.

5. Assignment of a social worker for all at-risk mothers to help them access resources and support during the first year, and for longer if needed. This would include parenting classes, counseling for childhood trauma, meetings with other parents, social events, and access to community support systems.

6. Counseling, drug treatment, classes on parenting skills, and job training to help people become committed, skilled parents, including incarcerated women who need guidance in attachment to reunite with their children. This would help stop the cycles of poverty and generations of troubled kids.

7. Changes in the policy of putting nonviolent offenders in prison, when treatment and intensive counseling could keep them connected to their children if there is a hopeful prognosis for change.

8. Training in attachment and the harmful effects of sudden separations for all social workers, judges, community workers, counselors, politicians, and those who work with children and incarcerated people.

9. Public, quality child care on a sliding-fee scale for all families.

10. Child care workers trained as professionals and paid accordingly. At present they are some of the least educated for the job and the lowest-paid workers in the United States. If we value our children, we must make this work highly respected and well paid.

11. Foster the consciousness that we are all the parents for all our children (recall the "village" idea introduced in the previous chapter), and that our current system—with its lack of maternity leave, health care, and public child care—is racist, sexist, and elitist.

12. Include experiential classes on parenting in schools, including time spent with younger students as well as infants and young children. Engage the male students in seeing themselves as future fathers who will have a huge impact on their children.

6 The Committed Parent

Beloved Child, I Am Here for You

> When I first held my newborn son, I looked at him with
> tenderness and wonder and thought to myself, you are a
> gift from God. I don't own you. I am here to help you find
> your way, to love you, and to let you go.
>
> —SUSIE RISHO, MOTHER OF THREE GROWN BOYS

Start with a Beginner's Mind: Be Open to Today

To experience a beginner's mind is to carry these questions in your heart and mind: *Who are you today? How can I be there for you? How do I support you in your journey?*

Being truly present for your child means responding to her as she is in the moment, not as you want her to be. If you find yourself operating on automatic in ways you don't like, then it's time to breathe and ask yourself, "What would I do if I were responding out of my heart and my wisdom instead of following old rules embedded in my being?"

Think of being present to your child as a form of meditation. It requires a quiet mind, an open heart, and the ability to step back and stay steady in the presence of the inevitable hurts and fears of a growing child.

Your cheers for her growing power, your arms to hold her when she falters, your smiles to welcome her and kind words to soothe her are all part of acknowledging how much you mean to your child and how deeply she lives in your heart. As a therapist I see over and over that our basic longings are the same. Whether it's a professional athlete or a kid playing summer league baseball, a girl wanting her mother's approval or a little boy afraid of the monsters under the bed, the fear, hurt, and longing all translate into the same message: "I wanted my parents to help me, cheer for me, tell me I was okay, and show me that they cared."

I hear repeatedly how chronic criticism, indifference, half-hearted approval, unpredictability, and harsh words build hurt upon hurt like bricks in a wall that blocks out joy and secure relationships. As one woman put it: "All my life I've had a constant undercurrent of anxiety. I have a wonderful marriage with a kind husband, but I still get anxious when people raise their voice. The legacy of my mother's unpredictable screaming and losing her temper is still inside me."

SHOW YOUR CHILDREN THAT IMPERFECTIONS ARE PART OF LIFE

Being present for your children includes letting them know you are comfortable with your humanness, and that means your flaws and foibles. Parenting offers redemption because you don't have to do it perfectly. In fact, you couldn't do it perfectly no matter how hard you tried because there's no such thing as perfect. Your "perfection" means being able to apologize and show that you can laugh at your own foibles. You can spill the milk, get frustrated on occasion, say that you need a break for yourself. Likewise, your children don't have to stack the blocks perfectly, smile on command, or clean their plates every night.

It's natural that you will occasionally be distracted, upset, or pre-occupied. You could say, "Sweetheart, I'm sorry I'm so distracted. I'm worried about my work and I know my mind keeps wandering. It's not about you." This will help allay the child's fears that she did something wrong.

If you find yourself flaring up, or feeling impatient, call a friend, get a hug, go outside, have some fun, or take a break, even if it means swapping child care with someone or getting a sitter.

Maintaining a balance between giving and receiving is key. The successful couples I interviewed for *If the Buddha Married* all said that they kept their relationship a priority during the early parenting years. These couples were often a team as parents, both doing household tasks, spending time with the children, and giving support to each other. Part of your humanness is to acknowledge your needs. A self-sacrificing martyr tends to create guilt or con-fusion in a child. Being responsible to yourself is a wonderful model.

EXERCISE: HOW ARE YOU PRESENT FOR YOURSELF?

Being present for our children starts with being present for our-selves. We have a significant impact on our children simply by being who we are.

These questions will help you open yourself to reflection, be-cause you can't change or accept what you can't see. Don't criticize yourself; just reflect.

You can do this exercise on your own or, preferably, share your answers with another person:

1. How often do you experience joy, curiosity, and wonder?

2. What is your capacity for physical pleasure, celebration, adventure, and taking on new challenges?

3. How do you expand your knowledge and interests to keep your vitality and curiosity alive?

4. How close or distant do you feel in your relationships with your colleagues, family, and friends? What is this like for you?

5. Think of a time when someone was especially kind or helpful to you. Describe what was said or done. Notice your feelings and body sensations, your breathing and sense of well-being, as you remember this event.

6. Think of a time you were with someone who ignored your need for help or were disconnected emotionally. Describe the event and notice your feelings and body sensations as you recall it.

7. How are the two experiences described in items 5 and 6 different?

8. Now describe a time when you were completely present with your child—either playing a game together, having a conversation, listening to her anxieties, or helping her shop for new clothes. Notice the feelings and the sensations in your body.

9. Describe three ways you create distance or disengage in relationships. For example, these could be half-hearted listening, minimizing a child's feelings, or interrupting your child by answering the phone. How often do these things happen? What are they really about?

10. How do you calm yourself, relax, feel pleasure? What do you say to yourself that helps soothe your upset or worry?

Create a Welcoming Home

Being present means providing a warm and pleasant environment. It doesn't require fancy furniture and beautiful decor. It means a welcoming place where your children feel at home, safe, and relaxed.

Recently I visited my niece Alissa, her husband, John, and their eighteen-month-old son, Noah, in a solid old apartment in a New Haven duplex. As I looked around I saw a cozy little nest in a corner of the living room with a thick rug and big pillows, a little blanket, and a big squishy soft lamb where Noah often curled up with his blanket and a toy.

Growing children need their own places for quiet or privacy. This includes the freedom to give personal expression to their rooms, clothes, and decorations. It's not about having an image of "house beautiful," but rather it's about a child feeling the right to their own life.

I've heard many clients say that they had a constant knot in their stomach for fear of getting scolded for doing something "wrong" in their parents' perfect house or fearing their parent would go ballistic over a coat left hanging over a chair, or a few crumbs on the kitchen counter. On the flip side, some children's homes are so chaotic, dismal, and unpredictable that the children are embarrassed to bring friends home and find the atmosphere depressing.

As parents and caregivers, look at your home through the eyes of your children. What can you do to make your home a welcoming place for all of you? You could invite your children to talk with you about the atmosphere in your home and together make some changes.

DON'T EMBARRASS YOUR KIDS

Being there for your children means you don't embarrass or demean them in front of their friends. Just as we wouldn't like a cutting remark or a cute story being told about us against our will, children don't like it, either. Also, don't talk about children as if they are not present. Again, think of how it would feel to you to be in a three-way conversation and have someone talk about you as if you were not there.

IMPERMANENCE IN PARENTING

Parenting is an endless experience of impermanence because all children are different and because they keep changing. One child turns to tears if you so much as raise your voice with a hint of disapproval; another child has a cheerful disposition that shines through your moments of irritation or fatigue.

Being there for a child requires us to ebb and flow, to give and take, to come close and create distance, to set limits and step back, to be helpful yet let the child make his best effort without us. One day we're rocking our child to sleep, another day we're watching with a jumpy stomach as he walks to the school bus stop for the first time. One day we're hearing about his first date, another day we're confronted with finding out he's experimenting with drugs.

TUNE IN TO RED FLAGS

While some parents are hypervigilant, others tend to minimize problems, overlook red flags, and wait too long to reach out for help when their children are troubled. They often have thoughts such as, "It's normal for that age, it will pass. It's no big deal." While it might be true that "this will pass," it's crucial to talk with your kids regularly.

You may need to take time to be with your child so that he can talk about what's going on as he gets older and check for depression, drugs, a hurtful relationship, or trouble at school.

It's also crucial to get help for the child as well as yourself, especially if you are getting distraught, preoccupied, and having harsh reactions to your child. It's tempting to want to punish or be shaming and critical, but if a kid's getting into trouble it's a big red flag. It could signal depression or suicidal feelings. Set limits or provide consequences, but not to the exclusion of understanding and care. This is where our love is tested: we don't switch it off when our child disappoints us. We are still the parent—older and wiser. The heartbreak of teen suicides often reveal children who feel isolated, ashamed of their behavior, unable to take control of their lives, and afraid that there was no one to understand.

It is a challenge for any parent to know when to push for a conversation and when to step back, when to be concerned, and when to let things ride. Talk with other parents, get wise advice from school counselors or therapists, read articles, and know that at some level your child wants you to be there and to care. He may not show it or say thank you at the moment because the pride of wanting to feel strong or independent gets in the way. But your kids need you. Be there.

7 Ego and Essence

How to Recognize the Difference

The True Expression of Nonviolence Is Compassion Based on . . .
genuine human relationships—real feeling for each other,
understanding each other—we can develop mutual trust and
respect. From that we can share other people's suffering and build
harmony in human society. We can create a friendly human family.

—THE DALAI LAMA, "COMPASSION IN GLOBAL POLITICS"

When we live out of essence, we interact with people by listening, putting ourselves in their shoes, and responding with understanding. When we live out of ego, we act out of our conditioned self and react to our child's behavior based on rules and beliefs from our past and our personal needs, whether conscious or unconscious, helpful or not.

The conditioned ego is constructed of thoughts and judgments: good, bad, lovable, unlovable, worthless, worthwhile, right, wrong. Our conditioned beliefs often crowd out our common sense and our ability to observe, be present, enjoy our child, and come to reasoned conclusions.

The Benefits of Living from Essence

Millions in our arms we gather, to the world our kiss be sent.
—SCHILLER, "ODE TO JOY"

When we live from the *I Am*, the place of essence, we drop the labels and bring fascination and curiosity to ourselves and our children. *I'm neither good, bad, smart, stupid, funny, dull, nor lazy. I just AM—experiencing what is going on in the moment, bringing my presence fully to the experience.*

Most of us slide back and forth between living out of ego and living out of our essence. The more we recognize these two states (the more sensitively we are attuned to ourselves), the more we become aware of the messages we are sending our children. This takes us deeply into understanding our motivation, fears, desires, and agendas for our children.

TRAITS OF BEING IN ESSENCE

Use this list for self-exploration.

1. Assume original goodness rather than original sin, which doesn't exist as a concept in Buddhism. We're simply at levels of being aware, awake, and tuned in.
2. Talk naturally, although it's fine to coo with infants. Be direct, clear, and plainspoken.
3. Show happiness and smile naturally when you greet your child after being apart. Make warm eye contact with your child.
4. Attune to your child's needs to be close or to be separate.
5. Find ways to have fun with your child. You are free to say what you would like to do, and not be obliged to do things you really don't enjoy if there is a choice.

6. Learn from others. Ask for help when you are confused, need assistance, or want suggestions. You can't possibly be expected to know everything about parenting.

7. Take time for yourself, and use your support system to take over when you need some time for yourself.

8. Allow your child to struggle (but not too much) in the interest of learning. Don't rush to do for your child what he can do for himself.

9. Apologize but don't grovel when you are insensitive, unfair, or unkind. Make sure to let your child know it wasn't her fault and she didn't do anything to deserve it.

10. Accept the ever-changing relationship you have with your child as his needs for independence, separateness, and other close friendships change the nature of your relationship.

Don't measure your self-esteem by your child's success or failures. He is not on this earth to shore up your self-esteem. We need to help our children manage the ups and downs of life, not to protect them from hurt or disappointment.

For example: I'm caught in my ego when I feel upset that my daughter didn't get a part in the school play. The upset stems from many concepts and ideas: I don't want my daughter to feel badly. I want to be able to tell my friends of her success. I want to feel the pride of watching her in the play. From essence, I accept the *what is* of the situation: she didn't get the part. That's life. I encourage her to sort through her feelings and get a perspective on the situation and still feel good about herself. The point is that from essence my focus is on her, and my self-esteem is not tied up in her accomplishments.

EXAMPLES OF LIVING OUT OF THE EGO

1. Thinking in terms of good, bad, right, wrong, instead of simply accepting *what is*.

2. Difficulty tolerating strong emotions because they trigger your own buried feelings. For instance, you might immediately try to quiet an angry, sad, or even happily excited child rather than be present.

3. Having little capacity for empathy or ability to attune to the feelings of your child because you are distracted or preoccupied with yourself.

4. Difficulty seeing the need beneath the surface of a behavior. You might react to a child's behavior as irritating, a nuisance, or difficult without seeing the underlying need. The child may want attention or feel angry, hurt, hungry, tired, or lonely.

5. Difficulty acknowledging your own part in the child's behavior—that is, perhaps your inattention, control, intrusiveness, or volatility contributes to a child's whining, rebelliousness, depression, or being explosive or unable to concentrate.

6. Seeing the world only through your own eyes. *If it worked for me, it should work for you. If it doesn't, something is wrong with you.*

7. Feeling threatened by differences. You're uneasy when your child has different interests, beliefs, needs, and goals in life than your own. This can lead to judging and coercing your child rather than getting to know him.

8. Measuring the "worth" of yourself and your children by external standards such as grades, looks, popularity, beauty, status, money, accolades, or power over others.

9. Constantly letting others know of your child's achievements as if it is a reflection of yourself or defines your child. Developing a surface or superficial personality so that others perceive you as friendly, kind, good, and smart. If you adopt an artificial persona, your child will feel separate and less safe to be real with you.

10. Feeling rigid and defensive and making negative remarks about others, especially those who are different.

UNDERSTAND THE EGO'S COVER-UP

Ego can be cunning and sweet, and can appear to be caring while hiding its self-serving agenda. We cloak our own desires in apparent kindness: "Dear, I think you'd be happier going to the park rather than the beach." What we really are saying is, *I want to go to the park rather than the beach, but I'm afraid to say so directly. I want it to appear that you want to go and obscure the fact that I'm manipulating you to have my way.*

WHOSE NEEDS ARE BEING MET?

....

A question that can often serve as a reliable "reality clarifier" for parents is this: *Whose needs are being met?* Am I thinking about helping my child find out who she is, or am I thinking of *my* image and the approval of others?

....

An example that comes up repeatedly in therapy is about parents, most often mothers, controlling what their children wear. One woman expressed it this way: "My mother bought all my clothes and seldom asked what I wanted to wear. She'd want me to wear these cute little dresses when I wanted to wear pants. It was as if I was a little object to look cute for her and her friends."

This is confusing for the child because it appears that the mother cares. After all, she is giving her daughter lots of attention. Unfortunately it is all about the mother's need to have her daughter look a certain way, and not based on knowing her daughter or taking her desires seriously. While a parent can set limits about dressing appropriately, we honor our child by giving her a choice. This gives her a voice and a sense of competence. Every time the child picks out what she wants to wear, she is expressing herself. Multiplied in hundreds of small ways in different situations, giving a child as many choices as possible builds confidence and a feeling of warm connection to the parent.

When we recognize our hidden agendas and scripts, it helps us understand how we covertly or overtly create either connection or contention in our relationships with our children. Even if children don't know consciously whether we're parenting more out of ego than out of essence, they feel it in their bodies, and in their minds, which intuitively know the truth.

> *We are all struggling, none of us has gone far. Let your arrogance go,*
> *and look around inside.*
>
> —KABIR

GIVE YOURSELF MERCY AND KINDNESS

We're all just standing where we landed in life—made up of our genetics, experiences, conditioning, and personalities. You give understanding and empathy to others to the extent that you have kindness and mercy for yourself. It's an ongoing process because it means accepting this moment as it is.

Practice living from essence by asking yourself the following questions:

1. What do I really need? What is missing in my life? What are my dreams for myself?
2. What pain, fear, or lack of confidence am I covering up?
3. Would it help me feel safe to tell someone how I really feel?
4. What would it feel like to repeatedly ask, *Whose needs are being met—mine or my child's?*

MY MOTHER AND THE PIANO

Here is a personal story that illustrates the confusion that arises when a parent is caught up in their ego needs. My mother was caught between two opposing needs: one was to see me get married to a "good" man, the other was for her to appear in a positive light to her friends. This was in total conflict with my need shortly after graduating from college: all I wanted at that time was to buy a Steinway grand piano.

I was living at home for the summer, working to save money for a piano. Instead of being proud of me for my focus, dedication, and hard work, I could see that my shopping trips to regional piano stores made my mother extremely nervous. Following a lot of sideways remarks, she finally blurted out, "What if you meet a man who doesn't want such a big piano!" After reeling from the punch I said, "I wouldn't want a man who didn't want such a big piano." I was relieved at some level because I finally had a window into her nervous reactions to me.

Shortly afterward, while my parents were away on vacation, the feared seven-foot Steinway was delivered to our home—hardly something that could be hidden. I laugh now as I picture my mother coming into the living room, eyes popping, calling to my father with alarm, "Kenneth, Kenneth, come see what Charlotte's done!" You'd think I was a puppy who just did it on the floor.

A few days later, the scenario was very different. My mother's good friend Kitty, a local piano teacher, dropped by and immediately sat down to try out the beautiful piano. Her pleasure in the touch and sound shone in her face. "You must be *so* proud of Charlotte," she said. Without a pause, my mother responded, "Oh, yes, we are." My initial reaction was something like, *You two-faced hypocrite*. But I also had a sense of relief at seeing my mother unmasked. Seeing into her world, so unconnected from mine, also left me feeling both sad and lonely.

This story may give you some idea of the resulting feelings of confusion, anger, hurt, and loneliness that parental agendas can cause in a child. It pitted my love for playing the piano against my deep desire for my mother's love and approval.

....

When a parent's self-esteem and image are tied to their child's behavior and success, it can result in a loyalty conflict within the child: *Do I please my parents, or lose their approval by pleasing myself?*

....

EXERCISE: FROM SMALL MIND TO BIG MIND

Here is a simple exercise I have used thousands of times that can shift you out of self-absorbed upset into a broader perspective that keeps you calm. Practiced regularly it becomes automatic.

1. Small Mind: Bring up thoughts or images of feeling agitated and upset. *This is terrible. How could he do this? I should have done something different.* Focus on thoughts of *my* personal upset, *my* child, *my* problem, and notice how your body feels.

2. Shift to Big Mind: Take a deep breath and change the language from "I" and "me" to "the." "I am feeling *the* upset of a mom alone with a crying baby, just like thousands of other moms right now. I am feeling *the* tiredness of not having enough sleep. I am feeling *the* frustration of having the same old argument with my teenager again, just like millions of other people. I am not alone, and this is not a tragedy. It's the *what is* of parenting, of life. It is just a moment in time."

3. Notice how you feel physically and emotionally when shifting from small mind to big mind.

As you practice going from a narrow focus of "my big problems" to a broader view, frustration dissolves into awareness: this is a human experience shared by many others. The mind may gradually shift to gratitude. You may think, *I can be thankful I have a bed to lie on where I can hold my baby, I have food for dinner, and my partner will come home and we will get over our squabble. Oh yeah, didn't I read a book that recommended calming babies by swaddling them and hold them sideways? I should go check it out.* A calm body equals a calm mind that can think of solutions.

TONGLIN MEDITATION

A variation on the Small Mind–Big Mind practice is to add Tonglin meditation. It starts by using the steps above to shift to "big mind." Then, while imagining others going through what you are experiencing, breathe in their frustration, grief, or hurt, and let it move within you, and breathe out a blessing to all of you. You can either do this with words or in a sense of love and care.

The first time I read about Tonglin meditation, I thought, *No way. Breathe in everyone else's frustration? Isn't mine enough?* But when I eventually started doing Tonglin, my sense of being alone faded dramatically. It was magical, and it prepared me for a great challenge to come. The feelings of frustration that swirled inside my chest and torso were somehow neutralized because I was embracing them instead of fighting them. As they transformed into a blessing, I felt a sweetness in my heart, and often a tear came to my eye.

This practice was my saving grace when my daughter was dying. A few days before she passed on, I went to a beautiful restored historic hotel in Marietta, Ohio, to meet my friend Pat. I arrived early and was immediately drawn to the shiny black grand piano in the corner of the lobby. I asked the woman at the reception desk if I could play since there was no one else around.

As I played "Danny Boy" with my eyes closed, my mind drifted to images of other mothers who had lost children or were sitting by their dying children—from illness, starvation, bombs, accidents, and wars—throughout the world. The tears rolled down my cheeks and I felt something ease inside as I repeated the song many times while feeling connected in spirit to the grief of countless other women. I breathed in their pain, connected it to mine, and sent out my blessing to us all.

Quite unexpectedly, I was suddenly filled with gratitude: Ginelle and I were at peace with each other, I'd had time to prepare for her passing, she was in a sunny nursing home instead of a hospital—the way she wanted it to be. She had also had the warm company of her biological sisters and mother, and we were all together caring for her and for each other.

Even now, as I recount that vivid memory, I feel a tear along with a sense of warmth inside—a feeling of peace beyond words.

8 Why Did I Do That?

Help Children Connect Feelings and Experience

> Emotion as a fundamental integrating process is an aspect of
> virtually every function of the human brain. As a collection
> of massive amounts of neural cells capable of firing in a
> chaotic fashion, the brain needs an integrating process to
> help it achieve some form of balance and self-regulation.
>
> —DANIEL SIEGEL, M.D., AND MARY HARTZELL, M.ED.,
> PARENTING FROM THE INSIDE OUT

*W*hy *did* I hit the dog? Why *am* I so worried about the class
outing? What *is* making me pick fights with my sister? We help children (and ourselves) develop awareness and a sense of mastery by
showing them how to recognize, notice, and understand how feelings, thoughts, and behavior go together. We do this by responding
to the underlying needs and feelings that fuel their actions instead of
just reacting to their surface behavior. For example, showing off may
signal a need for closeness. Talking back can be a cover for feeling
left out.

We can ask questions directly: "I'm wondering if you're mad about something. Feeling hurt? Worried?" We help a child explore what's really going on inside him so he can name and express his needs, fears, and feelings.

Sometimes adults react to little children as if their feelings are cute or unimportant. Adults laugh or call the child silly. I urge you not to do this. A child is often completely serious when she says something that strikes adults as amusing, and laughter or dismissive remarks can go right to a child's heart and leave her feeling humiliated, just as an adult might feel. They also deflate a child's joy, excitement, and curiosity. Little children are incredibly vulnerable to and affected by our reactions, which need to be empathetic, understanding, and compassionate.

As a Parent, Ask Yourself: Who Am I? What Do I Feel?

To help children identify their feelings, parents first need to identify their own. This involves asking yourself, "What is going on inside of me?" It is also necessary to recognize your own experiences of shame, humiliation, and hurt.

Link your feeling to the events in your life. Ask yourself: *Am I feeling crabby right now in response to a sharp remark my boss made? Because I wasn't invited to a special gathering? Because I just got stuck with a huge bill for fixing the car? Is this an old reaction that is connected to my childhood? Am I trying to bury my feelings or not tell anyone because I feel embarrassed and ashamed?* We can also ask, *When did I go numb and stop feeling anything? Am I afraid or avoiding a painful situation or conflict?*

Helping children explore their behavior and identify their feelings is an ongoing process that requires the parent to engage with them in exploring what's going on inside.

WHY DID I BITE MY SISTER?

Very often a child (or adult) does something out of character but has no idea why. As a personal example: When I was about three years old, my whole family—mother, father, sister, brother—was sitting in the living room, reading or quietly playing games. Suddenly, as if propelled by an unnamed force, I walked across the room and bit my sister Lenore on the arm. I had no idea why I did it.

My sister cried out, my mother expressed shock, and I was summarily put into my crib upstairs and left alone. I felt totally bewildered by what I had done. A swirling ball of shame welled up inside me, and in my loneliness, I picked up the large baby doll in my crib and threw it as hard as I could onto the floor. I never played with baby dolls again. I wanted the earth to crack open and swallow me up—a sensation that became sadly familiar. What I needed was connection, not isolation, and some help unraveling the feelings that had propelled me to attack my sister.

> In helping a child understand her own behavior, a first step is to remember that the aggressor is usually hurting and expressing a need. It doesn't help to shout or punish because it only leads the child to feel worse about herself.

As I replay that scene in my mind, I ask myself, "What would have helped?" After my mother's shocked response, it would have been useful if she had taken me aside and asked, "What's going on with you? Do you know why you bit your sister?" She could have helped me by gently probing: "Are you angry at her? Or at us?" The question that would have brought a torrent of tears would have been, "Do you think we love her more than you?" That was exactly what I thought. I needed someone to see how unhappy and hurt I often felt.

It would have been crucial at such a point *not* to rush in with a dismissive comment such as, "That's silly, of course we love you both the same," because this would have negated my experience and left me feeling alone, instead of helping me feel understood.

The next step could have been to encourage me to say why I felt that way—what was festering inside of me? It was the fact that mother had made Lenore a beautiful long dress with red stripes and little stars earlier that week. I had also overheard her tell her friend Helen that Lenore was cuter than me and easier to sew for because her belly was smaller.

If my mother had listened, repeated back what I said—showing that she was engaged with me instead of being defensive—and said, "I can see why you felt that way," it would have been like manna for my spirit, because understanding would have eased my feelings of being alone and ashamed.

After that, my mother could have looked me in the eyes and said, "Any time you feel hurt or upset, you can come and tell me. I want to know." She might have said, "I'm sorry for what I said to Helen. I can see why that would hurt your feelings." She could have told me, and not in a glib or superficial way, why I was special to her and that she did love me.

Then she could have dealt with the issue of my biting my sister so I could reengage with Lenore. She could have asked, "How could you work it out with your sister?" If I offered to apologize, great. If not, it wouldn't have been right to force it because it would have meant lying to my sister. My mother could have said, "Her feelings are probably hurt, too, and bites hurt." My sense is that once I had felt understood, it would have been easy for me to apologize sincerely. We also could have talked about what I could do to make it up to Lenore.

Mom also could have spoken with Lenore and encouraged her to tell me how she felt. "You need to tell her or she won't know." She could have then taken me to Lenore, put an arm around each of us, and said, "Charlotte has something to tell you." I could have said

I was sorry for biting her. Lenore could have spoken up as well: "I'm mad that you bit me. It hurt." That way we would all have been reengaged, everything would have been processed, and I would not be remembering this scene sixty years later. Unfortunately a pattern became entrenched whereby my sister would run to my mother crying that I had hurt her. I would automatically get shamed and blamed even though I was two years younger. Lenore would be cast as the victim and I would be the bad one and feel awful. What generally helps children in conflict is for parents to stay out of the middle and say to the children, "I know you can work it out."

> Understanding helps children feel loved. Kindness teaches kindness, compassion teaches compassion.
>
> Punishment and separation create anger, shame, and hurt, and engender a negative cycle of interaction.

Helping a child to understand his own behavior instead of responding to our initial impulse to change his behavior through punishment and separation is at the core of peaceful parenting, and of bringing up children to have a positive sense of self.

WHY ARE YOU KICKING THE DOG?

Here is another example. David, age eight, kicks the dog. His father scolds, "You must not kick the dog. That's bad." David kicks the dog again. His father yells, "Go to your room, and come out when you feel sorry for kicking the dog!" The downward cycle has begun in the form of a power struggle. David is feeling forced to say something he doesn't feel, and thus digs in his heels to defy his father. He thinks, *You can't make me.* And indeed, his father can't.

David broods in anger, which crumbles into hurt and shame, and he still has no idea why he kicked the dog. Nothing has been learned. An unnamed fury arises inside him, and later in the day he kicks the dog again. This time, his father, in frustration, hits David, and yells, "How do you like it when someone hits you? You think you'd learn something by being alone in your room. Well, go there again until you do."

When children are sent to their room to feel sorry for what they have done, what they usually learn is how to muster up defenses to handle the isolation and overwhelming feelings. Because David has no one to help him and feels alone, he switches to survival mode and just tries to cope with his awful feelings. He might use any one of a number of strategies children use to divert bad feelings: doubling up, playing with toys aggressively, reading, rocking, hitting his head against the backboard of his bed, breaking toys, digging his fingernails into his arm, devouring a bag of cookies hidden under the bed, playing violent video games, or going numb—anything to avoid facing the dreaded feeling of being cut off, alone, and ashamed.

What does the child learn? *I'm bad and I'm not lovable.* This extends to, *I'd better not tell my parents when I'm in trouble because then I'll get in worse trouble and I'll be alone again.*

To get on the right track to help the child change, parents need to help him learn what's going on inside, so he can change his behavior from the inside out.

....

When you feel the impulse to yell at, hit, or punish your child for his behavior, take a moment and remind yourself: Peace *is* the way. I am the parent and he is the child. How can I handle this in a way that keeps us connected, keeps his self-esteem intact, and helps foster more positive behavior?

....

Let's replay the scene. In our "peace *is* the way" replay, David kicks the dog. His father sees this and says in a calm, steady voice, "Hey, it looks like you're really mad. What's going on?" He steps between David and the dog and turns his attention to helping David figure out why he kicked the dog. He makes it safe by focusing on David's real problem rather than judging his action. This diverts a power struggle.

When David doesn't come up with any answers, his father might suggest some possibilities. "Are you feeling angry about something?" Pause. "Hurt?" Pause. Maybe David doesn't like the dog, or feels jealous, or maybe the dog's behavior was frustrating him. Maybe the trigger occurred earlier in the day, perhaps at school. The idea is to help the child figure it out himself without prying or making the conversation feel intimidating.

After the conversation about school wanders around for a while, David finally tells his father that his friend Jack got chosen to be on the soccer team and he didn't.

His father listens and responds, "And you feel really bad about that." (The parent stays with the child's experience and doesn't ask for details, which would break the flow of the conversation. The parent only comes in when the child is stuck and needs some ideas.) Here's how the rest of their talk might have gone:

David: "Yeah, it wasn't fair. I'm as good as he is."

Dad: "It wasn't fair because you believe you are as good as he is."

David: "I *know* I'm as good."

Dad: "So you want to know why you weren't chosen?"

David: "Yeah, well ... it's probably about that fight I got into on the field."

Dad: "You got into a fight."

David: "Yeah, Jimmy and me got into a fight the day before. He was calling me names and I got really mad. I didn't hit him very hard. But he went to the coach."

Dad: "You felt bad about being called names, and hit Jimmy." (The child is relieved not to be immediately scolded for hitting.)

David: "Yeah."

Dad: "What names did he call you?"

David: "Mostly he said I was a loser."

Dad: "Do you feel like a loser?"

David: "For not getting on the team," he says sadly as he drops his head.

Dad: "You really wanted to be on the team?"

David: "Yeah." A tear rolls down his cheek.

Dad: "Looks like you're also pretty sad . . ."

David: "Yeah."

Dad: "Um-hmm." (Pause.) "It's hard to get left out. I've felt really sad when that's happened to me." (Dad validates the child's experience, and shares his own.)

David looks up at his father and feels relief.

Dad: "Have you thought of what you might do about the situation?"

David: "What can I do? There's nothing *to* do." He sounds defeated.

Dad: "Oh, I think there are some possibilities."

David: "Like what?"

Dad: "How about you think about it for a while, then we can talk about it again . . . maybe later this evening." (In this case, David is not ready to come up with a solution, so his father gives him time to think and offers to continue the conversation. Remember, the goal is learning. It's

important for the parent not to work harder than the
child.)

Dad then returns to the situation with the dog. "So, do you
have an idea about why you kicked Benny?"

David: "When I came in he was eating and he didn't come to
see me."

Dad: "You were hoping Benny would wag his tail when you got
home?"

David: "Yeah."

Dad: "That was another disappointment."

David: "Yeah, I even called him and he didn't come. Then
I kicked him."

Dad: "Any idea how that felt to Benny?" (He shifts gears to
helping David feel empathy.)
David starts to cry.

Dad: "You feel bad about kicking Benny?"
David nods.

Dad: "Do you have any ideas about what you could do to make
things better with you and Benny?" (This gives David a
chance to restore the relationship and to feel better about
himself.)
David perks up. "I could go throw the ball, or take him for
a walk. Maybe both."

When David picked up a ball in order to play with Benny, he was
brought to tears by the eager look and wagging tail that greeted him.
Because David had been treated with kindness, his heart had softened and he was able to feel remorse for hurting the dog. It was an
experience in forgiveness he never forgot.

Later, his father spoke with him about restoring his relationship
with his teammate, Jimmy, and talking to the coach.

Notice that this process included:

1. Listening to the child and maintaining contact.
2. Responding to the need or hurt underneath the behavior.
3. Helping the child connect his needs or feelings to the behavior.
4. Helping the child be aware of the impact of his behavior on others.
5. Repairing the relationship with others: apologizing if the child is ready or able to, then giving back something to make amends or show he cares.

In this case, David also repaired his relationship with Jimmy and the coach.

While this process takes time in the short run, in the long run it often preempts power struggles, fear, or anger erupting in the household, not to mention saving the child from going through life feeling detached, bewildered by his behavior, acting impulsively, and having difficulty in relationships.

Your ability as a parent to meet a stressful situation with calm and understanding helps your child internalize the same ability to regulate emotions in difficult situations.

When children feel heard and understood, they are likely to calm down and find solutions for themselves. They can move from fear and shame, which constrict the mind, to acceptance and relaxation, which free the mind to come up with solutions.

In these two examples, the child was old enough to know it was wrong to bite or kick. With tiny children or toddlers, a parent can gently take the child's hand and say, We don't hit. Hitting hurts. Parents can also indicate disapproval with subtle body language, but it's also important not to use icy cold searing looks.

What Children Learn When They Feel Understood

The process might go something like this:

- Something's going on with me. I'm upset.
- I'm not a bad person, even though I did something wrong/ mean/dishonest.
- I don't have to keep it a secret. I can go to my mom or dad and they'll help me.
- I can figure this out.
- I can make things right again.

The ability to reflect on oneself and know we can repair the hurts we cause others is a skill for life. It gives us a deep acceptance of our humanness and is golden in relationships. It prevents the build up of hurt and resentment that is so damaging to all relationships.

It can be very difficult for some people to believe that understanding a child who has been hurtful to others will be effective, especially people who think that the best way to teach children is through stern lectures, punishment, or harsh consequences. But I have seen understanding work again and again.

From a Buddhist perspective, it makes complete sense. Understanding is experienced as love, and when we feel loved, we are willing to explore our human failings, knowing that we are still lovable and that people will not leave us for making mistakes. To feel known, understood, and accepted is to be reconnected to the pulse of life as it flows through us. We stay in the circle, connected to others. It's the essence of compassion. It's the practice of love.

EXERCISES FOR PARENTS

To help children connect their feelings to their actions, parents and caregivers need to be able to do the same thing with their own feelings. The following exercises will help parents reflect on their past and current behavior.

Take time with these memories so they come alive inside of you. Notice how you feel in your body when you recall the situation. Talk about this experience with another person.

RECALL A TIME WHEN:
- You made a mistake or were hurting and someone was understanding and kind to you.
- You made a mistake or were upset and someone yelled, was harsh, put you down, or shamed you.
- You were kind and understanding to another person when they were insensitive to you or when they made a mistake.
- You shamed or made another person feel guilty for being insensitive to you or for making a mistake.
- Someone tried to force you to apologize or say something that didn't feel true to you (in other words, they were teaching you to lie).
- You wish you had been more understanding with your child.

Now replay the above scenes as you wish they could have been. Notice how you feel in your body. Talk with someone about the experience.

If it feels appropriate, go back to your child, bring up the situation and tell him your thoughts. For example, *I've been thinking about how I got mad at you for losing your jacket, and I wish I had handled it differently. Here's what I wish I had said.* Don't grovel, just be matter-of-fact and friendly. This is guaranteed to get your child's attention and help him learn to reflect and apologize as well.

CONNECTING BODY SENSATIONS TO FEELINGS

Often our physical state provides us with clues as to where our distress is coming from. For example, a sudden tightening in the chest often signifies fear, a stomachache often signifies anger, as in, *I'm sick of you doing that.* Beneath the anger there is often an unexpressed need: *I needed you to talk with me in a nicer tone of voice,* or, *I wanted you to hug me when you left.* It usually comes down to: *I need to know you care. I want to know you love me.*

EXERCISE: WHAT DOES YOUR BODY HAVE TO SAY

1. Do a body scan. Close your eyes and imagine a little you with a flashlight going through your body noticing where your body feels relaxed, tense, shut down, open, energetic, or dull.

2. Practice noticing the sensations in your body throughout the day. Where do you feel tight, or constricted, or aching, numb, tingling, prickly, aching, cramping? Just notice, bring your focus to that area, breathe into it, and be aware of the sensations.

3. While you notice the sensations, see if you can identify any feelings (emotions). Then think about what is going on in your life. If the stomachache, tight chest, or headache could talk, what would it say?

4. Scan your life for the past week: what are you denying, minimizing, avoiding, keeping secret? What needs to be brought to the surface and dealt with?

When you get into the habit of checking in with your body, of noticing the sensations and finding out what's bothering you, you grow far less likely to blame others, become impatient, or lose your temper. This will feel good to you, and those around you.

OPENING THE WAY FOR CHANGE

Let's return to the four noble truths of Buddhism. When you have time to reflect, ask yourself, "What am I demanding be different than it is?" In other words, how are you resisting the truth of the moment? Then ask yourself, "How is my demand creating these upset feelings and behavior?" Lastly, look for the need or fear beneath your demand and upset feelings.

> When sudden impulses to be harsh arise, take a breath, slow down, and say to yourself once again: Peace is the way. I am the parent and he is the child. I need to be helpful and not fall into his emotional state. When I stay calm, I help my child learn how to regulate his or her feelings.

If you've already blown your stack, tell your child, "I apologize for yelling at you. I imagine that was very scary for you. It wasn't your fault. I need to take a break and cool down." (This also sets a great example for the child in his own behavior.)

Have complete mercy on yourself. Beating up on yourself or groveling to your child will not help you change or repair a situation. What's needed is reflection and kindness to yourself along with a willingness to explore your behavior and to ask, What was going on with me? What do I need? What is that trigger about? This will open the way to change.

9 Wow! I Climbed the Mountain

Having Fun Together Inspires Learning and Adventure

> The child who is decked with prince's robes and who has
> jeweled chains round his neck loses all pleasure in his play;
> his dress hampers him at every step.... It is no gain, thy
> bondage of finery, if it keep one shut off from the healthful
> dust of the earth. If it rob one of the right of entrance to the
> great fair of common human life.
>
> —RABINDRANATH TAGORE, GITANJALI

Children have an amazing capacity for learning and challenging themselves. Parents play an enormous role in igniting this potential. A child's ability to learn and grow is enhanced when she is joined by relaxed, inspiring parents or teachers who provide a wealth of varied experiences. Cooking, drawing, building things, sports, dancing, singing, gardening, making hideouts, acting, crafts, making up stories, and biking are all activities that increase imagination, coordination, lung capacity, fine motor skills, and concentration. Parents also inspire children by having their own active lives: working, taking a class, fixing things, helping out in the community, talking about books they like.

Taking pleasure together in the natural world is especially important: it helps children develop a love for nature and feel the excitement of exerting themselves and stretching their limits.

One day I was sitting on St. Mary Peak in the Bitterroot Mountains, at 9,300 feet, taking in the awesome 360-degree view. To my delight, three little girls appeared over the horizon, followed by their parents. Their attractive mom and dad were smiling, obviously enjoying themselves, and there was a sense of ease and connection among them all. As they settled down on the craggy rocks nearby, the father opened his backpack and out came a cornucopia of comforts: fleece jackets, a thermos (of hot chocolate?), an abundant lunch, and treats.

We got to talking, and I was astonished to find out that the girls were four, six, and seven. Four years old! Some kids complain about walking three blocks at that age. And this was a 2,800-foot ascent, four miles up and four miles down—a solid hike for anybody. How did they do it? I wondered. None of the girls was whining or fussing; in fact, they seemed proud of themselves and secure in the shelter of their family.

....

When learning is paired with pleasure, connection, and a sense of accomplishment, it forms a lasting imprint on the brain that encourages a child to take on other challenging tasks.

....

Parents help immeasurably when they impart a sense of adventure—*Why not? Let's try! It might be fun.* Challenges are more exciting than scary when there's no inner critic or fearmonger harping away. It's okay to make mistakes or do a mediocre job because the point is to stretch, laugh, explore, breathe, and have a good time.

It doesn't matter what you do—the important thing is that the parent help the child explore and find his particular talents and strengths and take on the role of guide and teacher rather than judge and jury. It's also important to prepare for outings with children by having enough food and the right clothes, taking breaks, not going too fast, and focusing on the pleasure of the journey. It's okay not to finish; the point is to be together as a family and have a good time.

Learning a New Skill Feels Good

Life takes on vitality and joy when one feels the tingle of a new idea, the excitement of figuring out a problem, and the satisfaction of making music or developing a skill. Think of all these activities as contributing to a huge neural network in the brain. Any one area of learning contributes to strengthening the entire maze of connections. *From people skills and sports to academic studies, physical work, and music—everything contributes to the whole.*

A sense of mastery helps a child (and an adult) learn to hang in there through frustration and confusion in any setting. *I've done it before: I stuck to it, I persevered, I figured out something hard, and I can do it again.* Parents play a part through encouragement, modeling, and providing the resources to make it happen. One father spoke of having a stack of scrap wood, nails, and a hammer in the backyard for his son who loved pounding nails and putting pieces of wood together, sometimes for hours at a time. One couple took their daughter on numerous trips into parks and woods when she showed a love for hiking. In both cases the parents followed the natural inclinations of their children.

Avoid Gender Stereotypes

Sex roles limit people. I recently cringed when I saw a commercial advertising a drive-and-crash circular speedway for little boys and a pink and blue castle with a prince and princess dancing together for the girls. It seems we never get beyond these terrible stereotypes and cultural conditioning. This is a huge disservice to all children, and it does nothing to help them learn to live together.

Boys don't need violence to play and girls don't need to wait for a prince to come. I have the same response when picking out birthday cards for young boys and girls. Stereotypes abound. Take a look at these seemingly innocuous parts of our culture and think about what is being taught—or, more accurately, drilled—into the minds of parents and children.

Alfie Kohn, the author of *The Brighter Side of Human Nature: Altruism and Empathy in Everyday Life*, makes a strong case that aggression is more a function of socialization and context than an innate drive. He quotes Ashley Montagu: "It is not that the brain is 'wired' for aggression, but that neural elements in certain parts of the brain can be readily organized by experience to function in behavior we call aggressive."

Boys and girls are different, but there are also many differences within each gender. In parenting for a peaceful world, we need to question all assumptions about boys being "wired" for aggression and violence, and girls naturally being kind, thoughtful, and longing for a prince.

It is a huge challenge for parents to go against the tide of sex-role stereotypes in American culture, starting with colors and toys, but it's unrealistic to think that children who are constantly exposed to images of violence and aggression will not be affected. Conditioning happens through repetition.

To help your children find out who they really are, let them lead the way toward whatever toys, songs, and games they are drawn to, as well as how they like to dress (within reason). As a therapist, I've heard countless stories of parents stopping children from following their inclinations because "boys or girls *don't do that*." I repeatedly hear of little girls being forced to wear dresses when they want to wear jeans, and little boys being pushed toward action figures and acting tough and playing football when they preferred art or music or tennis. It's crucial to realize that little boys feel fear and have a need for affection and warmth just as little girls do. One father tore up a pillow given to his son because it had a little bit of pink on it. "I don't want him to be effeminate!" he said adamantly, justifying his assault on the pillow.

We need to ask ourselves what we mean by being "effeminate" or a "strong woman" and what stereotypes we are inflicting on our children. Why not encourage gender-neutral toys such as blocks, Legos, drawing pads, rubber balls, farm animals, or books?

I remember a mother who glowed with pleasure when she peeked into the bedroom at our house and saw her son rocking a baby doll wrapped in a cloth, his face a portrait of serenity and happiness. She quietly stepped back so as not to interrupt his pleasure.

On the other hand, we can go overboard. I remember a friend swearing that her daughter would *never play with Barbies*—she didn't want to reinforce those stereotypes. Of course that made Barbies prized possessions. By contrast, a Mennonite father said that while he was taught values of nonviolence, as a boy his parents allowed him a cap gun, which helped him fit in with other boys. What we're looking for is a balance between guiding our kids and being careful not to overcontrol in ways that give more power to the toy in question.

When I go to my high school reunions, I usually stay at the home of my friend Jim. It always makes me smile to see the soft dolls and pink walls in his daughter Judy's bedroom . . . along with numerous trophies and a photo of Judy, a small, slender woman, being inducted into the Wrestling Hall of Fame. I asked Jim how Judy got started.

"When I was teaching my boys to wrestle, Judy said, 'Teach me, too.' I was surprised for a moment. There were no girl wrestlers when I was in school. But then I thought, Okay, why not? She took to it and became a world champion." What a tribute to an open-minded father!

When I was little, embroidering was another form of play. Mom would iron outlines of cartoon figures or flowers on dish towels and offer a box of colorful thread for us to sew with. On several occasions my brother's friends would see us embroidering and hesitantly ask to join in. My mom didn't miss a beat. "Sure," she said. Then another boy gingerly joined in, and there we all sat in a semicircle embroidering—a fond image that still brings a smile to my face. (Among other benefits, sewing helps children develop fine muscle control and concentration.)

LENA AND THE BIRDS

My friend Lena, age three and a half, can recognize and name about seven birdcalls—more than I can—because her knowledgeable mother often takes her out on their deck where they imitate the bird sounds together. Ponder for a moment everything Lena is learning. First, by listening deeply and sorting through the complex sounds of the birdcalls, her capacity for hearing is increasing and developing one part of her brain. Imitating the sounds of the birds is developing another. She is also learning to identify different birds by sight and pair them with the birdcalls. And she is developing her capacity for memorization.

Does it matter if a child can name a birdcall? Not especially, but it matters a great deal that Lena has learned to listen intently, pair a sound with sight, develop her vocal cords by making the sounds herself, and find pleasure in learning while feeling a close bond with her mother, as well as with nature.

I've seen other warm connections between parents and children playing tennis, riding bikes, fishing, boating, playing sports, and making music.

Parents and caregivers do children an enormous lifelong favor when they help them to explore a full range of activities and play, which become pleasures to draw on through the years. The best barrier against an aging brain, cognitive decline, depression, or loneliness is to develop a large repertoire of interests, including physical exercise, that bring delight to our lives, soothe our feeling of loss, and keep the blood and oxygen circulating in our brains and bodies.

TIME FOR FREE PLAY

Although families inspire their children to grow and stretch, unstructured, unsupervised time is also a crucial part of helping kids learn to create, cooperate, and enjoy themselves. Fun and play are grossly underrated for both children and adults. As a child who did nothing but play until I reached first grade (half days at that), I believe that the things my friends and I learned from running in the woods, playing hopscotch and hide-and-seek, and sewing were excellent forms of learning. We also tended our little animal burial ground in the woods, went to movies, had a little garden plot, made puzzles, or created little plays based on the musicals we saw in movies. It was a great education, before we even entered the classroom.

The capacity for joy we instill in children bodes well for our later years—playing doesn't have to be only for the young. Late one summer I got a call from my sixty-year-old friend Steve. "Hey, it's a gorgeous day. Want to float the river?" he asked. I looked at my watch and thought of the totally messy kitchen I had planned to clean up. I calculated the hours and minutes I had before an appointment. "Let's do it," I said, with a burst of happiness. My kitchen remained a mess, but my body still feels ecstasy as I recall the sun glistening on the water, the blue heron taking flight, Steve's infectious happiness, and the incredible sense of peace I felt on the last float of the summer. As parents, keep your joys alive because in doing so you give a lasting gift to your children.

HOW PARENTS CAN INSPIRE THEIR CHILDREN
TO STRETCH THEMSELVES

1. Children want to be around parents who are fun to be with. When an outing or event feels exciting and parents are short on criticism and long on patience and humor, young children are likely to want to join them.

2. Passion is contagious. When parents take obvious pleasure in music, sports, building things, sewing, cooking, or painting, children pick up on their energy. As a young girl I always wanted to go hiking with my father because he was so at peace in the woods. It felt as if the forests and mountains were his natural home. The tensions that sometimes flared at home dissolved when he put on his hiking boots. There was warmth, safety, and, well, it was exciting. I felt included in something special.

3. Make physical exercise and being adventuresome part of your family values. When children start walking, running, making weekly visits to a swimming pool, or having some kind of regular activity at a young age, it becomes a natural part of life.

4. Parents can invite the children to take part in planning family time. While they don't have veto power, they can have a voice.

5. Nudge but don't force. A nudge gives encouragement, but a child should not be pushed beyond her ability. That sets up resistance and often a sense of failure. Don't use criticism or shame to motivate a child.

6. Have conversations instead of lecturing. If kids show resistance to doing something, have a conversation to get at what's really going on. My friend Kerri, an avid hiker and former smoke jumper, told me about camping with her nieces, who were upset about all the bugs. Kerri said, "Let's have a talk about it," and asked them, "What don't you like about the bugs?" Each one got to share her

feelings, including Kerri, who pointed out that they mostly didn't hurt you—even a mosquito bite was not a big deal—and that they all play a part in nature. The conversation ended up on a positive note, with the children agreeing to notice the different kinds of trees and bushes and count the different kinds of bugs and talk about the part they play in nature.

7. Know when to let go of a plan. Julie, age five, was all dressed up for her first dance performance when she went sobbing to her parents and climbed in her mother's lap. "I don't want to go," she said in utter desperation. "I wanted to learn to dance, not perform." After a few reassurances—she'd do fine and she'd feel good afterward—it was clear that she was still truly afraid. "Honey, you don't have to go. You don't have to perform," her mom said. Her father agreed. "It's fine if you don't perform." These wise parents freed Julie to keep taking dance lessons and decide when she was ready to perform, which was several years later.

....

You make peace with your child when you don't set rigid agendas that are tied to your own self-esteem or self-image. You know you are in your ego when you become insistent, apply pressure, or get mad at the child for not following your script.

....

8. Listen to children when they say "That's enough." Forcing a child to do something beyond her exhaustion point, either mental or physical, can create an aversion for the activity and create resentment of her parents.

I've heard stories of a daughter being forced to play tennis beyond her exhaustion point, a young girl who broke her leg when a gymnastics teacher pressured her against her will to *try one more time*, and a little boy who hated playing games with the family because he was sent to his room or shamed when he started making mistakes out of fatigue. He was accused of "not trying."

If you see real fatigue setting in, or your child sends you a message that he or she is losing focus, it's time to stop with a cheerful spirit. I remember a picnic when I was lying out on a beach under the Southern Cross in New Zealand with a family and their two young daughters. The minute the girls started bickering, the father said, simply, "It's time to go home." There was no lecture and no harsh words. They swooped up their stuff and were gone in five minutes. This wise father was aware that the children had reached their limit.

9. Keep in mind that life is not a competition. We live in a highly competitive society. However, if you are raising children to take pleasure in various activities, don't keep score, count miles, or expect a perfect performance, as if you care more about attaining some goal than about the child. The point of these activities is to stretch, learn something new, and have a good experience together. That sets in place the lifelong belief that you can enjoy doing something even if you aren't very good at it.

10. Some children will take to competition on their own. They will want to excel, and will work very hard. Your job is to lay the groundwork, get them good teachers, create opportunities and let their own enthusiasm take over. Again, from a Buddhist perspective, we cheer for our children, but we don't attach our sense of worth to their achievements.

11. Notice what sparks your child's interest and where he excels. On the other hand, if he doesn't take to certain experiences, ease up. One kid's hike is another kid's art project, guitar lesson, kite flying, biking, or swimming.

12. Offer the one sport and one music option. Many parents require their children to take part in both sports and music—a fantastic combination for the brain. Beyond setting this general

requirement, the child gets to choose. Allanda's son, Charlie, resisted the idea of music at first. He tried playing the clarinet and didn't like it. He tried singing in a choir, but didn't like that either. But then he heard someone play guitar, and that was it!

13. Know when to help a child work through fear. When a child is afraid or daunted by a new activity, a lot of encouragement and a big nudge can be enormously helpful. Here's an example: When Andrea and her husband moved to a college town, their son Marty, who had excelled in tae kwon do, found that that his new classes used a different approach than he had learned, and he would have to start over. He was devastated and wanted to quit. Andrea nudged Marty to try, knowing how much he had loved it. He resisted until she had him speak with the tae kwon do teacher, who took Marty aside to assure him that he knew it was hard, but, after all, part of martial arts is doing what's hard and moving through fear. Eventually Marty agreed to try, progressed quickly, and in six months he had moved up several levels. His old spark and confidence had returned. Persistent nudging and encouragement, combined with the teacher's understanding, helped him eventually face his fear.

14. Cheer for your kids, go to their games, give them your attention. There's nothing like having dad, mom, aunt, grandpa, sister, or brother up there in the stands. No one can ever take your place. You matter forever!

As you can see, there is not one fixed approach that works for all children. One will delight in her first dance performance; another will freeze up in terror. Your job as a parent is to listen deeply, be understanding and know when to help your kids push through their fears and when to back off. It's an exquisite combination of instilling fascination, a willingness to try new activities, and steady practice. Most of all help your child find what sparks her interest and joy.

HELP CHILDREN KEEP THEIR SENSES ALIVE: AVOID "NATURE DEFICIT DISORDER"

Raising children to feel awe and wonder at the natural world, to feel interconnected with it, to value clean air, water, earth, and forests, is to give them a life-sustaining gift.

Partly in response to contemporary humans' increasing separateness from nature, a field of study called ecopsychology has evolved to help us explore the depth of our need for connection to nature and the immense cost of losing contact with it. Ecopsychology also explores the relationship between people and planetary well-being, which are intricately connected. It's about our connection to nature and our dependency on it.

At the heart of Buddhism is knowing that everything is interconnected: all systems within our bodies interface with all aspects of nature. We are not separate beings in any way. The air we breathe travels around the world, the water we drink has been on the planet for millennia—traveling in the rivers, clouds, and underground streams. *To be whole is to be in contact with nature because we are an intrinsic part of nature.*

To raise children who want to protect the natural world and its creatures, we start by helping them to appreciate and love it in a way that leads them to want to protect it. This starts in the earliest stages of a child's life, as we recognize our infant's and toddler's natural capacity to live through their senses.

In the words of Robin Moore, a North Carolina State University professor and director of the Natural Learning Initiative, "Sensory experiences link the child's exterior world with their interior, hidden, affective world. Since the natural environment is the principal source of sensory stimulation, freedom to explore and play with the outdoor environment through the senses in their own space and time is essential for healthy development of an interior life."

....

From the trillions of cells interacting in our bodies, to all the amazing tastes available to us, to pondering our total interdependence on water, sunlight, trees, and the foods that grow in the earth, true wealth is the capacity to be constantly amazed and grateful for these everyday wonders of life.

....

In a brilliant, touching, and timely book titled *Last Child in the Woods: Saving Our Children from Nature-Deficit Disorder*, Richard Louv sounds the alarm about our current generation of children, many of whom live in a virtual world and have few if any direct experiences with nature. As Louv, chairman of the Children & Nature Network, points out, they might know *about* the deforestation of the Amazon jungle, but they've never wandered in the woods or sat by a stream. For many, television, computers, and electronic gadgets have eclipsed running in the woods, putting up a tent in the backyard, playing in sand, climbing trees, listening to birds, or generally taking pleasure in nature.

LOSS OF SENSORY CAPACITY EQUALS LOSS OF JOY

We take for granted our capacity to experience smell, taste, sight, sounds, and touch. Yet, according to Louv, the current electronic-centered lifestyle of our children is resulting in a loss of capacity for physical sensation, and with it the capacity for awe, wonder, joy, and pleasure—and they don't even know it is happening. The implications of this are daunting to imagine, especially as one ages.

Losing our connection to nature and leading a sedentary lifestyle have also been linked to obesity, depression, and other diseases. As Louv writes, "You'll likely never see a slick commercial for nature therapy, as you do for the latest antidepressant pharmaceuticals."

FEELING SAFE IN NATURE

In my thirty years of helping clients imagine a safe place, nearly every one of them gravitates toward a place outdoors in a woods, by a river, or on a beach. As they recall the smells, sounds, sensations, colors, the heat of the sun and the sensuousness of a breeze, they go into a deep state of relaxation. We practice cues to help them "return" there at will to lower their stress level. When your mind is conditioned to feel at peace in nature, you have a natural resource for soothing yourself.

Losing the capacity for awe and wonder and being touched by beauty is like losing part of ourselves. I went through a period of feeling dissociated from people and nature in my early thirties; it was like looking at the world through a plastic shield. I could see flowers, trees, squirrels, lakes, and people, but it was like seeing them through a Plexiglas wall. I had no visceral response to them. The only thing that occasionally took me out of my detached state was being in water.

I've often wondered if the separateness I felt was akin to what is experienced by a young person who spends most of his time at a computer, watching TV, or continually texting friends. I wonder if a decreased ability for sensory pleasure leaves children with an emotional disability, a disconnect that will permeate the rest of their lives. What happens when someone has a diminished capacity to tap into sounds, colors, touch, tastes, and smells—the very sensations that connect us so deeply to the earth, to beauty and to each other? The people who are happiest in their later years are those who can experience joy, awe, and wonder along with close relationships.

That experience of being unable to feel connected to people and nature was one of the most painful of my life. I could fully understand why some people use drugs or opt for suicide—anything to feel something; anything to escape an empty world.

Fortunately, waiting for me was the legacy of a childhood of climbing mountains, playing piano, swimming, having my own little garden, biking, and walking in the woods with my botanist grandmother. I realized that I was coming out of this time of anxiety and disconnection when, by surprise, a feeling of happiness arose in my chest as I looked at a rose—the velvet red-orange petals unfolding, the heady fragrance, the sharp thorns, the shiny leaves. My period of disconnection had been like losing a best friend, a dear one, my umbilical cord linking me to a primitive part of my existence. This may sound dramatic, but there is mounting evidence that disconnection from nature affects our mental and emotional well-being in ways we do not fully comprehend.

FROM LOSS OF NATURAL PLEASURE TO COUNTERFEIT STIMULATION

When a child loses his sensory capacity for connection with nature, he may also lose the capacity for contemplation, relaxation, and comfort with stillness. In general, when we can't go deeply into the human experience, we turn instead to counterfeit stimulation—computer games, TV, the Internet, texting, tweeting, everything that is fast, and stimulating. We can't sit still.

The more we become dependent on constant stimulation the more quickly we feel boredom and become helpless to find sustenance in quiet ways—reading, walking, sitting, watching a sunset. We also become less able to self-motivate and be creative—play in the leaves, have a pickup game of baseball, put on costumes. The problem with increasing stimulation is that it never satisfies in the long run. It's like never getting quite enough to eat. The hunger never abates and the craving gets more desperate. The person feels increasingly helpless to feel satisfied and happy, as if he were losing control over his own life. This feeling also contributes to depression and anxiety.

Fortunately, there is a growing awareness of the risks of losing our capacity to feel embedded in nature. (God bless Michelle Obama for growing vegetables on the White House lawn and inviting children to help with the planting.) I've been thrilled to see schools include garden projects, summer hiking programs for children, and public service announcements telling parents to get their children out to play for an hour a day. Even so, it will take persistent efforts on the part of parents to push against the growing trends toward being plugged into electronics.

HELP YOUR CHILDREN GET BACK TO NATURE

Whether you live in an apartment or a home with a yard, there are many ways to be in nature. If you need more guidance, look into your community's resources. Here are some ideas:

1. Carry infants and tiny children in a sling on your chest and take them outside with you. Your heartbeat is nature itself connecting to your child.

2. Spend time with toddlers in a yard or in parks where they can play, run, and dig in the sand. Take them on hikes using a back carrier. Jog while pushing children in strollers.

3. Build or buy a sandbox, and take your child to the Goodwill store to pick out sandbox toys. Let your child be creative, even if he picks out something that seems odd.

4. Choose a nursery school, or preschool, with an outdoor space. Find out how often the children are allowed to go outside; do they go out in the winter, too? Ask about the curriculum: does it include stories about nature?

5. Take your children outside in all seasons, weather permitting. This includes walking in the (light) rain when there isn't a risk of lightning.

6. Give all children swimming lessons. This is both for safety and to connect the child to the element of water, which is intrinsic to who we are. (Swimming will be useful later in life, too, for exercise and therapy.)

7. Help your child plant seeds and watch them grow. As an alternative, let your child pick out a plant. Don't turn it into a losing situation, as in, "See what happens when you don't water your plants!" Instead, make positive comments such as, "The plant has a new leaf coming out. See that!" If you plant an herb, show the child how use it in cooking.

8. Fence in an area if possible so your child can play outside on his own.

9. See that your child has unstructured time in nature. Have your child play outdoors an hour a day if at all possible.

10. Send your kids to a camp in the summer that focuses on hiking, crafts, physical exertion and team building. Many communities offer different kinds of inexpensive day camps that include outdoor activities. For example, I recently visited Camp Watanopa, near Missoula, Montana, which I went to as a child. I saw a video of kids learning teamwork by doing rope courses, using a climbing wall, having water fights, playing sand volleyball, and canoeing. It's a simple, no-frills, low-cost camp for boys and girls, and many states and regions have camps like this.

11. Help your child collect the different leaves you see on a walk. Bring some home and press them in a book. I still find the remnants of flowers and leaves my grandmother occasionally pressed in a book.

12. Have your child help you arrange a bouquet of flowers.

13. Take your child to a zoo, to the woods, to state and national parks.

14. Go camping. If you don't have the equipment, borrow some from friends who do and ask them to show you how to use it. Better yet, go together.

15. Get a tent for the backyard where children can play and have sleepovers.

16. Keep a family journal when you go on outdoor trips. I have several such treasured journals from childhood vacations. You could make a list of all the animals you saw, where you hiked, and the names of mountains and streams and rivers. When a child is old enough, show them maps and brochures of where you are going.

17. Read *Sunflower Houses: Inspiration from the Garden* by Sharon Lovejoy. (The subtitle is "A Book for Children and Their Grown-Ups.") Lovejoy describes how she and her children created a summer playhouse out of living sunflowers with a roof of morning glories. The book has lots of similar ideas for small projects.

18. Rent Ken Burns's *The National Parks: America's Best Idea* and have a family viewing session over a few weeks. Along with bringing home the wonder of these special places, it can teach your children about the continuing need for preservation.

To keep children engaged on a car trip, make a little tote bag of wrapped treats or magnetic checkers, or something to read, with labels that say things like, "Open when you see a white horse," or "Open when you see license plates from ten different states." This will help keep your children's eyes on the outside, where they might also notice the landscape. Stop and read historic markers and visit national monuments. Prepare children for trips by showing them pictures and teaching them the history of parks, cities, farmlands, and landmarks and monuments.

And for you, the parent, set your worries aside for a moment and notice the bark on the trees, the different plants in your neighborhood, the birds, the new leaves in spring, the wonder of an opening flower, the joy in your child's face. Share this amazing experience with your partner, friends, and children.

10 Deep Listening and Loving Speech

And when old words die out on the tongue, new melodies break forth from the heart.

—RABINDRANATH TAGORE, *GITANJALI*

I was about to do my son in. I was so mad at him. Then I said to myself, "Use the skills from the parenting class!" It was hard, because they felt so foreign, but I did. I stopped lecturing and started listening. I got calm and let him talk and tried to understand where he was coming from, and it was amazing—he worked his problem out all by himself . . . without my incredible wisdom. Every parent should have such a class. We really learned what it meant to listen, and it has made a huge change in our family life.

—KERA, MOTHER OF SIX GROWN CHILDREN

....

When we show empathy and understanding to our children, they learn to give empathy and understanding to themselves and others.

....

Buddhist writings focus on friendliness, kindness, understanding, and compassion, or what we often call empathy: the ability to put ourselves in someone else's shoes and attune to their feelings.

A basic vow of Buddhism is to quiet oneself enough to listen to both the words and the spirit of another. *Listening without interrupting, correcting, contradicting, getting highly excited, questioning, spacing out, or giving advice is one of the deepest spiritual practices anyone can explore.* It requires us to be calm and receptive, to move beyond our ego and enter into the world of another person. It conveys a feeling of love.

It is a form of meditation to breathe deeply, drop back and let go of the ego's persistent desire to put the focus on the self: *I know what you should do. I had that happen to me. I have the answers. I am the wise one.* As Kera said, "*I stopped lecturing and started listening.*" And, as so often happens when we listen, the child finds the solutions to her own problems.

....

When we listen deeply to children, they learn to hear themselves and find their center, their voice, and their own solutions.

....

Separation Creates Anxiety

> *The experience of separateness arouses anxiety; it is, indeed, the source of all anxiety. Being separate means being cut off, without any capacity to use my human powers. Hence to be separate means to be helpless, unable to grasp the world ...*
>
> —ERICH FROMM, *THE ART OF LOVING*

Here is an entry from my diary at age fourteen. "When I grow up I'm going to really listen to my children so they feel understood. I hate the way mother says, 'Oh, you don't really feel that way,' or dad has this low persistent shhh whenever I get upset. Young people have real feelings and they're big. I don't think grown ups understand this. I don't want my children to feel lonely the way I do. I am writing this so I won't forget."

While my parents were great role models for taking part in numerous activities, persevering, and feeling competent, I ached for someone to ask me about my day, or what I felt, or what was going on with me. While I excelled in piano and school, I felt a deep loneliness coupled with a fear of talking with people. Since we didn't have real conversations at home or talk about feelings, needs, hurts, or what was going on in our lives, I had no idea of how to do this with others. I always felt as if I might be intruding.

CHILDREN ARE LITTLE PEOPLE WITH BIG QUESTIONS. · HONOR THEM.

A basic question to ask yourself is, "Are my words creating separation or are they creating connection?" Start by simply asking a child, How's it going? What's fun for you? What toy do you like? How was your day? What were the roses, and what were the thorns? These questions invite a child to reveal him- or herself. Likewise, there are ways to talk, set limits, and correct a child without being dismissive, inattentive, shaming, and insensitive.

It may only take a few negative experiences of a child being humiliated for her to give up asking a parent questions. As an example, at age six, I asked my mother, "Is it possible that there could be another little girl exactly like me in the world?" I had spent considerable time pondering this question while looking at the family globe. My mom smiled and said in a fluffy kind of way, "Well, there are probably other little girls just as silly as you." I felt deflated, hurt, and angry. I rarely asked her another cosmic question. Fortunately I could go to my father and grandmother with these big questions that were so important to me.

When you ridicule a child's questions, you demean and humiliate her and send a message that it's not okay to be inquisitive. When you take a child's questions seriously, it leads her to feel safe with you and safe to ask questions. Questioning is at the core of being wise in the world. When a child feels heard and understood, it makes her feel respected and deeply cared for. In addition, when you don't know the answer, you can say. "I don't know. Let's see if we can find out?"

LOVING SPEECH IS ABOUT BEING REAL AND AUTHENTIC

We are playing the instrument of who we are whenever we talk with our children. Our tone of voice, volume, the speed of our words, their directness or indirectness, whether we make eye contact, and our level of truth or deception are all apparent. Our words can convey ease, tension, fear, distraction, or ambivalence.

People may speak with a relaxed, centered voice, or a tight voice that makes them sound anxious or afraid. Some parents use baby talk with their children or speak in a high-pitched, nicey-nice tone of voice even when the child is past the baby stage. If you tend to alter your voice when speaking to your children, you might ask yourself why. Better yet, experiment by exhaling deeply and speaking in a more natural way.

Part of being authentic is dropping down inside and allowing your words to arise in response to your child rather than rattling them off like a tape-recorded message.

LOVING SPEECH AND ANGER

Haim Ginott, author of the classic *Between Parent and Child*, urges parents to recognize their anger before they blow up and lose their temper at their children. This starts with recognizing that you are frustrated or annoyed and voicing it without attacking and shaming the child. *I get angry when you leave your toys all over the living room. I'm angry when you agree to rake the yard and then take off to be with your friends and don't tell me.*

Focus on Anger Prevention

Anger prevention comes from consistently setting natural and logical consequences for our children's actions so that the rules do the talking and preempt frustration. It's best if the policies are explained to the child and agreed upon as much as possible. When there's a policy that toys go into a box and have to be earned back if they are left in the living room, there's no need to lecture or shout at the child. Just stick to the policy. If the child runs out of money and begs for more, give a clear, friendly response: "You'll get your allowance on Saturday." We build expectations and consequences into the structure of family life so that we are not constantly nagging, pleading, or losing our temper.

BE AWARE OF THE POWER OF YOUR WORDS

Our mindful use of language and tone of voice is a reflection of our awareness, attunement, and warmheartedness. It is the song we sing to our child on a daily basis.

I have listened for more than thirty years as clients recount, often with tears and anger, the cutting words and actions that denigrated, shamed, humiliated, and belittled them when they were children. They have also talked of the confusion created by candy-coated words that appeared to be nice but really were intended to manipulate, bribe, and coerce them to do their parent's bidding. As one woman said, "Everything was coated with syrup. It all sounded nice, but it felt so awful most of the time. There always was an agenda or criticism underneath."

On the other hand, the positive descriptions from children and young adults I interviewed was repeatedly along the lines of: *They really listened. They didn't freak out. I knew I could go to them. They helped me figure things out.*

EXERCISE

Go through the following list on your own or with another person. You might want to write out answers if you do it alone. Take your time and go as deep as you can.

Part 1

1. How did your parents treat *each other* in terms of listening and understanding? Think of specific examples both positive and negative. How did it affect you at the time? How does it affect you now?

2. How did your parents treat *you* in terms of listening and understanding? Think of examples both positive and negative.

3. Describe positive interactions you've had with your child.

4. Describe negative interactions you've had with your child. Specifically recall critical, apologetic, nagging words and phrases you have used. What do you wish you had said or not said?

5. Imagine asking your child to tell you if you have been scary, shaming or left her feeling badly. What do you think she would say?

Part 2

1. Drop down inside. Imagine yourself as a newborn without any words in your mind or body. Then imagine how they

became conditioned into your head. What was said, done, not said, not done, or implied?

2. Imagine that you existed prior to taking on those words. Imagine how you would be today without them. (This concept is taken from a workshop on quantum consciousness by author Stephen Wolinsky.)

DEVELOPING EMPATHY FROM WITHIN: MAKE FRIENDS WITH YOURSELF

The first step to having empathy and compassion for yourself is to realize that your thoughts and behavior stem from your conditioning. They are not your essential spirit—the one energy, the flow of life that permeates everything.

Keeping this in mind, with a sense of friendliness toward yourself, remember how it feels to be scared, to whine, sulk, lie, be sneaky, get excited, be sad, depressed, lonely, or worried. Tap into the body sensations. Then go underneath these behaviors and think of the need or fear that motivated them—such as, I wanted to be noticed, cared for, feel important, feel loved, and so on. The more we can empathize with a child's behavior, the more we can be helpful and understanding instead of reactive and angry or frustrated.

ACTIVE LISTENING 101

I have worked with many parents on the basic skills of listening, and they are amazed at the differences they see in their child's reactions. Even if you can only slow yourself down and feel empathy fifteen or twenty-five percent of the time, you and your child will benefit.

The best way to calm a child is to meet him at his own emotional level. If he is upset, respond by saying, "Oh, you're upset." If the child is sad, respond by saying, "Oh, you seem sad."

Even if it feels strange, simpleminded, or silly, try making a simple empathetic remark and see what happens.

That's all you have to do most of the time. If parents are anxious about having feelings, they typically rush in to be reassuring—to give advice, lecture, and, well, "freak out." Reactions like this are more about the parent's ego and anxiety than about the child.

EXERCISES FOR EMPATHY

1. Put yourself in your child's shoes. If you're upset with your child's behavior, ask yourself, Why would I lie, tattle, make up stories, be afraid to go to school, or want to throw myself on the floor and scream? Remember a time you've done exactly that, or something similar.

2. After listening, you can show empathy by saying, "Yeah, I know, I have a hard time with that, too, like when people leave me out or when I feel I've messed up."

3. Ask open-ended questions, such as, "How was that for you?"

4. Help your child to problem-solve. Ask him, "Have you thought about what you might do about it? What might help you figure it out?" "What kind of help might you need?" This tells the child that you have faith in his ability to solve problems.

5. If your child is floundering, you might say, "I have some thoughts about that. Do you want to hear them?" If she says yes, say what you're thinking. If you get a "yes, but," back off.

6. Give advice as a last resort and be clear and honest when you do. Instead of "you should" sentences, you can say, "Here's what I'm thinking might work . . ."

7. Notice which responses work best for your child. Children are very different: some open up easily, others need more time, some are highly sensitive to criticism or even suggestions, while others relish your help.

8. Know when to say something, and when to let it be. If your child

is talking about a difficulty and tends to exaggerate and make a big deal out of daily events, listen and say very little. Think about what needs to happen so that your child feels more secure. If it is a chronic situation, you could address it directly: "Jamie, I'm aware that sometimes you add things to a story or say things that don't seem true." Then give a specific example. You could ask, "Do you have any idea why?" Or you could say, "I know when I've done something like that it's to get people to like me more."

MORE THOUGHTS ON EMPATHY

- Avoid repeated lectures. Kids will tune you out. Ask yourself, Has my lecture on this subject worked? Am I caught in my ego, trying to pressure my kid to be a certain way? What is this about for me?

- To sort out what belongs to you and what belongs to your child, I urge parents to go to Byron Katie's Web site, TheWork .com, and download the "Judge-Your-Neighbor Worksheet" and the accompanying material to help you work on yourself. It can help you question your judgments about your children. For example, she poses the following questions: Take a thought that is getting you riled up such as, My son should be getting better grades. Then ask yourself, "When you believe this thought, does it create peace or stress?" "When you believe this thought, whose business are you in?" "When you believe this thought, how do you treat others?" "How would your life be without this thought?"

- When you have something important to say, make sure you have the child's attention. Slow yourself down, make eye contact, and get down to her level. Speak slowly and see if you are getting a response.

- Don't make talking the center of your relationship. You want to have easy time, fun time. You don't want your child to think—*Oh, God, not another deep conversation*.

- Don't pry into feelings, invade a child's inner life or overanalyze. Kids reveal themselves when they feel safe, usually in a relaxed moment.

- It's often helpful to explain the rationale for family rules and why you do things a certain way. At the same time don't let your child get you on the defensive, rationalizing or overexplaining. That gives them too much power. You are the adult. You don't need to justify yourself. There are times when it's right to say, "That's what I've decided. End of discussion." Keep it simple, age-appropriate, firm, and as relaxed as possible.

- Notice the times when your child is most open to talking. For example, Carla waited up for her teenagers when they started dating. Carla said, "I'd be tired sometimes, but they were open to talking. I learned so much about what my children were going through in their lives during those special times."

- Schedule special times with your children. Another parent, Steve, regularly scheduled lunch dates with each of his kids. "It was a time to have a relaxed conversation, find out what was going on in their lives, and ask questions about their plans, such as how were they doing with their friends, how were they going to handle a particular situation, or what courses were they thinking of taking next semester."

GUIDELINES FOR WHAT TO AVOID WHEN TALKING WITH YOUR CHILD

There are some words and phrases that cut directly into the emotional memory of a child and create feelings of insecurity that can haunt your child, often for a lifetime. It is best to avoid them at all times.

1. Avoid saying anything that creates shame or cuts into the child's sense of worth (for example, "You're useless/worthless/more trouble than you're worth/ stupid").

2. Don't threaten abandonment or leave a child alone as a punishment. It strikes terror into a child's heart because you are the source of their life. It's sometimes tempting to say, "I'll leave you in the store if you don't stop it." But don't say it.

3. Be especially careful never to make hurtful statements such as, "I don't know why I ever had you kids," "My life would be so much better without you," or "I wish you had never been born." These are lethal to the self-esteem of children. In conducting deep therapy—including hypnotherapy—with individuals who have tenacious addictions or feel suicidal, I often find these beliefs buried at the core of their being. They can become a highly destructive part of a child's personality and can even lead to the belief that *I don't deserve to live.*

4. Avoid labels like "stupid," "smart," "good," "bad," "great," "fantastic," "loser," and so on. They set you up as the judge and create separation.

5. Any phrase that starts with "you" is likely to create distance between you and your child, such as, "You're ridiculous," "You silly girl," "You shouldn't have done that," or "You're so difficult."

6. Avoid dismissive responses such as, "Oh, you don't really feel that way," or, "I'm sure she didn't mean to hurt your feelings," or, "It will be better soon." These responses imply that your child shouldn't feel the way he feels and often result in children feeling ashamed of their inner experience.

7. Be mindful of your child's body language. If he appears to look down, look away, shut down, tap his fingers or feet, mumble, try to get away, consider what you said to him. You can name what happened. "I noticed you looked down when I just spoke. Did

I hurt your feelings? Is this feeling too heavy? Would you like to stop?"

8. Don't use physical force to get obedience or compliance, especially when you are triggered yourself—"You'll do what I say, damn it!" It's not helpful to make sudden moves out of anger or with a cold, angry face.

9. Remember, apologies are golden. You can apologize if you cross a line and say something hurtful out of anger or frustration. But this wears thin if it occurs repeatedly. When you apologize, don't grovel or say you're sorry out of guilt. This will often make a child feel worse.

EXERCISE: BREAKING HABITS, DEEPENING OUR AWARENESS

Every time we make a commitment to be more aware of ourselves and change our reactions into responses, we give our children two gifts. First, we are kinder and more understanding. Second, our child sees us as a parent who is growing and changing. The gift to ourselves is the increasing ease within and a more relaxed relationship with our children. Every shift in your behavior makes a difference.

PART 1: MEDITATION ON MAKING SMALL CHANGES

Meditation is being aware. Pick out one or two of the following responses or habits you'd like to change. Then, for several weeks or months, notice when you do them and check for the underlying need or feelings. Keep a daily journal.

1. Interrupting.
2. Contradicting: "You're not ugly. I didn't say that. You're not bad at math."

3. Correcting facts while the child is telling you about an event.
4. Asking for facts, times, and other details when a child is telling you about an experience. (This interrupts the flow, takes her from the spirit of the story into her head.)
5. Criticizing.
6. Repeating the same old lectures.
7. Scolding: "You should be ashamed of yourself."
8. Starting sentences with "You.": "You're silly. You're pushy. You're demanding."

PART 2: OBSERVATION, SELF-EXPLORATION

Notice when you do any of the above and also note your child's reaction to it. For self-exploration, keep a journal, using the following questions:

1. What was going on with me?
2. Was I anxious?
3. Did I feel defensive?
4. Do I have an underlying anger at my child?
5. Am I afraid of his feeling upset because I think it reflects on me?
6. What is it that I'm not accepting about my child? How do I want her to be different than she is?

A TALE OF TWO TRIPS TO THE DENTIST—WITH AND WITHOUT EMPATHY

1. *Without Empathy*

Mom: "It's time to get ready. We have to go to the dentist."
Dennis: (*Upset.*) "I don't want to go. My teeth are fine."

Mom: "Come on, you'll be okay." (*This statement lacks empathy. Mom is not responding to Dennis's fear, which creates shame about having those feelings.*)

Dennis: (*Starts crying.*) "It's gonna hurt."

Mom: "Oh, it won't hurt that much. Don't fuss." (*Mom doesn't tell the truth, or take Dennis's concern seriously. She is abrupt and hurried.*)

Dennis: (*Keeps crying.*)

Mom: "Don't be a baby. Be a big boy." (*Mom continues to shame Dennis for feeling the way he feels. She doesn't realize that her agitation is stirring up his fears. And besides, he is a little boy.*)

Dennis: "It is going to hurt." (*Cries louder. Dennis's fear has increased because he feels alone in the absence of understanding.*)

Mom: (*Angrily.*) "Dennis! Do you want to have your teeth rot and fall out like Aunt Harriet's? Then you'll have to have them pulled and get false teeth!" (*Mom is desperate, so she puts out dire threats to control the situation.*)

Dennis: (*Screaming.*) "I don't care! I don't want to go!" (*As Mother's agitation rises, so does Dennis's. He's feeling more alone and more afraid.*)

Mom: "You've got to go. There's no two ways about it." (*She tries to calm herself.*) "If you don't cry, I'll give you some money for a treat." (*She tries bribery to get him under control.*)

Dennis: "I don't care! I don't want to go!" (*Money is no compensation for the fear that is getting bigger every minute.*)

Mom: (*Frustrated.*) "Do you want a spanking?" (*As if any kid wants a spanking.*) "If you don't stop fussing, you're going to get one."

And on it goes. Escalation. No peace.

2. With Empathy

Mom: "Hey, Dennis, it's time to get ready to go to the dentist."

Dennis: (*Adamant.*) "I don't want to go. My teeth are fine!"

Mom: "I know, honey, it's a drag. I don't like going either." *(Mom validates Dennis's feelings and shows that she understands. She joins him and stays connected.)*

Dennis: "Why do I have to go?"

Mom: "The idea is to *keep* your teeth fine." *(This is a reasonable answer with a positive twist.)*

Dennis: "I still don't want to go."

Mom: "Yeah, I know. But it's just one of those things we do to stay healthy."

Dennis: "Is it going to hurt?"

Mom: "It does hurt sometimes, but today is just an exam and she'll poke around a little, but no shots." *(Mom tells the absolute truth.)*

Dennis: "Are you sure?"

Mom: "Yes, I'm sure. Here's your coat, honey. Oh, they may take X-rays too." *(Mom prepares him for what will happen, and moves the situation forward by handing him his coat.)*

Dennis: *(Takes the coat, and they head for the bus stop.)*

Mom: *(On the bus.)* "The name of your dentist is Susie Raintrope. You can call her Dr. Susie. She works with kids every day." *(Mom personalizes the experience by giving a name to the dentist to make it less likely that Dennis will be afraid of an unknown adult who can hurt him.)*

Mom and Dennis sit quietly on the bus looking out the window.

Dennis: "Mommy, what are X-rays?" *(Dennis is now getting interested in what is going to happen.)*

Mom: "It's like taking a picture of your teeth and gums so they can tell if there are any problems. They put a little piece of cardboard in your mouth and you have to hold it still for a few seconds."

Dennis: "Does it hurt?"

Mom: "It can be a little uncomfortable, but it doesn't hurt bad. And it's quick, and then you get to see the pictures of your teeth." (*Absolute truth, no extra words.*)

Dennis: "How do you know she'll show them to me?"

Mom: "I'll be right there and I'll make sure she does."

The conversation continues. The boy feels safe and protected by his mother.

Note that both mothers want the same thing for themselves and their child. They both care. They want a peaceful trip to the dentist and they want their child to have healthy teeth. The difference is a matter of skill and practice. Once a child starts screaming and the parent gets agitated in return, the tension often escalates. If a parent uses empathy from the start and remains calm, there's likely to be less agitation to manage.

> Listening in a relaxed way, and staying empathic, is soothing to a child and literally makes them more mature and intelligent. We all think better when we're relaxed.

"I UNDERSTAND": AN EXERCISE IN FORGIVENESS AND LETTING GO

"I understand" will help you deepen your self-acceptance, which will naturally extend to your child and all others in your life. It is a deeply healing exercise I have used for years in my practice.

In Buddhism, the way of transformation is to bring kindness and understanding to the parts of ourselves that have been selfish, unkind, or insensitive, and to become aware that we were asleep, unconscious or unaware. You can do the exercise with another person while one person reads aloud, taking time for you to go through the steps, or you can do it alone.

1. List one or more personal traits that feel troublesome or out of control. You can include past behavior that still brings up feelings of shame, guilt, hurt, or anger. These could include the habit of dishonesty, of being a doormat, of losing your temper, of being hard on your child, or of engaging in an addictive behavior. They might also include things like being bossy, interrupting, making bad decisions, selling yourself short, or not taking on new challenges. Bring up specific images or scenes that illustrate these traits.

2. For today, pick out one particular trait or scene that brings up physical and emotional discomfort. Take a discomfort reading from one to ten, with ten the worst discomfort you've ever felt. Take time to tune into your breathing and enter a relaxed state. Breathe into your heart area and remember to let the breath all the way out and to pause before inhaling again. Say to yourself several times: *I am willing to bring kindness to this part of myself.*

3. Bring up the image of the behavior or trait that disturbs you right now. Feel the sensations in your body and notice the thoughts in your mind. Take your time.

4. With your eyes closed, imagine seeing yourself engaging in the behavior that troubles you. You may appear at your current age, or you may drift back to yourself as a child. Look into the eyes and heart of that part of you and notice what you see: fear, anxiety, need, terror, hurt? How old were you when that behavior took root? Let that part of you know that you are here now, and you see into her.

5. Start by telling that part of yourself, *I understand. I understand why you did that.* Talk slowly, as if the words are arising from your heart. You may not consciously understand, but some part of you hears it. As you continue to say *I understand*, see what comes to mind. Expand on this by acknowledging that you understand why your behavior made sense at the time. For example:

> I understand why you drank so much as an adolescent. It's how you buried your pain about being abused.

> I understand why you get so quiet. It was how you avoided being shamed.

> I understand why you are always being good. You're afraid your mother or father might fall apart.

> I understand why you shoplifted. You were trying to give yourself something special after your father left.

> I understand why you ate so much. You were trying to fill up the loneliness.

> I understand your resentment of your child. It's hard to give more love than you were given.

Be aware that tears often arise when people give themselves understanding. It's a response to the heart opening. It is natural and healing.

Repeat the reasons why you understand until you start to feel a sense of compassion for yourself. If nothing comes, continue anyhow. Give yourself time.

Now say to yourself with all your heart, *I will never put you down for that again.* Then imagine how that would feel in your life, to never belittle, berate, or scold yourself for that behavior.

6. Ask the part of you that you are talking with, *Do you know it's the year 20——and I am now _____ years old? You are part of me and I am part of you.* Then look in that younger person's face and see what you see. Usually the part of you from the past does not know that there is a grown-up you. You can be reassuring. *Yes, we've made it out of that house. We're grown up now and can do what we want. We've come so far since then. I am here to take care of you.*
7. Then elicit your wise, adult self and say, *I understand why you did that, but now we are going to learn better ways to get what we need.*
8. Take a few moments to come out of the trance state, gently, quietly. Be with whatever happened and allow it to be absorbed.
9. At the time, and in the days that follow, write down all the things you can do differently to fulfill your need or longing without harming yourself or others. If you are in a group, talk about your experience with other group members.

"I UNDERSTAND" EXERCISE: SHORT VERSION

> *My religion is kindness*
> —THE DALAI LAMA

Whenever you start to scold, shame, or berate yourself, stop the momentum of self-harm by saying, *I understand. I understand. I was trying to fill a need for love, power, understanding, or to feel good.* (Or make up a phrase that works for you.)

Then breathe, exhale, and see what arises in terms of understanding.

This can also be helpful with your kids. Whenever they start to act up or become defiant, say to yourself, *I understand*. Then think of what would make you act that way. Hopefully, this will calm you down so you can be more effective in handling the situation.

This takes us away from any impulse to use punishment, which does not work for children, just as it does not work for adults. In watching numerous videos of the Dalai Lama, what is most compelling in his interactions with others is his openhearted friendliness. This is what draws people to him, and what draws our children to us.

11 | You Soothe Me, I Soothe Me

Helping Children Manage Their Feelings and Impulses

> Once the wave realizes that it is only water, that it is nothing but water . . . it has transcended all kinds of fear, and perfect Nirvana is the state of non-fear.
>
> —THICH NHAT HANH, THE HEART OF UNDERSTANDING:
> COMMENTARIES ON THE PRAJÑAPARAMITA HEART SUTRA

> The brain itself is social. . . . One person's inner state affects and drives the other person. We're forming brain-to-brain bridges— a two-way traffic system—all the time. We actually catch each other's emotions like a cold.
>
> —DANIEL GOLEMAN

....

Our actions play a huge part in creating the reactions we receive from children. Children are not a fixed entity; their brain development, and capacity for emotion, learning, and joy are all part of the dance we share together.

....

Self-Regulation and Compassion

As parents, we provide a wonderful gift for our children by helping them learn to have, recognize, contain, and manage their waves of emotions and feelings.

To understand emotional regulation, think of a scale from minus ten to plus ten, with zero being steady and calm. A person with a history of family chaos, yelling, and violence is likely to have much greater extremes and sudden reactions than someone from a relatively stable family. For example, a few words of criticism or disagreement and the person with a history of trauma might spike immediately to an eight—stress hormones are secreted and adrenaline starts pumping as if there is an emergency. The capacity to reason and make good judgments is severely compromised.

By contrast, for someone who is self-confident and comfortable with feelings, the reaction to the same situation might be a one or a two. The body stays calm, the person can think clearly and make reasoned decisions. In other words, it's not so much what happens in the world that affects us as adults, it's our interpretations and hardwired reactions to them that holds sway over our lives.

One could understand emotional self-regulation as having emotions that gently rise and fall, rather than spike and crash. In other words, we can have them, but they don't have us.

The Lifelong Benefits of Emotional Self-Regulation

We are more intelligent when we're relaxed. A well-regulated emotional system enhances our ability to learn, focus, concentrate, cooperate, and stay centered. It lays the foundation for seeing from a broad perspective, making informed decisions, and remaining levelheaded when we are criticized or others disagree with us.

This naturally extends to social skills that require the ability to listen, to be open to others, and to work together for the common good. A relaxed mind can quiet down, listen, ponder, and allow wisdom to arise.

SELF-REGULATION AND EMPATHY

Richard Davidson, a psychoneurologist, found in MRIs (magnetic resonance images) of monks who practice Buddhist compassion meditation that meditation created definite, lasting effects on the brain circuitry related to empathy. I would love to have seen these monks working in a child care center to see how they managed the strong emotions, needs, and conflicts of small children. My hunch is that their deep sense of delight in these young lives and their inner equanimity would have a calming effect on the children.

Self-regulation generates empathy and compassion, and thus is highly relevant to the creation of a more peaceful world.

A *Newsweek* article titled "Adventures in Good and Evil" (May 4, 2009) states that "People who are emotionally secure, who view life's problems as manageable and who feel safe and protected tend to show the greatest empathy for strangers and to act altruistically and compassionately." Various studies have found that emotional stability, trust, and security were highly related to compassion and to helping others. In the words of Phillip Shaver of the University of California at Davis:

"If only people could feel safer and less threatened, they would have more psychological resources to devote to noticing other people's suffering and doing something to alleviate it."

ADD AND ADHD

ADD (attention deficit disorder) or ADHD (attention-deficit hyperactivity disorder) are real, although I would call them a "condition" rather than a disorder because there are so many positive traits of people with this syndrome of behaviors. It is estimated that approximately seven percent of the population has some aspects of ADD or ADHD. While many people tend to overmedicate these conditions, others tend to dismiss them as behavior problems or lack of good parenting, which is not true.

ADHD is characterized by a constellation of behaviors that can include: inattentiveness, being easily distracted, lack of focus, difficulty reading, restlessness, fidgeting, blurting out remarks, acting impulsively, difficulty finishing projects, and excess nervous energy. The symptoms may vary from child to child. They can also include high energy, creativity, persistence, wildly creative thinking, warmheartedness, and generosity. As someone who has navigated through life with many of these symptoms, especially being extremely slow to process written material, I can testify to how important it is to name the condition and get help in the form of strategies and, sometimes, medication or lifestyle changes. Because I was finally diagnosed, I was granted double the allotted time to take my psychology boards, otherwise I never would have passed, and it would have meant a Ph.D. up in smoke. There are many strategies you can learn as parents to help kids with ADD or ADHD. The first is to realize it's a brain condition that can't be changed by admonishing a child to pay better attention or stop being messy or lazy. It's also important to become an ally to the child and not take their behavior personally. Another is to channel the enormous energy in useful ways. As we all know, one mother took her child with ADHD for swimming lessons, and he went on to win eight Olympic gold medals.

WHEN IT ONLY LOOKS LIKE ADD OR ADHD
Children who live with highly unregulated parents who explode, cry, are negligent, are extremely anxious, get moody, are unpredict-

able, and are emotionally distant often show symptoms that look like ADD or ADHD.

Although some children have a genetic predisposition for ADD and ADHD, in other children these symptoms appear not as a result of genetics but because no one has ever helped them learn to regulate their emotions. If a child has been exposed to constant TV, fast-moving violent movies or video games, and lacks the stabilizing benefits of parental involvement, good food, physical exercise, creative play, time outdoors, and the development of talents and interests, he may well appear to have ADD. If his home life is characterized by neglect, shouting, cursing, crying, and inconsistency, his internal world is likely to mirror the chaos around him. *Remember, it is primarily through interactions with parents that children learn to regulate their emotions.*

In schools, teachers often mistake a restless, distracted child as being ADD or ADHD when the child's behavior is actually a reaction to the material being too difficult, too easy, or too boring, or the lesson doesn't fit the child's learning style, or the child doesn't feel liked by the teacher or other students. In addition, it may be that a spirited, active child is not getting regular breaks and enough physical exercise. Before making a diagnosis it's important to get a profile of the child's life that includes all of the above concerns.

BILLY BECOMES A "GOOD" STUDENT

This brings me back to Billy, my grandson, whom I spoke about in the Prologue. After his mother died, a new person entered his father's life. She heard Billy screaming in the night about killing people—something he often did while playing his video games (simulated killing, that is). This led to a dramatic change in the household. All the violent videos were removed, the TV was only turned on for certain programs, and the caffeine-and-sugar-laden Mountain Dew disappeared. The family instituted a game night, and Billy was given a regular bedtime in his own bed and a laundry basket for his clothes. Order replaced chaos and homework became a priority.

When I visited a few months after these changes, Billy was more relaxed, patient, and better able to concentrate than I had ever seen him. He went from being a below average student to a very good student, but more importantly, he felt better about himself. We sat together in the car in the rain listening to Louis Armstrong sing "What a Wonderful World" while we chatted away, waiting for his school bus. He talked about how good it felt to be on top of his schoolwork, to have more order in his life. And, by the way, the strategies that worked for Billy can be invaluable for all kids whether or not they have ADD or ADHD.

Anger, Rage, Fear and Grief: Make Friends with Them All

....

In this section I include more extensive ways for parents to make friends with all emotions, including happiness and joy. This is key to helping children be able to self-regulate—that is, to both have and contain strong feelings. What we want to avoid is emotional dysregulation, where emotions are either buried or out of control.

....

Separate anger from rage. Anger often signals that someone is invading your territory, verbally, physically, or emotionally. The reaction, whether spoken or not, is generally, "Stop. Back off. That's not okay." Rage, by contrast, is when a person taps into their shame and blows up, spewing blame and wrath on other people rather than reflecting on himself. Rage is not useful, effective, or helpful in relationships. Parents who explode with rage are wise to get help.

Anger often signals an unmet need: *I want you to care, to listen, to notice me.*

I remember as a teenager bursting out at my parents with, "Why can't I be upset? What's wrong with that?" I hated my father's persistent *ssshhh* whenever I raised my voice or got upset. I desperately wanted to be heard and know that my feelings were okay.

There are long-lasting effects to emotional dysregulation—that is, emotions that go out of control. For example, people who were traumatized in childhood often become highly attuned to the slightest hint of anger because it triggers physical memories of violence—stress hormones are secreted, breathing gets shallow, muscles tighten, and the body tenses for fight, flight, or freeze. In other words, a slightly raised voice can be experienced as a dire threat.

One time in a therapy group with survivors of profound abuse, a woman began criticizing aspects of my personal life. She was crossing a line and I said so. She persisted. Our voices got intense and I tapped my fingers on the floor as I said strongly, "You get to question anything I say or do when I'm in this group, but you don't get to tell me how to live my life." Shortly after that the conversation stopped abruptly, followed by a highly charged silence. I had never been that angry in a group and worried that everyone might be scared and leave. I turned to the group, took a deep breath, and said, "Okay, what's going on with everybody?" There was a long pause.

"That was wonderful!" a woman said with an elated look on her face. "You were both *really* mad but you never called names and no one got a black eye or a bloody nose." In her thirty-eight years of life, she had never seen anger contained. It had always exploded into rage and physical harm.

REGULATING ANGER: SOME QUESTIONS TO EXPLORE:

1. How was anger expressed in your family?
2. Did you get punished, scolded, or put down for expressing your opinions, especially if they were different from those of your parents?
3. What happens in your body when you start to feel angry?
4. What thoughts generally trigger your anger?
5. Can you go underneath your anger and find an unmet need? Did someone forget about you? Did you feel hurt? Misunderstood? Unfairly treated?
6. Do you bury your anger? Do you shut down, act friendly, mumble, and try to ignore it? Does your anger sometimes explode? Does it lead to excess use of alcohol, other drugs, food, or come out in physical symptoms?
7. What's the angriest you've ever been?
8. Does your anger come out in sarcasm? Harsh remarks? Digs?
9. How would you describe your ability to remain nondefensive in the face of criticism or someone else's anger?
10. How do you and your partner (or close friends) handle anger or frustration? What is the model you set for your children?

MAKE FRIENDS WITH FEAR

While we want children to be courageous and strong, it need not be at the expense of expressing their fears.

This is especially important for little boys, who are taught to be tough and deny fear, which often results in feeling alone, ashamed, or angry. To express fear and have someone hear you is to feel connected, validated, and safe. We all have fears; we just have to learn how to manage them.

Some people are brought up to squelch their fear. Other people are paralyzed by it. The thought, *I'm afraid*, translates to, *I can't do it. It's too much for me.* It's incredibly helpful when parents show children that you can do something even though you're afraid.

There is usually an inverse ratio between fear of trying something new and excitement. At first, the fear is high and the excitement is low. *However, the more we try new experiences and live through them, the more our fear subsides and our excitement rises at the prospect of a new challenge.*

....

Effort and determination to take on challenges and move through fear builds confidence and core strength in children.

....

PARENTS CAN HELP NORMALIZE FEAR

Casually mention fear when it arises. A mom can tell her child that she has fears about going back to school after working for so long. Yet she still goes. She then can relate that it's not so hard after all. She can say she's nervous about talking with her boss, and then tell her child how it went. Parents—yes, this includes fathers—can tell stories of when they were afraid but kept trying and eventually succeeded. The idea is to help children repeatedly take action even though they are afraid.

One mother told a story about her teenage son applying for his first job at a local store. When he told her how nervous he was, she replied, "That makes sense. You've never done this before. I get afraid, too, when I'm doing something new." Instead of becoming a cheerleading team—*You'll do great!*—she met him at his emotional level and normalized his fear. She wandered around the front of the store until he emerged from the interview, and his face lit up. "He hired me on the spot."

I've spoken with seasoned classical musicians who get nervous before every performance, but they perform well because they have practiced diligently and have a long history of performing well.

Just as musicians practice in order to play well, parents can educate children to be safe instead of afraid. *Here's how we cross the street. We watch the light, look for cars turning the corner, and we walk pretty fast, but we don't run. Let's try it together, then see if you can do it on your own.*

....

When we take situations apart and teach skills step-by-step, we help children replace fear with competence and knowledge.

....

Avoid an automatic "no." Consider saying, "Have a good time." It's like a vote of confidence. Many children want to ride their bike alone to the store, hike in the woods, or go downtown with a friend, Instead of giving an automatic "no" to spirited, adventuresome children, parents can ask relevant questions to see if the child is prepared. Then, whenever possible, say "Yes!"

DON'T LIMIT HAPPINESS AND JOY

Just as parents become containers for children's anger and fears, they need to be open to expansive feelings of joy.

Some parents feel uncomfortable with a child's effervescence and big spirit. A man I interviewed told me how his parents repeatedly squashed his feelings of joy. "If I got excited, really happy about a new discovery or something that had happened to me, I'd get this bland, 'That's nice, dear,' kind of response, as if they were trying to calm me down, or as if I were too much for them. On the other hand, my Aunt Lou would smile, ask questions, laugh, say, '*That's wonderful,*' and make me feel good. She was playful and encouraging."

I spent fifteen years living in what I called stoic land—Minnesota, the land of Scandinavian and German descent. I often had the sense that my feelings were too big, my happiness too expansive, and, well, that it was practically rude to have a strong opinion about anything. It was always a relief to visit New York City, where I immediately felt that I fit in.

One time when I was visiting a family in Minnesota, the teenage son burst into the room with a huge grin. "I really nailed it today in our baseball game," he said. He was reveling in his expansive feelings. But his joy evaporated when his mother quickly said, "Now don't get a big head." I wonder if the mother noticed the change in her child's face and the way his body slumped as he left the room.

HELP CHILDREN ACCEPT SADNESS AND GRIEF

Some parents have learned to be stoic or tough and believe that crying is a sign of weakness or being a baby—especially for boys. They may make comments such as "Grow up," the proverbial "Big boys don't cry," or, "Stop crying or I'll give you something to cry about." Or the comments may be more subtle: "Come on, it's not that big a deal. You'll be okay," or "It's not that important. You'll get over it."

....

With regard to creating peace, when we push boys to think that tough, strong, and dominant are manly qualities and that tears, feeling hurt, and thoughtfulness are girlish—meaning negative—we also push them toward aggressive behavior and disrespect for women.

....

When children have no language for their more vulnerable feelings, they often get channeled into anger or aggression. Schools, religious organizations, and community programs could make a huge difference if they took an in-depth, searching inventory of the ways they push both boys and girls to deny huge parts of their emotional capacity in order to fit into stereotypical male or female roles.

It's okay to let your child know you are sad, or to see you cry or experience grief. You don't want to overwhelm a small child with uncontrolled grief, but you can let them see your tears, so long as you say, "It's okay, I'm just sad. I'll be all right."

As children learn to identify their inner experience—*I'm feeling sad, angry, scared, disappointed*—they gain mastery over the landscape of their emotions. Naming feelings gives children a language that permeates every aspect of their lives and positively affects their ability to learn, concentrate, focus, and be at ease in relationships. It also teaches them to say, *I want, I would like*, and *I need*.

The less we fear our inner experience—anger, hurt, shame, pain, need, sadness, confusion—the more at home we feel in our emotional and physical bodies. It's a language for seeing deeply into ourselves and others, and contributes to living at peace because it takes us away from fear.

ASK CHILDREN FOR THEIR OPINIONS

This may seem like a strange section to have in a chapter on handling emotions, but when we create a family life where children feel valued, understood and regarded as intelligent, we naturally foster emotional regulation. A wonderful way to do this is to ask your children's opinions on various topics, including questions of right and wrong.

For example, when you read an article in the paper about a court case involving an ethical question you could ask your child, "What would you do if you were the judge?" You might ask a young child to tell you about a favorite teacher, and what makes him special.

My father frequently posed questions that made me feel deeply respected. When we were moving from Missoula to Ann Arbor, my parents decided to sell our house "By Owner." A friend from church called and said he knew some people who were interested. The people eventually bought the house and the friend, who happened to be a realtor, asked my father for a commission. My dad told us about the situation and asked, "What would you do? I didn't hire him, I thought he came to me as a friend." This led to a great discussion between him and us three older kids. I loved that he wanted our opinions. A few days later he said he had agreed to split the commission with the man.

When I questioned why he'd decided to pay him since he didn't hire him, he gave me a wonderful reply. "I know I don't have to, but he's been a friend, it makes it easy for us, and I like the people who are buying the house." Most important, he went on to say, "It's not always about sticking to one's guns. I thought it over and it felt right to me."

There was so much wisdom in his answer: Namely, there are many sides to every situation, it's good to stay on friendly terms with others, you shouldn't always feel bound to follow the letter of the law, and it's good to base a decision on what feels right.

AVOID A THOUSAND NO'S

No! Stop! Don't do that! Watch out! That's bad. You can't. A *Redbook* article on parenting said that parents say "no" to toddlers up to four hundred times a day. Reflect on yourself. How would it feel if people repeatedly said to you in an irritated way, "No. That's wrong! Don't do that! Stop! No, you can't!"

The shift from endless no's to friendly diversions and alternative suggestions is like changing the radio station from loud harsh music to something relaxed and fun. An abrupt "no" is like a door being slammed. As a parent, the more you find alternatives to "no," the more harmonious the atmosphere in your home will be.

ALTERNATIVES TO SAYING NO

There are many alternatives to saying no by which you can make the point and still set limits for a child.

1. Distract small children. If your little child is trying to pull off your glasses, pick up another object and say, "Look at this." You don't need to say no; just shift attention to something else.

2. Keep objects out of reach that you don't want the child to touch. Put covers over outlets and clear off tables when you have exploratory toddlers.

3. Try not to scream when they start playing with the controls on the stereo system or something they're not supposed to touch. Pick them up, and validate their interest: "Those knobs are really interesting. I like turning them, too. But, sweetheart, they aren't for kids. Here's something you can play with that also has dials to turn." Then put the stereo out of reach.

4. Go from "No" to "Yes, when." Instead of "No, I'm too busy," you can say, "Yes, I'd love to, as soon as I finish writing this letter." Instead of no to inviting her friend over, say, "Yes, after you get your room cleaned up," or "Yes, after you've had a nap." A time limit will feel manageable to a child. Instead of "No, I won't buy that toy, those designer jeans, or that expensive iPod," you might say, "That's not something I feel inclined to buy, but maybe you can figure out a way to earn the money or find it used or on eBay. I'd be willing to help you find some work around the house and I'll contribute what I would have spent on a less expensive one."

The kindly, unspoken message is, Kiddo, you've got to *earn* luxury. This also teaches delayed gratification: you can't always have what you want when you want it.

....

An overblown sense of entitlement is counter to making peace in the world. It reduces our capacity for empathy by putting the focus on "what I want." We mistakenly measure our happiness by acquiring things instead of deepening our connections with others.

....

5. If you have household policies, stick to them and don't back down. "The policy is that you can't go to a movie on weeknights.

I won't change my mind, so please stop asking." Use the broken record technique. "I hear you and the answer is still no." End of conversation. Don't allow the child to engage you in explanations or a long conversation. You don't want to encourage whining and nagging. Remember, you are helping him learn to regulate his impulses and attachments: "No, I can't afford that." "No, I can't go out tonight, I need to do my homework."

6. Childhood development includes children testing their parents. It's about power and a need to know the limits. It's easy for a parent to feel triggered when a little child smiles with that smirk that says, "I'm going to do what you told me not to do." It's like a dare. Don't take it personally and don't react. Swoop up the child, laugh, or distract. If the child get's you to react or blow up, it gives him far too much power. If you stay calm, set a limit, or use humor, you stay in control.

EXERCISE 1: CALM PARENTS, CALM CHILDREN

Here are some phrases to say to yourself when you start to feel reactive/upset/angry/punishing around your child. Don't forget that the first step is always to take a deep breath and exhale fully.

1. I'm the parent, she is the child.
2. It's my job to be older and wiser.
3. I'm triggered (I want to get back, retaliate, teach him a lesson, punish). I need to calm down and not do any of these things.
4. I'm reacting like a kid.
5. Slow down. Don't react. There are other ways to handle this.
6 This too shall pass.
7. If I can calm down, it will help him calm down.
8. Find a phrase that is soothing to you and say it repeatedly.

When my daughter was in trouble as a teen I must have said, "The Lord is my shepherd, I shall not want" a million times. For me it meant, I shall not want anything to be different than it is. I accept what is. It helped me tap into the vastness of time and be aware that this was just a passing drama. What phrase or thought might work for you?

EXERCISE 2: A PRACTICE FOR STAYING CALM

Because we tend to forget all the techniques we know in the moment when we're triggered, we need to practice apart from the situation.

1. Bring up a recent situation in which you got reactive/upset. Feel the upset in your body.
2. Take a stress reading—give yourself a rating from one (low) to ten (high).
3. Use one or more of the phrases in Exercise 1 above, or one of your own along with taking gentle deep breaths.
4. Replay the scene. What is your response now?
5. What is your stress level now?
6. Practice, practice, practice. To change an automatic reaction, continue to practice on a daily basis. You are slowly grooving a new reaction into your brain. It takes time. (Also see the information on EFT—the Emotional Freedom Technique—in the Resources section.)

REMEMBER THE BUDDHIST BLESSING

Throughout the day say a version of the Buddhist blessing: *May all children be happy, may all parents be happy. May I be happy! May I learn to calm down!* Add your own words as you imagine the energy of your blessing going out to people around the world.

I2 Upset Prevention for You and Your Child

We have been talking about empathy and understanding, and helping children self-regulate. This chapter describes small, commonsense actions and routines we can use on a daily basis to foster a sense of well-being that helps prevent upsets. This chapter reflects the daily care and devotion I found in families where there was generally a sense of harmony and kindness toward one another.

Remember that the circuitry in the brain is dynamic, interconnected, and affected by our actions and emotions. When there is a steady stream of stability, connection, kindness, and fun, we are deeply affecting a child's brain and emotions.

As an example, I still have a pleasant memory of being three or four years old, riding in the grocery cart and enjoying my little box of animal crackers. I felt a deep sense of contentment as my mother smiled at people, chatted with the grocer, and carefully looked at the vegetables and fruits, mumbling to herself about the prices. I knew when we went to the store I'd get my animal crackers and I always looked forward to going up and down the aisles seeing all the colors and shapes. That sense of contentment is still with me when I go to a grocery store, reflecting the power of a parent's small consistent actions and pleasant countenance.

1. Have regular rituals in your home, especially with young children. This includes eating, reading, bedtime stories, helping with chores, and talking about the day. These routines provide connection points your child can count on. They also provide consistency. You don't discuss bedtime, helping set the table, or Saturday morning chores. This is the routine and that's it. It doesn't have to be one hundred percent rigid, but it does need to have a relaxed consistency. There can be exceptions for special occasions.

2. Make sure your child has had enough to eat throughout the day, to keep her blood sugar stable. This includes taking stabilizing snacks if you are going to be out for a long time—whole wheat crackers, fruit, cheese.

3. If your young child seems stressed or is reaching out to you, pick her up so she feels safe again. Touch is calming. When parents react with indifference or irritation to a stressed toddler, she usually gets more distressed. (Think of what you need as an adult when you feel stressed.)

4. Keep your word. If you said you would take your child to a friend's house at 3:00 P.M., be on time. Don't keep your child waiting while you talk on the phone or straighten up the kitchen. If you have to be late, tell your child in advance and keep the next agreement.

5. Give your child as much freedom as possible to explore, move around, and be active. Even when shopping, allow the child (with clean hands) to touch things that are safe. I remember watching a little girl touching soft fabric in a yard goods store with a look of deep pleasure, until her mother screamed, "Don't touch that! Don't touch anything!" as if she had set off a bomb. We need to help children understand that some things are okay to touch, and other things are off-limits. Kids can do limited exploration. Just make sure they're being respectful of others.

6. Limit sweets or cut them out altogether. Children often get upset because they are in withdrawal from sugar. The same goes for caffeine. Find treats that don't create withdrawal or cravings.

7. Make sure your child has enough sleep and quiet time. More and more children (and parents) are living with a lack of sufficient sleep. The consequences are huge for health, mental capacity, and emotional stability.

8. Don't drag your child around on long shopping trips or stay too long in museums or anyplace that results in exhaustion or irritability. Take breaks, keep excursions short and sweet, and look for early signs of fatigue in little children. Don't wait until there is a meltdown. My beloved grandmother frequently took me to museums as a young child of five or six. She had a great sense of when to take a break. We'd sit down together and she'd pull a book out of her purse and read to me or go to the cafeteria for something to eat. I don't remember ever getting tired or bored.

9. Make sure your child gets physical exercise on a regular basis. Playtime outside is preferable: throwing a ball, running, playing hopscotch, tag, and other sports, including unstructured play with friends. This is preparation for developing a healthy lifelong habit of regular exercise.

10. For very young children, limit screen time, loud noise, constant music, or constant agitation in the household. Find some of the old Woody Guthrie or Burl Ives children's songs to play. Whatever you buy, listen to them to make sure they are not agitated and overly stimulating, especially for toddlers and very young children.

11. Provide age-appropriate blocks, construction sets, weaving materials, art supplies, cloth to drape over chairs or make hideouts, latch hooks, wood scraps, things that can be taken apart, and other things that lead to creative play and the development of dexterity and fine motor coordination. They engage your child's

mind and body and help them feel satisfied, competent, and relaxed.

12. Play games with your child such as concentration, checkers, or store. Shift to more challenging games as the child develops. Also allow time for children to play on their own, and encourage independent interests. Some families have a game night once a week.

13. Stick to the limits. At bedtime, for example, read a story, say good night, and if the child gets up, silently put him back in bed. It's normal for children to occasionally test you by pushing the limits. Respond by quietly sticking to the limit—no lectures. There are also times to negotiate a new limit—such as a new bedtime, bigger allowance, and so on, but not as a response to whining or throwing a tantrum.

While the above list might appear daunting at first, upset prevention takes less time and effort in the long run than being preoccupied and distant. Most of all, it keeps you close and connected to your child. And remember, you don't have to do it perfectly— a pretty good job will do a great deal to bring a warmth and friendliness to your household and relationships.

13 The Amazing Sounds of Silence

Helping Children Live out of Their "Knowing Place"

> Mohammed's son pores over words, and points out this
> and that, but if his chest is not soaked dark with love,
> then what? The Yogi comes along in his famous orange.
> But if inside he is colorless, then what?
>
> Kabir says: Every instant that the sun is risen, if I stand in
> the temple or on a balcony, in the hot fields, or in a walled
> garden, my own Lord is making love with me.
>
> —KABIR 42, FROM *THE KABIR BOOK*, VERSIONS BY ROBERT BLY

*W*hen we go to our graves we will value the times when our
hearts were soaked dark with love, when we stood in an open field
warmed by the sun, a soft breeze caressing our face, or when we
gazed into the eyes of a tiny child, a friend or lover, who looked back
at us with a smile of delight. In these wordless moments, we sink
deeper into our hearts, and "know" the essence of life.

In *Daughters of Copper Woman*, a Native American creation story
by Anne Cameron, people speak of the "Knowing place." It's the
place beyond words where body, mind, and spirit flow together. Our

senses are alive and receptive, and our body knows how to react without thinking. This often happens when playing music or sports, making love, or spending relaxed time with someone who is dear to us.

In Buddhist terms, we are in the present moment, the place of simply *being*.

Young children naturally live in the present guided by their sensory awareness. They feel drawn to an object, they touch it, smell it, put it in their mouth. They don't think, *I see that red block, I am now crawling over to it, I am now picking it up and putting it in my mouth.*

> *Is there enough silence for the word to be heard?*
> —QUOTE AT THE TOP OF THE *FRIENDS OF SILENCE* NEWSLETTER

What do we want our children to hear? Think of the song of a bird, the crunch of fallen leaves under foot, the purring of a kitten, the silence of clouds moving across the sky. Think of the subtle qualities of art, music, writing, and sports that elicit feelings of motion, space, awe, and wonder. The more we feel stillness in the midst of motion, the more we experience being connected, engaged, "in the zone." Think of the solutions that come to our minds effortlessly when we step back from thinking and allow answers to rise up from our knowing place. *Silence and knowing flow together.*

....

As parents it is our job to be present, yet also to get out of the way and allow our children to find their inner voice, their core self.

....

For many parents, getting out of the way means biting their tongue, holding themselves back, taking lots of deep breaths, and possibly having a phrase to say to themselves, such as, "Whose problem is this?", "It's not do or die," or "May all parents find patience."

Trusting silence and trusting children to act out of their knowing place is about surrender as opposed to control. It's about not forcing children to make up reasons and stories about why they want to do something. The reason closest to the truth is usually as simple as, "because I want to," and sometimes that's all that matters.

To help children flow from their natural selves, allow them the freedom to play, create, invent, babble, build towers with blocks, dance with scarves, make up games, put on little plays, and make rhythm instruments with sticks and pans. Children can often entertain themselves for hours if we allow them to follow their instincts, play freely, and get dirty. Of course there are limits. You're not obliged to have mud in your living room or paint spilled on your rug, but the more tolerance you have for disorder, the more your child will explore his own spontaneous world. You can also provide a place for a mess, if possible.

Trust in evolution and remember that you don't always need to teach, demonstrate, suggest, or do anything. Just provide the raw materials and be a friendly presence.

The more children learn to love life on their own, the greater the capacity they will have for entertaining themselves, being creative, and living life without boredom. Just check in occasionally, and take pleasure in the wonder of your creative child. If you do participate, offer but don't insist, or let it be when you get cues from your child that she wants you to join her.

ELEVEN MILLION BITS OF INFORMATION A SECOND: THE UNCONSCIOUS FLOW

According to Tor Nørretranders in *The User Illusion*, the impulse and the decision to do something occurs internally before the thought reaches the mind. You look at a row of different flavors of ice cream and out come the words, "I'd like mint chocolate chip." Any attempt to explain why would require you to make up a story. Try to answer the question, Why are you wearing what you are wearing right now? It's difficult to put these impulses into words. Your preference simply reflects your knowing place or your basic nature, or, sadly for some, your conditioning—I *should* wear that, eat that, say that. Notice if your mind gravitates toward making up a story to explain what you are wearing, then notice how it feels to say, because I felt like it.

RECOGNIZING YOUR BASIC NATURE

To bring up a child free from arbitrary censors and critics is to allow her the flow of her basic nature or "knowing place."

Children synthesize millions of bits of unconscious information that lead them to pick out a red bike, the light blue jeans, the mystery book, or decide to see a particular friend. Imagine that all these little decisions *matter* in terms of their life flow.

Recently I spoke with a friend who plays the flute. "I could never imagine playing an instrument where I didn't use my breath," she said. By contrast, as a child when I tried to play a flute or clarinet I found trying to blow into an instrument completely frustrating. I knew by age four I wanted to play the piano. We were both expressing our basic nature. There's no explanation beyond that.

In raising children, you can foster a clear sense of who they are when you let them find their basic nature. This is best done without interjecting your will unnecessarily, but instead by encouraging them to develop a clear mind for exploration and creativity, unhampered by excessive *should*s, *must*s, and *can't*s.

This doesn't mean that we treat children as if they are fragile or give in to their every whim. It's about allowing them control over a multitude of small decisions that helps them find out who they are. We can still say "It's time to set the table, turn off the computer, go to bed, or come with the family on a picnic."

DON'T CONFUSE YOUR CHILD'S "KNOWING PLACE"

Andy, age ten, wakes up on Saturday morning with the thought *I want to play with my friend Charlie.* He remembers how much fun they had the last time they played together. This idea is the result of the millions of bits of information converging in Andy's mind. But, because his parents prefer that he play with Jim, whom they regard as a better student and thus a better influence, they start cajoling Andy to change his mind.

His mother contradicts his impulse. "You haven't seen Jim in a long time. He sure is a nice kid. I saw his mother a few days ago and she said Jim was hoping to see you."

She is throwing words and thoughts into Andy's knowing place. This creates confusion: now Andy has to manage the clutter of his mother's words competing for air time with his own desires.

This overt manipulation puts Andy in a no-win situation. If he goes along with his mom's wishes, he goes against himself. If he stays true to himself, he feels guilty and afraid of losing her approval. If this happens repeatedly, it can result in a lifelong anxiety about making decisions. He will always feel the conflict, "Do I please myself, or do I please other people?"

....

It is important for parents to notice their motivation and ask themselves, "What's my real agenda? Is it for me or my child?"

....

If Andy's parents were completely honest and spoke their minds, they would say something like this: "We'd rather you not play with a kid who is average in school. We want you to play with Jim because he gets very good grades and we're hoping he would influence you to work harder. And his family has better standing in the community. In other words, we want you to be more like Jim."

Of course, most parents don't want to talk like this because they can hear how undermining it is. They would rather hide from their judgments by saying, "We're thinking of Andy's best interests." The unfortunate result of these covert agendas is that, one way or another, they often cause the child to believe his parents are disappointed in him—that he's never good enough.

QUESTIONS FOR PARENTS. DROP INTO YOUR SILENCE AND HEAR DEEPLY INTO YOURSELF.

1. Notice when you give hints. What would you say if you were open and direct?
2. What's motivating your frequent "suggestions"? What is your underlying agenda?
3. Do you want your child to excel in order to show your own parents that you did a good job raising him?
4. Is your self-esteem or sense of well-being tied to your child's performance, popularity, or image?

Dropping hints and urging a child to go in a certain direction may seem benign, but over weeks, months, and years, constantly questioning a child's wishes undermines his self-confidence and sows confusion, stress, guilt, and often anger that creates distance between the child and the parents. This is not to say that you don't encourage diligence, hard work, and developing one's talents, but you let the interests or direction in which these efforts are made belong to the child. And if you have something to say, be direct. "We'd like you to bring your grades up, and we're concerned." Even then, it might be better to say, "We notice your grades are slipping. What do you think is going on?"

It all comes back to the Buddhist concept that we create our own suffering through our demands that people be different than they are. As parents we create suffering in our children by thwarting their basic nature and trying to mold them into an image instead of getting to know them.

HELP CHILDREN THINK ABOUT ETHICAL QUESTIONS

Here's a situation where the silence of two mothers' egos helped their daughters solve an ethical dilemma and also fostered tolerance and understanding.

Mary and Jessie, both mothers of second-graders, shared an apartment. A neighbor child, Sandy, often came over to play with the girls until Sandy's mother, Darlene, found out that Mary and Jessie were lesbians. Darlene said that Sandy could no longer play at their home, although the girls could come play at her house. What to do?

Mary and Jessie sat down with their daughters, Maya and Ruth, and explained the situation. It led to lots of questions and a discussion of fear and prejudice. Neither of the moms put Darlene down or said she was wrong. Nor did they tell their daughters what they should do.

The girls both thought it was stupid of Sandy's mom, but after mulling it over for a day, they decided they would still go to Sandy's house because it was fun and they liked Sandy. A couple weeks later, Maya blurted out to Sandy's mom, "Why don't you like our moms?" Darlene got red in the face and looked extremely uncomfortable. The visits dwindled away after that; Maya and Ruth made the decision themselves. These wise mothers allowed their daughters to weigh the questions, live them out, and come to their own decisions at the age of seven. They did not make anyone out to be bad or wrong, and helped their daughters understand the irrational nature of prejudice.

....

Young children are capable of making important decisions when left free to think issues over for themselves, especially when parents step back and stay neutral.

....

SILENCE AS PART OF FAMILY LIFE

Silence isn't just turning off the TV or cell phone and not talking. Think of silence as stillness, a relaxed body and mind, a state that allows us to listen for our center, our Knowing place. Constant noise and stimulation pull our focus away from ourselves and keep us on the surface of our lives, while quiet allows us to go inside and find out who we are.

Silence is also what gives life to sound. Just as music is a dance of silence and sound, we can listen more consciously after a time of quiet. When we're going to pitch in and clean up the house we can put on lively music to energize us. When we want to rest, we can have something soothing, and then, for a while, we can return to quietness so that we can listen to ourselves.

Parents help by creating an atmosphere in which a child can feel safe and comfortable with silence or without background noise. They may need to begin with themselves.

Buddhism teaches you to give up some little habit or dependency to find out more about yourself. The point is to notice what comes up for you when you take a break from TV, alcohol, excess shopping, overwork, texting, new clothes, caffeine, or long periods of time on the Internet.

Many people experience something akin to withdrawal. They feel jumpy inside—nervous and restless. You may feel an urge to eat, or a need to call someone or check your e-mail. Painful thoughts and memories that have been drowned out by constant stimulation sometimes arise. As with any skill, it takes practice to relax into silence and stillness. It takes a willingness to be with whatever arises in the silence.

As you get more comfortable with stillness, it can feel like passing into a depth of peace and pleasure that feels new. You hear the intricacies of a piece of music, see the exquisite petals of a flower, savor the taste of food, or feel the joy of having a heart-to-heart conversation with someone dear to you.

Try to build quiet times into the family's schedule by limiting TV viewing, having days off from texting, or designating a time when everyone sits in the living room together quietly, perhaps reading or writing in a journal. It's not about asking children to "do nothing," it's about helping them develop an ability to focus and quiet down.

On my family's summer camping trips, we had a tradition of setting aside an hour after lunch when we were all to be quiet. We could sit in a camp chair or lie on a cot and read, embroider, carve, write, or sleep. One time, as I began to feel drowsy while lying on a cot I closed my book and gradually became aware of the sounds around me—squirrels, birds, bugs, the wind in the pines. As these layers of sounds crept into my hearing range it was as if they crept into me, the presence of nature mingled together with my presence. That lovely experience was made possible by my parents setting a time for quiet. And more than fifty years later this experience is still with me. I love to stand completely still in the woods and listen for a long time.

Silence is the breath, the source, the beginning and the end. It's the pause between notes, the sleep between our days, the stillness in our being that gives meaning to the music, harmony, and rhythm of our lives. It provides the possibility of a heart soaked dark with love. Give this gift to your children.

Afterthought on Silence

If you feel so moved, subscribe to the *Friends of Silence* newsletter, which features a lot of great quotations on silence. Just reading it is an experience of calm. Send a donation of $10.00 or more to Friends of Silence, 11 Cardiff Lane, Hannibal, MO 63401, or check out friendsofsilence.net.

14   If the Buddha Taught School

May all people have access to education.
—AN ADAPTATION OF THE BUDDHIST BLESSING

Education is life itself.
—JOHN DEWEY

My hope is to inspire parents, teachers, caregivers, and policy makers to become a voice in bringing education up to the ideals put forth more than a century ago by John Dewey and other progressive educators. They envisioned a democratic education that prepared children to contribute to society and learn from real-life experiences. This approach is echoed in what we call progressive education—it supports creativity, originality, a love of learning, and real-life learning situations. Children are helped to learn in their way, at their pace. Shaming and humiliating students is totally counter to this approach to education, and many do not focus on grades or testing, although children often do very well on standardized tests. The focus is on cooperation, working together, and respect for each other—the underpinning of peaceful relationships.

....

One of the structures of our society that stands in the way of raising children to make peace in the world is our system of education. Overall it is racist, sexist, culture-bound, and classist. It perpetuates inequality.

....

> *What is true of every member of the society, individually, is true of them all collectively; since the rights of the whole can be no more than the sum of the rights of the individuals.*
>
> —THOMAS JEFFERSON TO JAMES MADISON, 1789

Education for All: What Will It Take?

Buddhism reminds us that we are all interconnected, which means that the well-being of each of us is tied to the well-being of all of us. In other words, everyone needs to be given access to education—young, old, rich, poor, girls and boys, people of all nationalities, incarcerated and homeless people—anyone who can be lifted up through learning. When everyone is included, it's like weaving a tapestry in which all the individual threads are strong and contribute to the integrity of the whole. As it is now, we see the extremes of privileged children stressed to the breaking point trying to get into elite, pressure-cooker schools, against a huge background of millions of children not completing high school and being relegated to a world of alienation, exclusion, and often despair that is masked by addictions and antisocial behavior.

Giving everyone access to a useful education is practical. A person who graduates from high school and learns a skill is far less likely to harm others or draw on society's resources than someone who doesn't make it past the ninth grade or learn a skill that leads to a job. Likewise, older people who have access to community classes are more likely to feel stimulated and engaged with life, which contributes to their emotional, mental, and physical well-being.

In practical terms, helping everyone to have access to a useful, stimulating education is a way of addressing racism, poverty, class, and privilege. It's not enough to hire better teachers, add more tests, and fix school buildings. We need a philosophy of learning that supports families and creates safe communities while making education useful to the students it serves.

....

Relevant education for all is at the center of healing many of the deep chasms in our society. It is the way we make peace within our own country. That is a crucial step toward making peace in the world.

....

What Does Effective "Education for All" Look Like?

Here are some questions for policy makers, educators, and parents that could become part of a dialogue. Some questions may apply to you personally in how you relate to your children. Others may help you consider how to be a voice for improving education or relating to your children's teachers.

1. What is the purpose of education?
2. How is the true purpose of education reflected in our school programs and curriculum?
3. How do we make education relevant, inspiring, and helpful to different groups of children, and, at the same time, expect excellence from them?
4. How do we measure learning? How relevant are current forms of testing?

5. How do we identify inspiring teachers, support them, learn from them, and have them supervise and train new teachers?

6. How is our belief in improving education reflected in our funding for all children? In other words, how can we change our funding policies so that children from poor neighborhoods get the same skilled teachers, materials, and opportunities for learning as students from privileged communities?

7. How can we inspire children to maintain a lifelong joy for learning? How do we inspire children from at-risk areas to believe they can learn and go to college?

8. How can empathy, compassion, cooperation, and a social conscience become an integral part of education?

9. How do we foster a mind-set of thinking for the common good—"us thinking"?

10. How do we help children develop a capacity for critical thinking?

11. How do we build character and integrity in children?

12. What social structures need to be created in troubled neighborhoods to prepare children to succeed in school and be safe when simply getting to and from school? How do we involve the families?

Think about the above questions as you read the following story.

BORED, SO BORED: LARRY'S STORY

When I hear teachers lament about the policy of teaching to the test—what some call the "drill and kill" approach—I think of my older brother Larry, a brilliant guy who spent sixteen years in school daydreaming through classes and getting mediocre grades. My mother would come home from parent-teacher conferences where she always heard the same remarks: "It's a shame he doesn't work harder. He's so bright . . . but he spends a lot of time looking out of the window."

Neither my parents nor his teachers ever considered that the reason why Larry was daydreaming and not doing his homework was that school was lifeless and irrelevant and that he was bored out of his mind. There was nothing to challenge him at any level. My parents who had a hands-off policy toward our performance at school, never pressured him to work harder for the sake of grades.

Here's Larry's version of the story. Notice the points he makes about the problems with standardized education and testing, and consider how we are squandering our greatest natural resource— our young people—with traditional approaches to education that often exclude teaching critical thinking, social studies, and conflict resolution, as well as learning from real-life experiences.

> *I was bored, so bored. When I had those math papers to do—fifty of the same kind of problems—I'd do them while I was in another boring class like history, while the teacher was droning on out of a book . . . or not do them at all. It seemed so useless. Most of school was just memorizing, and you could see where it was going—to prepare for a test. But it didn't mean anything. It had no purpose. After school we'd hike, go fishing, ramble around, and bike all over the place.*
>
> *I read a lot out of the* World Book Encyclopedia *at home. I learned a lot of geography that gave me a sense of the world, which I didn't get in school.*

Larry's grades were usually B's and C's, except for calculus and physics:

> *I'd get A's because . . . well, you'd write an equation that might be useful. It had real-life meaning. One time I got a D in math even though I*

got straight one hundreds on every test. But I didn't do the homework.
It was just grunt work and nothing creative.

After dragging himself through college, Larry volunteered for the army because he feared being drafted after starting his master's degree. Due to his near-perfect math scores, they shifted him out of boot camp, trained him in electronics, and sent him to the Philippines. While he was there he met up with a group of researchers from MIT (The Massachusetts Institute of Technology). They were so impressed with his skills that they offered him a full scholarship to MIT as part of a research team exploring transistors, the precursor to the computer chip.

Unfazed by the status of the offer, he continued with his plan to study forestry. He stayed true to himself, whether it meant not doing "grunt" homework or turning down MIT to follow his chosen career.

Here was a brilliant kid who wanted to do something useful, meaningful, creative, and relevant, but who appeared to be a mediocre student. The army was quicker to pick up on his intelligence and put it to use than the public schools had been.

One might think that this is a story exclusive to the past; after all, it happened fifty or sixty years ago. Unfortunately, I interviewed kids who related similar stories: school was all about learning the facts, memorizing them, spilling them out on a test and then forgetting them.

While there are many excellent approaches to education, the outdated practice of using rote memorization—the least effective form of learning—persists. Our shortsightedness is also reflected in cutting classes in the arts, physical education, literature, and social studies in our scramble to improve test scores in math and science. Such cuts are coupled with piling on more and more homework with questionable usefulness and assuming that multiple choice tests truly measure a student's aptitudes. These practices keep us locked into an old system that is kind of like using candles to read by instead of turning on a light bulb.

Moreover, while policy makers talk about improving the academic standing of the United States in the world, they drastically cut programs that identify and respond to gifted kids, especially since the start of the No Child Left Behind program. I sometimes think that the government needs to have a Department of Common Sense. In other words, if you want to promote excellence and raise our standing in the world, don't cut programs that nurture the brightest students.

The end of the story is that Larry got straight A's in graduate school at the University of California at Berkeley because, in his words:

It was a high-level ball game. You were working on defining real-life problems and figuring out ways to solve them from many angles.

Larry's weakness in public school became his strength as a professor:

My students were like me—bored stiff with math. But I made it come alive by applying it to the real world. I helped it mean something.

....

If we take Larry's words—"relevance," "meaning," "alive," "real world," "many angles to solve a problem"—and contrast them with "grunt work," "boredom," "rote memory," and "meaningless," we have a pretty good idea of what helps education to be either effective or ineffective.

....

We actually know a lot about what works in education. In order to create solutions, however, we need a spiritual awakening—we need to *truly care* about all children and their families. This includes a commitment to give all children equal access to quality education. Children from destitute areas can and do become prepared for college when given high expectations along with programs that feel exciting, useful, and relevant. I include some shining examples at the end of the chapter.

Education for the Twenty-First Century

We're in a new age of information technology, knowledge of the brain and its functions, along with an awareness of the power of an integrative approach to learning. We need to match our curriculum and approach to education to reflect this knowledge. Here are some concepts to be aware of in the contemporary education landscape.

1. **"Powerful emotional engagement leads to lasting learning."**
   —Jean Harlan, Ph.D., author of *Science Experiences for the Early Childhood Years: An Integrated Affective Approach*

With each science experiment in Dr. Harlan's book (now in its ninth edition), she cites a learning objective, such as to be *amazed* by crystal formation; to feel *powerful* with a lever's help; to *delight* in bouncing light beams; to find *satisfaction* in balancing.

When education is experiential and stimulates wonder, creativity, humor, and critical thinking, it is more likely to be retained and applied. Think of some of the most effective learning experiences in your life—in and out of school. What was the setting? What emotions did you have? What was the relevance to your life?

2. **Brain Integration**

Our traditional ways of teaching subjects separately—math, music, spelling, physical education, science—reflect old ideas about the brain, namely, the mistaken notion that we have different compartments that perform different functions. An exciting aspect of recent research shows that the brain is actually highly integrated and "plastic," meaning that it's capable of training one part to take over a skill or function when another part is damaged. As a simple example, we know that singing the traditional A-B-Cs song helps kids memorize the alphabet better than just reciting the letters.

The brain is a living network. Everything affects everything else. When you "light up" one circuit of learning, it sends electrical impulses to other areas. In other words, singing or playing a musical instrument is closely tied to language. It also stimulates our capacity for math and writing, just like a brisk walk that increases our heart rate is likely to help us think more clearly.

From a personal perspective, when I recently took on the daunting task of cutting upward of one hundred and fifty pages from this book's manuscript, I was initially overwhelmed. Time for exercise. After doing the weight/strength machines at the gym, followed by running up the mountain in the cold air as fast as I could go, I came home with a vigorous "slay the dragon" feeling. Okay, no nonsense, do it! Similarly, if I play Bach on the piano first thing in the morning, I am more centered and focused for writing.

If we were to integrate our knowledge of the brain with education, we might have kids singing and dancing or doing aerobic exercises at the beginning of each day to stimulate the brain. Just like the A-B-Cs song, we might think of all the ways to combine singing and dancing with learning other subjects. Likewise, we would use many approaches to learning with an emphasis on affective, experiential learning. We would also repeatedly have faith in a child's ability to learn by setting expectations for success.

3. Gain a Global Perspective

In our fast-changing, high-tech world, students need to develop a global perspective on other cultures and societies instead of assuming that the United States sets the standard and that our ways are the best. We need to understand ourselves as part of the whole, with much to learn from other cultures. This has become increasingly relevant to many jobs and careers and will help students later in life as well.

4. Learn across Subjects

Art, music, math, computer technology, science, social studies, literature, and people skills need to be experienced as important parts of becoming an innovative thinker. It's called teaching across subjects, not as separate topics but as interrelated ones. For example, how can we combine reading labels in a grocery store with math?

5. Connect with the Community

To be highly effective, schools need to include a broad range of interactions with people and organizations in the community. As one example, a teacher had her students make paintings to hang at the local homeless shelter. The children first did a project to learn about poverty—what leads people to become homeless, and what the community is doing, or not doing, to help. It was a powerful experience for many of the children.

6. Teach Critical Thinking Skills

As a parent, one of the most powerful skills you can teach your child is the capacity for critical thinking.

Critical thinking is the ability to look at a theory, claim, advertisement, or idea and evaluate it on many levels. Where did the idea come from? Who is promoting it? Who is selling the product? Who benefits from it? Who gains power? Who is left out? Is there a hidden agenda? What do you learn if you "follow the money"?

Young children can be taught critical thinking through looking at advertisements. They can learn to see the intent of the ad—for example, whether the product being sold is supposed to make them feel more popular, fit in, or be happier if they have it. Help them explore: What's the con, and what's the pitch?

When I was a teenager my father showed me the book *How to Lie with Statistics*. It left a lasting impression. He was obviously amused and intrigued by the way it showed how misleading charts and percentages can be. For example, quoting "a fifty percent improvement" might mean that there was an increase from two people to three people out of one hundred who were helped by a certain product or treatment.

Critical thinking is also about teaching children to trust that nervous feeling in their gut that tells them, *This person seems weird—I don't trust him.* A parent can help by not discounting a kid who doesn't want to hug Uncle Charlie or Kiss Aunt Connie. Validating a kid's experience helps fine-tune a questioning mind that sees through hype, propaganda, seduction, and misinformation, which pervades mainstream media. It also protects children against exploitation by those who profess to have all the answers, by charismatic leaders, or by those who want to seduce them.

....

A capacity for critical thinking is highly important when it comes to raising children to make peace in the world. It helps them see through propaganda, hype, and seduction.

....

7. Understand the Pygmalion Effect

> *What we at Harlem Children's Zone have learned over the years is that great expectations yield great results.*
>
> —GEOFFREY CANADA

Understanding the "Pygmalion effect" underscores how a positive attitude toward your child affects his or her performance. (Pygmalion in Greek myth was a sculptor who fell in love with a beautiful statue he had carved.)

Repeated studies have shown that teachers' perceptions of their students can greatly impact the students' performance.

Dr. Robert Rosenthal and Lenore Jacobson did a study where teachers were told that certain incoming students showed excellent potential. In reality, these students were picked at random. The researchers found that, "When the teachers were led to expect enhanced performance... then the children did indeed show that enhancement." They further speculated that these elementary school teachers might have unconsciously behaved in ways that facilitated and encouraged the students' success.

That's how subtle your messages can be and how your belief in your children's capacity to learn supports their belief in themselves. Over time, your positive beliefs in your children can get entrenched as self-fulfilling prophecies: I *can* learn this if I work at it, I *can* accomplish this difficult task, because I've done it before. Likewise when children are called lazy, incompetent, or stupid, the child internalizes this perception and may well act it out.

8. Homework: How Can Parents Be Helpful?

The fundamental question when it comes to homework is how you can be helpful without taking over your child's work or getting your own self-esteem mixed up with your child's school performance. I'll talk more about homework in Chapter 19, "My Parents Rock."

On a larger scale, however, homework as a concept is something that we as a society should question. There is little if any evidence that piling on more and more homework leads to a child's greater knowledge, intelligence, or quality of life. We need to consider what it does to kids' minds to ask them to devote hours to homework, especially if it is meaningless and repetitive with no room for creativity. It harks back to eighteenth- and nineteenth-century education that was directed at preparing children to be obedient laborers. Homework should include projects in the community, service to others, and practicing a musical instrument. It needs to have meaning and relevance.

I believe it's hard for many people to change their attitudes about homework because we have some underlying belief, possibly related to the puritan work ethic, that we need to suffer, toil, and tolerate drudgery. What if, instead, we adopted the belief that learning and dedication to hard work comes out of passion, fascination, and good teaching?

Upward Bound: Help Start a First Generation of College Students

I've spoken to a number of people from working-class backgrounds who went to college because one or more high school teachers sparked the belief in them that it was possible. As my good friend Pat told me, "I had never dreamed of going to college; no one in my family ever had. A teacher came to me and said, 'You're very smart and very good at writing. You should go to college." It was a big shift in my thinking, a totally new idea about what was possible. "Other teachers brought me clothes, one organized a club for students to visit colleges. It was so important to visit and see what college was like. It helped break down the mystique. When my family first drove me to the University of Illinois, I was very excited. My parents dropped me off on the sidewalk and wouldn't even come in the door. They were really frightened of the place. We came from a rural, isolated region and had very few experiences away from home."

If you want your children to make the breakthrough to college, start by talking about it when they are young. Make it sound normal. *I didn't go, but I want you to go. It will help you get a better job. It will be interesting. You can do it.* Don't make it a commandment to rebel against as in "You will go to college!" Take them to a college campus and learn about colleges yourself. Help them understand that they are smart enough, that success is more about finding what you like to do and how hard you work.

Do everything you can to bring a rich environment into your home. A hallmark of families with generations of college graduates is a love of learning, broad experiences in life, and the assumption they can do it.

EXERCISE

1. Recall an experience when someone had faith in your ability and think about how it affected your performance.
2. Recall an experience when someone had a negative view of your ability and think about the effect it had on your performance.

What If Your Child Resists Going to School?

If your child starts getting aches, pains, and stalls out when it comes to school, help her explore the possible causes. It might be about anything from being bullied to being shamed by a teacher, from not getting into the school play to having a fight with a friend. Be open and ready to listen.

If a child isn't doing well in school, several factors may be at work:

1. He doesn't learn well with the method that is being used.
2. She is having difficulties in her relationship with her teacher.
3. He isn't developmentally ready for a particular subject.
4. She doesn't have a strong aptitude in a particular subject.

5. He is highly anxious because of emotional problems from his past or in his home situation.

6. She is being bullied or having problems in relationships with other kids.

7. He is anxious, overstimulated, and agitated in the classroom.

8. The teacher has a conscious or unconscious negative attitude toward the child, who has internalized the negative perceptions.

Open the way to a conversation with your child to find out what's bothering him. *Hey Charlie, I notice you're not excited about school the way you used to be. I'm wondering what that's about.* With some children, it takes casual conversation to ease into talking about what's troubling them. It's usually best not to charge in with the difficult questions. It's likely your child already feels badly. If she feels you are on her side, she's more likely to feel safe to talk. The very act of being taken seriously and listened to can help a child feel better.

If your child is having trouble with a teacher, you might visit the classroom or have a conference with the teacher. When a parent approaches a teacher with goodwill, listens carefully, and doesn't automatically defend the child, it can open the door to understanding and lead to a shift in the situation.

WHEN YOUR CHILD TALKS ABOUT BULLYING

If your child tells you she is being bullied, pay attention. If she is resistant to going to school, or your child has sudden changes in sleep habits, moods, eating patterns, or difficulty concentrating, listen to her. Really listen and don't jump to immediate solutions, but stay engaged with your child. It may help to talk with the teacher or principal and include your child in the discussion. Don't give up. If it becomes extreme, consider taking your child out of that school setting. Likewise, if you see your child bullying others, get help. Bullying is usually a cover-up for fear, insecurity, and low self-esteem. It is also a learned pattern of behavior based on what the child has observed at home or in the media.

The type of school your child attends can have a great influence on fostering an atmosphere where bullying is rare if it exists at all. In terms of schools, Nicholas Salmon, a school architect spoke of working with teachers and staff to design schools that fit with progressive education and provide a kind of community setting where there was flexibility between grades, teachers, and subject matter. These schools stress strong ties between students, teachers, parents, and community. He commented that in these schools bullying is rare, and is dealt with immediately as a community concern for all people involved.

I spoke with Augusta Kappner, former president of the Bank Street College of Education. Here's what she said: "There was no evidence of bullying at Bank Street at all. Kids were taught by example and intellect about feelings and rights, and we developed the most caring group of kids I have seen. Kids came to understand that they too could be 'the other' and developed the kind of empathy that we wish the rest of the society had. Although parents came from different backgrounds and beliefs, we were clear about our expectations of respect for each other, and the children didn't seem to have a problem with it.

"There was/is indeed a lot of contact between teachers and parents but also a lot of contact between teachers and kids in and outside the classroom (overnight trips, etc.) and a lot of role modeling in problem solving. I remember the story a parent told me about visiting a potential high school with her Bank Street son. When he learned that the school required a course in ethics, his reaction was, 'Why would you have to have a course in ethics? Isn't that what we *do* everyday at Bank Street?!'

"I think the kind of hands on, project based teaching and

learning that goes on in most progressive schools has a better chance of modeling and 'teaching' mutual respect and developing *empathy*, which is the key variable. A capacity for empathy is what helps kids resist peer or mob pressure."

Dr. Kappner added, "Two things to keep in mind, however, is that Bank Street only goes thru eighth grade. It does not include high school. And recently the Internet has become much more persuasive for kids, so there can be actions that are invisible to teachers and parents."

Don't Overprotect Your Children

I frequently hear from teachers that parents automatically "protect" their children from the consequences of poor academic performance. Instead of asking how to help their child study, they pressure a teacher to raise a grade when it isn't warranted.

Similarly, in the case of stealing, bullying, or being rude in class, some parents refuse to believe their child is in the wrong; to them, whatever happened was "no big deal" and the teacher just has it in for their kid. As a result, the child follows the parent's attitude and learns to minimize, rationalize, and blame others for doing a lousy job. It's no gift to impart to your child a habit of blaming others or making excuses. It doesn't prepare him for the real world where, for example, if you leave your bike unlocked, it's likely to be stolen, or if you don't listen to your boss, you might get fired, or if you don't pay the rent, you get evicted.

One teacher told me he had informed parents that their eleven-year-old son was making inappropriate sexual remarks to girls in the class. The parents replied, "Oh, he's just a boy. It's natural." This child later got into more trouble for being physically and sexually aggressive with a girl. It also turned out that he was watching a lot of sexually explicit Web sites.

....

If you minimize, rationalize, or cover up for your child, you need to explore why you do it. Is it about your own self-esteem? Do you see your child as an extension of yourself? Remember that you are the parent, and you need to help your child take responsibility for his behavior.

....

When to Get Extra Help for Your Child

Sometimes when a child has difficulty learning, it has nothing to do with the teacher or the parents. The trouble may have to do with the way the child learns best, the fact that he's too anxious in class to concentrate, or it could potentially be a learning disability. Sometimes a tutor or special help is invaluable.

My daughter, Ginelle, was having a terrible time learning how to read when she was in first grade. She wanted to read—she carried books around with her and even pretended to read—but it just wasn't happening. After she was tested at a local university in the spring of first grade, the specialists suggested that I have a student tutor come to the house. Ginelle was delighted when this friendly "big girl" came to visit, and within eight weeks she was reading at grade level.

I will never forget her glowing face and bright blue eyes shining at me when she said, "Mommy, I want to read this book to you." Another ten weeks of tutoring and Ginelle was reading at third-grade level. Reading became a lifelong pleasure for her.

What does this tell us? Ginelle, like many children, needed a different approach to reading, as well as a calmer atmosphere. *She was able to learn when given the right help.* We can make enormous differences in our children's lives when we or the school provide special tutoring or special help. Ginelle developed a deep love of reading that frequently sustained her throughout her life. Just as we need the right tools for the job, or a correct diagnosis to find a cure, we need effective approaches to children's different ways of learning.

Teachers' Concerns About Their Students

Hats off to dedicated teachers. It is demanding work and requires being "on" every day. Teachers are often unfairly blamed for children's problems or expected to make up for a lack of learning in the home.

It was breathtaking for me to watch my grandson's kindergarten teacher shepherding five-year-old kids through project after project with warmth, clarity, and focus.

I also spoke with a group of teachers from the Lolo, Montana, elementary and middle school. Along with others I interviewed, they revealed a genuine delight in children, a love of teaching, and excitement about programs that stimulate children's interest. Many had attended various workshops to learn new skills and innovative ideas. They wanted programs to keep up with the rapidly changing world, and many had been frustrated with the focus on teaching to the test that has become so common since the passage of No Child Left Behind in 2001.

Teachers also expressed deep concern for children who went home to an empty house after school, possibly for the whole evening, while a parent held down two jobs to make ends meet. They spoke of the great need for after-school programs that go until 6:00 P.M., possibly later.

The following is a list of things they suggested that parents can do to help improve the parent–child–teacher relationship.

1. Stay involved and get to know the child's teacher.
2. Attend all PTA meetings.

3. Attend all your child's events—plays, presentations, sporting events, art shows. Bring the whole family so everyone is engaged.

4. Give your child a place to study—a desk or card table with decent lighting.

5. Don't have the TV on all the time. Don't have a TV in the child's bedroom. Limit TV and screen time (computers or other devices).

6. Help your child learn respect by showing respect and consideration for your child's teacher and for other people. If your child complains or is having a problem, come and talk with the teacher.

7. Talk with your child about school. What does he enjoy? What is easy? Hard? Fun? Little kids will often give monosyllabic answers, but that's fine. Encourage them. (Open questions, rather than "yes" or "no" inquiries, are best for getting beyond monosyllabic replies.)

8. Engage with your children, spend time together. Make learning a natural, everyday experience. If you can't be home after school, arrange for your child to go to a neighbor's house. You put a child at high risk when he is left alone for long periods of time with a TV or computer as the baby sitter.

9. Discourage girls from wearing highly sexual clothes and makeup to school. It can make them become objectified targets and vulnerable to predatory behavior from others. I'll talk about this more in the sexuality chapter (15).

10. Make it clear to your children that you expect them to follow the school's rules.

11. Don't sabotage teachers when they set limits or give reasonable consequences. Help your child understand the need for rules at school, and don't cast your child as a victim by encouraging him to blame others.

12. Don't get upset if your child is slow to learn something; it's normal to have different rates of learning.

13. Don't punish your child for getting low grades or having difficulty learning. Talk it over with your child and his teacher. Find out why and ask what can be done to help him. Don't make grades the measure of a child's worth.

14. Some parents reward children with money for getting good grades. This is an external reward for what needs to belong to the child. From a Quaker or Buddhist perspective, this detracts from the child's intrinsic pleasure in learning. In his book *Punished by Rewards*, Alfie Kohn cites study after study showing that rewards are not helpful or necessary for a child to learn. At the same time, some schools in poor neighborhoods, trying to jump-start kids to study have used money as a reward for doing homework and found it helpful.

Match the Child to a School That Fits

If you have a choice of private or public schools, remember it's the fit that counts. There are some excellent public schools as well as private ones.

Likewise, when your child is looking for a college, it doesn't have to be an outstanding one, it just has to be "good enough." Don't put your kid in a pressure cooker to go to "the best."

In his book *Outliers: The Story of Success*, Malcolm Gladwell lists the colleges that Nobel Prize winners graduated from. The list includes state universities and colleges as well as MIT and Harvard. He makes the point that it only needs to be a good-enough school, and that the main ingredient is a good fit, as well as the academic effort and time put in by the student. The goal is to help children become fascinated with learning.

In his book *Teacher Man*, Frank McCourt, writes about his thirty years teaching in New York City public schools. He eventually ends up teaching in an elite school where the students are vying to get into the top Ivy League schools. In McCourt's words, "in all my years at Stuyvesant only one parent, a mother, asked if her son was enjoying school. I said yes, he seems to be enjoying himself. She smiled stood up, said, Thank you and left. One parent in all those years."

Good News! Examples of Successful Programs

I include this section to counteract the pervasive belief that certain schools in poor areas are beyond hope. I hope to create a mind-set within all people that education and the future for children can be drastically improved by creating programs that address the needs of the children, the family, and the community.

May the following examples inspire you to believe that all things are possible when we do whatever it takes. There are many shining examples. You can search the Internet for "remarkable schools" or "turnaround schools" to read about them. I found it inspiring, and hope you will too.

A SUCCESSFUL APPROACH TO INNER CITY POVERTY: THE HARLEM CHILDREN'S ZONE PROJECT AND BABY COLLEGE

Baby College and the Harlem Children's Zone Project illustrate how education can be made successful for children in the inner city. I first heard of this wise and holistic approach on National Public Radio. Here is a description of the program from their own Web site (hcz.org):

> Called "one of the most ambitious social-service experiments of our time," by the New York Times, the Harlem Children's Zone Project

is a unique, holistic approach to rebuilding a community so that its children can stay on track through college and go on to the job market.

The goal is to create a 'tipping point' in the neighborhood so that children are surrounded by an enriching environment of college-oriented peers and supportive adults, a counterweight to "the street" and a toxic popular culture that glorifies misogyny and antisocial behavior.

The HCZ pipeline begins with The Baby College, a series of workshops for parents of children ages 0–3. The pipeline goes on to include best-practice programs for children of every age through college. The network includes in-school, after-school, social-service, health and community-building programs. . . .

For children to do well, their families have to do well. And for families to do well, their community must do well. That is why HCZ works to strengthen families as well as empowering them to have a positive impact on their children's development.

The results have been spectacular by any standards. According to the Web site:

- 100% of students in the Harlem Gems pre-K program were found to be school-ready for the sixth year in a row.
- 81% of Baby College parents improved the frequency of reading to their children.
- In 2009, HCZ overall served 21,280 individuals (10,462 youth and 10,817 adults).
- Nearly all children in every program scored at or above grade level in standardized tests.
- Nearly all children were accepted into at least one college and many received grants and scholarships.

....

We could save millions, possibly billions of dollars if we supported the kind of education that makes learning possible from birth onward. It would lower the number of high school dropouts, as well as the rate of addictions, crime, incarceration, antisocial behavior, depression, and suicide. It would also help us live closer to the spiritual teaching to love one another.

....

An afterword to the HCZ project is that, like many progressive schools for at-risk children, children are admitted by lottery. PBS showed a scene when the lucky kids names were called while the other parents, not so lucky, were left dejected knowing that they had to enroll their children in a dangerous, low-performance, inner-city school. This is a travesty. Imagine the uproar if children in rich white neighborhoods or children of members of Congress had to go through a lottery to decide whether they could go to good schools or to failing schools. From a Buddhist or Christian perspective, our approach to education needs to be grounded in treasuring the lives of *all* children and making our voices heard by our communities, legislators, and representatives.

ANOTHER SCHOOL THAT DOES IT ALL

The Ron Clark Academy fully embodies the values of education for the common good and emphasizes the importance of creative approaches to learning. The school, formerly in Harlem but now located in Atlanta, is for children in grades five through eight. Here are some excerpts from the school's Web site, which will give you an idea of its mission:

> . . . *students will be exposed to classes and programs where they will learn and be involved with photography, dancing, music produc-*

tion, the art of design, dramatic performance, and business leadership. . . .

Before going to Broadway shows, Mr. Clark had his students read the story, learn the songs, and research the architecture of the theater. Before going to the bowling alley, Mr. Clark visited himself, measured the lanes and used the dimensions on worksheets. He also used the bowling pins to teach fractions, and took the prices from the snack shop and used them in math class. On every trip, whether it is up the street or across the globe, the Ron Clark Academy will make every moment a learning opportunity because as Mr. Clark has learned children must have a connection to something before they will appreciate it.

When the children from the Ron Clark Academy danced and sang "Dear Obama" at the 2009 inauguration, I was delighted with their enthusiasm and impressed with the lengthy lyrics they had memorized. It was education come alive. History, music, dance, joy, creativity, and memory were brought to an idiom the children knew. The Web site continues:

Our international trips will be integrated throughout the curriculum, and exposing students to new cultures and situations are keys to our philosophy. In addition to the international trips, each class will travel on as many as 30 field trips each year to a world that they, in many cases, have never imagined. Art museums, Broadway shows, cultural festivals, and professional sporting events are just some of the ways that their eyes will be opened to the reality of diverse and rich cultures, sometimes within Atlanta, and sometimes around our country and throughout the world.

This living education is key to raising children to create a more peaceful world. When children learn from the inside out—by combining experience with history, the arts, thinking, seeing, hearing, feeling, observing, and creating—they develop a rich interior world that becomes a lifelong resource. It's like being multidimensional instead of two-dimensional, like having a full palette of colors to work with instead of one or two. It's the difference between hearing music as something out there and feeling it dance inside you, or seeing many sides of a question and not falling into simplistic, shallow thinking. It's about developing an awareness of the common good.

When creativity is encouraged and explored, life becomes more fascinating and fulfilling, and the mind and brain are more fully stimulated and developed. This aids with all learning, and helps improve problem-solving ability as well as the ability to grasp complex issues. Add to this the experience of students traveling to many parts of the world and learning firsthand about other cultures and traditions, and you tap into the roots of peace: genuine interest and curiosity, understanding, and knowledge of and empathy for others.

> We need to support these progressive schools, where education is aligned with helping children develop their minds, creativity, voices, and social conscience. When we work together in a community for the common good of children, they will learn to pass it on to others.

The Heart of Our Social Policies: A Time for Fundamental Change

I am rewriting this section as the last piece of the book to be revised. I am just two weeks and two days post–triple-bypass surgery and still reeling from the knowledge that I am lucky to be alive. So, if I sound impassioned, it's because I am. Some might say I'm going off the topic of parenting, but actually I'm going to the heart of what it means to bring a social conscience to raising all of our children to create a more peaceful world.

Parenting for a peaceful world is not just an isolated job for families. There is an integral relationship between families, community resources, and, ultimately, national funding policies. A strong humanitarian network for all our people, such as maternity care, quality affordable child care, parks, recreation, good schools, after-school programs, low-cost clinics, low-cost housing, safety on the streets, and a broad educational system are all essential to our children's lives. To have these resources available to all children of all races, classes and cultures is to give meaning to the concept of liberty and justice for all. These services also cost money and require a skilled and well-paid staff.

The availability of basic resources reflects the spending choices we make as a society. Every year I get a request from my grandson to buy magazine subscriptions to raise money for school supplies. This brings to mind the popular slogan from the Vietnam War era: "It will be a great day when our schools get all the money they need and the Air Force has to hold a bake sale to buy a bomber."

In the summer of 2009 it was heart-wrenching to read that funds were being cut for community swimming pools, physical education, music, driver's education, arts programs, after-school programs, and high school equivalency (GED) testing programs, to name a few. At the same time it was widely publicized that the United States spends one million dollars per year for every soldier sent to Iraq or Afghanistan. This brought to mind a famous quote from President Dwight D. Eisenhower: "Every gun that is made, every warship launched, every rocket fired signifies, in the final sense, a theft from those who hunger and are not fed, those who are cold and are not clothed." We need to ask ourselves, where do kids go when swimming pools close, and park programs and GED testing programs are shut down? What is the ultimate cost of these shortsighted, inhumane cuts in spending? What is it about our consciousness that allows such inequities to grow in our society? Why is it that we spend more money on prisons than schools?

Caring about all of our children necessitates that we drastically reduce our military spending and change our beliefs about military power. We in the United States make up 6 percent of the world's population, yet spend 41.5 percent to 48 percent of the world's total military budget. If things stay this way, it is inevitable that we will continue to see huge deficiencies in programs that help children grow and thrive. (Following the United States in percent of worldwide military spending, according to the Stockholm International Peace Research Institute, is China with 6.6 percent, France with 4.2 percent, and on down to Canada in thirteenth place with 1.2 percent.)

In his famous farewell address in 1961, President Dwight D. Eisenhower spoke of the grave implications of a "military-industrial complex" that overshadows our need to "use our power in the interests of world peace and human betterment." "In the councils of government, we must guard against the acquisition of unwarranted influence, whether sought or unsought, by the military-industrial complex." His fears have been borne out by a country controlled by corporate interests and military spending at the cost of programs for human betterment, particularly our public education system.

My hope is that every parent will read Eisenhower's speech, that it will be included in social studies classes in every high school, and that we will join together to break the taboo of talking about the choices we are making to support corporate interests and invest in the military establishment rather than in the needs of our people. (You can find the speech online by searching for "Eisenhower" and "military industrial complex.") Such a shift would appear radical in the United States, but it is already prevalent in the European Union and many other countries.

We need a fundamental shift in values, policies, and beliefs about our place in the world as a military power. Again, President Eisenhower: "Disarmament with mutual honor and confidence is a continuing imperative. *Together we must learn how to compose differences, not with arms but with intellect and decent purpose.*" Decent purpose involves moving from fear and control to cooperation and respect in all our dealings—personal, political, and in our corporate culture. In other words, the values that parents and teachers impart for raising resilient, cooperative, peaceful children should be reflected in the actions of our government's financial institutions and funding policies. From a Quaker-Buddhist perspective, this means returning to the concepts of right sharing and remembering that all life is sacred and to be treasured.

15 Sexuality as a Part of Life

> *In classic Buddhism, not unlike other world religions,*
> *sexual energy has often been regarded as a volatile force*
> *that can create complications and prove antithetical to*
> *holiness, solitude, and inner silence.*
>
> *In the broader Mayayana Buddhist approach, it is*
> *recognized that personal love can be a heart-opening*
> *spiritual experience.*
>
> —LAMA SURYA DAS, AWAKENING THE BUDDHA WITHIN

> *God is love, lover and Beloved.*
>
> —SUFI SAYING

*S*exuality is about touch, affection, warmth, energy, passion, and the amazing capacity of our bodies for pleasure and love. From a spiritual perspective, sexuality is about knowing, connecting, caring, respecting, and deeply treasuring another person.

Our sexual energy is one with our life force energy. When we experience sexuality as love, lover, and Beloved, it becomes one with the indivisible energy of All That Is. To experience the true wonder and power of sexuality, it needs to be liberated from all forms of domination, subordination, compulsion, fear, and duty. When we take the ego out of sexuality, it becomes one with the Beloved.

After talking to many couples for a previous book, *If the Buddha Married*, it became clear to me that their sexual relationships were deeply embedded in their emotional relationships; in other words, people who have warm, loving, knowing relationships tend to have warm, loving, knowing sexual connections. As a relationship deepens emotionally, it often deepens sexually.

Sexuality taught from the perspective of nonviolent openheartedness helps children feel at home in their bodies, and able to give and receive affection with others—the foundation for enduring satisfying sexual relationships.

In many religions worldwide, sexuality has been seen through the lens of male domination and female subordination. In the 1960s, with the arrival of sexual liberation and the feminist movement, sexuality began to be freed from shame and fear and to be explored as a life-affirming, natural, and powerful aspect of life for both men and women (as well those in same-sex relationships).

Typical of any time when we cast off rigid rules, it was an experimental era. Along with people becoming more comfortable with their bodies and their sexuality, people engaged in open relationships and experimented more freely with alcohol, drugs, and promiscuity, which sometimes became problematic. Still, there emerged the possibility of women being whole and powerful and becoming equal partners in their sexual relationships. Shared passion and physical pleasure began to be seen as life-affirming.

Sexuality and Equality, Sexuality and Shame

It is only through a deep sense of equality that we bring sexuality out of the depths of exploitation and humiliation and into a positive and spiritual aspect of life.

A fundamental part of making peace in the world is helping male and female children understand their sexuality as a natural, normal, and amazing part of life.

In moving toward a more peaceful world, we need to help children feel secure and comfortable in their bodies and have a positive yet responsible attitude toward sexuality. First, sexuality has to be liberated from its terrible, destructive associations with temptation, sin, uncontrollable forces, pain, obedience, violence, or something to be taken or given out of duty. It's not a commodity. To do this, parents need to explore their own history with sexuality along with their attitudes, fears, and feelings toward it.

It's easy to drift off into abstractions. But we also need to help children feel at home with touch, sensations, flesh, sweat, smells, sounds—*their physical selves*. We need to help them become comfortable with real bodies, not the airbrushed impossibly thin ones we see in advertisements and the movies. Comfort with one's body includes feeling free to touch, cuddle, hold, roll around in the grass, get wet, put your feet in mud, and take pleasure in your own body. And girls should be confident that being chunky or full figured or not a standard clothing size does not detract from their inner worth.

....

When children's sexuality starts with a positive relationship with their own bodies it becomes a connection with their natural selves.

....

Getting Comfortable with Sexuality

As parents, we set the stage for teaching our children about sexuality by exploring our own sexual attitudes and histories. If you feel uncomfortable with sexuality or in talking about it with your children, you're among the multitude of parents who feel the same way.

I would love to see schools, churches, and community organizations sponsor events at which parents could come together with a facilitator to talk about sexuality in their own lives, and to explore ways to teach their children about sexuality in the context of nonviolence and love.

As a young mom, it was my good fortune to be part of a community of parents, both single and married, who had picnics, parties, consciousness-raising groups, an alternative school, and provided child care for each other. Along with our families being friends, we also got together as parents to talk about child rearing, including sexuality. One night, we talked over just about everything: defining sexual boundaries, taking pictures of kids in the bath tub, rough housing with kids, how to go about monitoring children "playing doctor," bringing up the subject of sex, and of course the question of what you say when they ask, "How does the baby get started?"

One time we talked about the helpful and not helpful things our parents had said or done about bodies, relationships, and sexuality. These immensely freeing conversations validated our questions. I encourage you to have similar conversations with other parents (if you know them pretty well and you think they'll be open to it). You'll be amazed at how much more comfortable you become with these sometimes intimidating topics.

EXERCISE: EXPLORE YOUR SEXUAL FEELINGS

With a partner or another person, talk about the first time you became aware of sexual feelings. How old were you? How did you learn about sexuality? What questions did you wish someone could have answered for you? Think about your own parents' approach to the subject and whether you want to do things differently with your own children. (I have a sexual history form for men and women on my Web site that I have used in workshops and with numerous clients. It's designed for people to use in a small group or with one other person. One can explore it on one's own, but part of the healing power of the sexual history exercise is talking with another person.)

Teaching Sexuality in the Context of Human Values

Most of us remember the giggle-inducing, embarrassing lectures and movies we were shown in junior high school under the title "sex education." We had to get permission slips from home, teachers talked dryly or in hushed tones, and there was no conversation about relationships, feelings, responsibility, raging hormones, or pimples. Sexuality looked more like a plumbing diagram. Even so, the whole thing felt ominous. First we saw the movie on menstruation, then we learned, *this is how sex happens*, then you have a baby.

Sex Education: What Will It Be?

All children get sex education. The question is, What kind of sex education?

Never talking about sex teaches fear and uneasiness around sexuality. Having *Playboy* lying around the house teaches that women are sexual objects and it's okay for men to think of them that way. It denigrates women and men.

Making sexist remarks or putting down men or women teaches disrespect and inequality in relationships that will affect a child's understanding and experience of sexuality.

Teaching "just say no" limits sexuality to something to control and fear, until, as if by magic (after marriage), it's time to say yes and have pleasure and passion. Besides, for all but a few teenagers, it's not a very realistic prescription.

A parent whose primary emotional intimacy is with her child often creates ambivalence about the opposite sex in the child or young adult. On the one hand, the child feels special and needed. On the other hand, leaving the parent and forming a primary relationship with another may induce guilt. The buried anger at the parent often becomes directed at the grown child's partner.

TEACH POSITIVE ATTITUDES ABOUT SEXUALITY

Let your children know you are open to any questions they have about their bodies, their development, and sex. Conversations about sex can arise over time rather than having the big, heavy conversation. In successive conversations, keep it simple and as relaxed as possible. There are useful books on the subject and lots of information on the Internet.

- Help children feel comfortable in their bodies—running, playing in water, getting dirty, making faces, touching themselves, joking about pee pee, and farting.
- Be respectful in your own relationships and to your child.
- Keep clear sexual boundaries around your child—show affection and hugs, but don't require them. Physical affection needs to come out of warmth, not duty. Good night hugs and kisses are fine so long as a child is not coerced or not given a choice.
- Model comfort and ease with affection and touch in your own relationships.

- When your children are adolescents, teach them about birth control while simultaneously helping them develop values about responsibility to others, including not bringing a baby into the world you can't take care of.
- Teach them to have respect for people in same-sex relationships. Let them know that approximately three percent of the population is in same-sex relationships, and many others have experimented with same-sex relationships. Sexuality can be understood on a continuum.

ASSERTIVENESS HELPS MAKE SEXUALITY SAFE

Preparing a child to feel safe with her sexuality is also about helping her to feel safe to say "yes" or "no" to touching, holding, kissing, or any other form of physical affection from anyone, including you, the parent. It is the prelude to being able to feel she has the right to say, "No, I don't want to," when she is dating. Being able to say "no" creates the basis for saying an authentic "yes."

Similarly with boys, the more genuine their relationships are with their families, the more they'll have access to their feelings and won't feel they have to prove themselves through exploiting or using sex for power, and the more we help create a foundation for sex in the context of a caring relationship.

....

Deep sexual pleasure resides in feeling safe to be honest and open and to know your partner is committed to you.

....

IF SEXUALITY IS PROBLEMATIC, GET HELP

I have spent thirty-five years working as a therapist with the painful legacy of sexual abuse, violence, and neglect. Such abuse often leaves a person extremely uneasy or tense around sexuality. I encourage those who have been victimized to get help from a skilled therapist or join a group for survivors of sexual trauma.

Even though women in my therapy groups often had had multiple sex partners, it didn't mean they were knowledgeable or comfortable with their bodies or sexuality. In a survivor's therapy group, a woman once said, "I want to spend a group session where we're all like little kids and I get to ask any dumb question I want." Everyone loved the idea. It was one of the most memorable events in my career as a therapist. The women had innocence, curiosity, and desire to know! All of the women came from families with no direct, positive sex education and a lot of negative experiences of family chaos, violence, and sexual abuse.

Know that you will feel better if you talk with someone. I have incredible faith in the power of the human mind, body, and spirit to heal.

RED SEX, BLUE SEX: EVANGELICALS AND SOCIAL LIBERALS

A fascinating *New Yorker* article called "Red Sex, Blue Sex: Why do so many evangelical teen-agers become pregnant?" by Margaret Talbot echoed what I've heard from many parents. I highly recommend reading it. Search the Internet for "Red Sex, Blue Sex" to find the article online. Researchers found that sexual attitudes broke down into two distinct groups: the religious right or evangelicals (the red sex) and the social liberals (the blue sex).

One point of agreement between liberals and conservatives is the hope that their children will be responsible about sex. However, their definitions of responsible differ. In Talbot's words, "Social liberals in the country's 'blue states' tend to support sex education and are not particularly troubled by the idea that many teen-agers have sex before marriage, but would regard a teen-age daughter's pregnancy as devastating news. And the social conservatives in 'red states' generally advocate abstinence-only education and denounce sex before marriage, but are relatively unruffled if a teen-ager becomes pregnant, as long as she doesn't choose to have an abortion."

WHAT BLUE-SEX PARENTS TAUGHT ABOUT SEXUALITY

I spoke with many parents and their teenage or adult children who felt their parents did a good job of teaching about sexuality.

Echoing the Blue side, families taught that sexuality is a natural part of life and wanted to help their children make informed decisions for themselves. Their teaching centered around values, responsibility, commitment, and thinking through decisions. Most of all, they were realistic. None of them taught their children to "just say no" because they believed it was impractical and they wanted their children to feel free to bring them their questions, worries, or fears.

As one father said, "If we stress that they shouldn't have sex, then how will they be able to come to us if they have had sex or are worried about it or having strong urges? How can we teach them about sexually transmitted diseases? How can my daughter ask her mother to take her to Planned Parenthood so she will be safe, if all she's ever heard is 'Don't have sex'? There's so much fear in that kind of teaching, and we don't want our children to think sex is a terrible thing to be afraid of. I don't see how you can go from fear of sex to feeling good about it."

For liberals, wanting their children to experience sex in a caring relationship replaces prohibitions against sex. As one mother put it, "I didn't want my daughter or my son to have meaningless empty sex. I wanted it to be positive. We taught both our children that a positive experience was more likely to happen when they were older, felt close to someone, and had a commitment." Several of the parents didn't necessarily know if their children had been sexually active.

Some did. One parent said, "We don't want to intrude, and we want to respect their privacy . . . but we do talk about making good decisions."

PARENTS LINK SEXUAL RESPONSIBILITY TO
USE OF ALCOHOL

"My parents never said that sex or alcohol was bad, but that too much drinking can lead you to make impulsive decisions, and to be careful about that," said one young adult I interviewed. This family's teachings about alcohol and other drugs was similar to its teachings on sexuality: It's not bad, but it can be risky and one needs to be responsible. Some parents pointed out that underage drinking was illegal and they wouldn't allow their children and friends to drink in their homes, but some parents occasionally let their children have some wine or beer at home with the family. One college girl commented that she was glad for her introduction to alcohol in the family. "My freshman year I saw girls who had never been allowed to drink go to frat parties and end up drunk and in a lot of trouble."

One father who rarely drank told his daughter, "If you want to see what it's like to get drunk you are welcome to do that at home when we're here"—an unappealing idea to a teenager. The girl later told me that she had no desire to get drunk and thought what her father said was funny and a little weird. But it was much better than not talking about it at all.

Nearly every family offered help if their child got caught in a difficult situation. *"If the driver is drunk or you are drunk, call us. We'll come, no questions asked. We just want you home safe."* It is especially important to teach the girls that if a guy seems drunk or is being sexually aggressive or if she feels scared, to call, and to call right away. "We'll be there. We won't blame you. We'll understand. We were young once."

....

While it's good for parents to show trust in their children, it's important to be aware that they are young and their judgment can be shaky. So remember to make it clear *if all else fails, call home at once.*

....

One Quaker mother who had been happily married for forty-five years summed up how she and her husband imparted sexual values to their four children:

We taught them that sex was a deeply loving and spiritual connection when you are with someone you love. There's respect for the deep honor of the other person. We had a ceremony for each of our daughters when they started their menstrual cycles just as my parents had had a ceremony for me.

We wanted our kids to feel at ease in their bodies and with sexuality. It helped that they were all part of a swim team. They saw bodies every morning at 6 A.M., took part in swim meets, and had trips with their teams. It was a relaxed, natural, everyday kind of thing, although I'm sure they had attractions and feelings for each other.

The girls were treated just like the boys and it gave them a way to be together with a lot of respect for each other as equals. They went out on group dates with friends from their team. They'd have pizza, watch a movie, and hang out together. It met their needs as teens.

As a midwife, I talked with them about the difference between people having children because they were ready for a family, and others who were trying to fill up some empty place. We helped our children feel secure and strong, which is what a child needs to handle dating and sexuality. Three of them became proficient in martial arts, which gave them a lot of confidence.

We didn't let our girls date until they were sixteen. There was a lot of negative stuff going on in their high school—young girls being exploited and rated by the guys, who passed their ratings around. We felt protective of our children. In general, we'd explain our values and we expected them to live up to them.

I asked her if they taught their children to abstain from sex until marriage.

"No," she said. "Alan and I didn't because we had an eight-year courtship starting in high school, and it would have been unnatural. We didn't want sex to be this huge thing that was the center of everything. But we stressed commitment and using birth control."

....

"We taught our children that you have no right to bring a child into this world if you can't take care of him. It's not fair to the child or to yourself."

....

The results of my interviews were in complete agreement with the article "Red Sex, Blue Sex." Namely, it was clear that sex education, along with talking about responsibility and respectful relationships, is the best way to prevent early or unwanted pregnancies that so painfully contribute to a multitude of personal and social problems. It was also important to help children think about their future careers and plans for a good life, which would be devastated by an early pregnancy.

"JUST SAY NO" DOESN'T WORK

Prohibitions may work in the short term, but they don't teach children to think for themselves or learn to make informed decisions, nor do they express faith in our children. In the long run, they often backfire.

This doesn't mean that parents shouldn't impart values. But we are wise to remember that what you resist, persists. When the Reverend Ted Haggard stepped down as president of the National Association of Evangelicals, which represents thirty million evangelical Christians, he said, "The fact is I am guilty of sexual immorality.... I am a deceiver and a liar. There's a part of my life that is so repulsive and dark that I have been warring against it for all of my adult life."

Perhaps if we made sexuality less of a war with ourselves, less repulsive and dark, it wouldn't become so fractured within us. If we made it more of a positive human experience, if we didn't elevate abstinence to the highest ideal, sexuality would become part of the tapestry of our whole lives and not such a shadowy force to fight with. Buddhism doesn't talk about sin or call people liars, it simply teaches that people are at different levels of consciousness. As parents we need to help our children become conscious and grounded in their own values.

Evangelicals and conservatives often argue that if we provide sex education and birth control, we're "encouraging" teens to have sex. Yet the opposite has proven true in study after study, bearing out the adage that knowledge is power.

....

Children who are provided with sex education, a positive sense of their bodies, plans for their future, and access to birth control have later sex, more protected sex, more pleasure from sex, better marriages, fewer divorces and more stable children than those children who were given no information and told to "just say no."

....

If we hear this information not from the point of view of liberals or conservatives, but rather as parents who want the best for our children, we can join together in helping them learn about touch, bodies, sexuality, relationships, and responsibility to self and others. This helps young adults become the authors of their own lives, capable of complex thinking and making conscious decisions. Instead of just saying "no" to sex, children learn to say "yes" to all that leads to a fulfilling life.

16 Tune In, Tune Out

Living in a Media World

From a Buddhist and Quaker perspective, our heartfelt, authentic connections with each other are at the core of making peace in the world. How is this impacted by the electronic world?

It has all happened so fast. Televisions, computers, the Internet, cell phones, iPhones, iPods, text-messaging, BlackBerrys, Facebook, MySpace, Twitter, chat rooms, message boards. From three national television networks in the 1950s to hundreds of cable channels that play around the clock, to thousands of Web sites on the Internet, we've experienced enormous change in a short time, a veritable flood of electronic media. And it's all made life much more complicated.

Let's Start with the Positives

Being able to stay in touch with friends through e-mail, find old friends on Facebook, or search out information on the Internet is a positive thing. Another is that the younger generation, so totally at home with electronics, can teach their parents and grandparents to use e-mail, program a cell phone, or figure out PowerPoint. I enjoyed having my nephew Alex reassure me as I asked yet again for instructions on programming my first cell phone. "It's okay," he assured me, "you're doing good."

Instant communication is connecting us around the world. This has immense political implications. When millions of Iranians protested the election of 2009, CNN showed real-time images that protesters had posted on Twitter. While these images showed brutality, the event also reminded us of our commonalities. The protesters in the streets didn't seem so different from us. We dress alike, we often act alike, and we have a shared desire to stand against oppression.

Keep Worry in Perspective

As with any new trend, it's easy to worry about the consequences of so many new technologies. To put things in perspective, author Alfie Kohn imagined a conversation about the arrival of the printing press: "Pros: More efficient at disseminating ideas to many people; allows scribes to do other kinds of work; creates jobs for teachers once literacy becomes expected. Cons: Heretical ideas and inaccurate information will spread unchecked; children will spend too much time indoors reading these newfangled books; oral traditions will be destroyed and human contact will be diminished." It echoed an article titled "Adventure Books Appeal Especially to Boys," which my grandmother Emily Shope wrote for the Library Department of the Missoula Women's Club and *The Missoulian* sometime between 1920 and 1930. In the article, she voiced her concerns that the new movies would become substitutes for creative play and reading.

I had to smile at these examples, which are not so different from concerns about current technology.

Still, I believe there is cause for concern, as most of the positives carry some negatives.

The Internet makes it possible to access information on nearly every subject imaginable. It also makes it necessary to discern what is credible and what is funded by a company hoping to sell a product.

Technology can help parents and kids keep in touch. A dad can send a quick message to his daughter ("Hey, have a good game"). On the other hand, parents and children can be tethered together with ten texts a day, which doesn't leave any breathing room between them or may seem intrusive.

Parents can seek out medical information to help them be informed and make wise decisions. There is also the issue of discerning the accuracy and credibility of the information found on the Internet.

Blogs can be fun, but bloggers can also get mean-spirited and use their sites to spread bias, prejudice, or disinformation.

Even Pope Benedict has weighed in. In his 2009 message on the Forty-third World Communications Day, Benedict voiced concerns I have heard echoed by many parents and educators:

> *The concept of* friendship *has enjoyed a renewed prominence in the vocabulary of the new digital social networks that have emerged in the last few years. The concept is one of the noblest achievements of human culture. . . . We should be careful, therefore, never to trivialize the concept or the experience of friendship. It would be sad if our . . . on-line friendships were to be at the cost of our availability to engage with our families, our neighbours and those we meet in the daily reality of our places of work, education and recreation. If the desire for virtual connectedness becomes obsessive, it may in fact function to isolate individuals from real social interaction while also disrupting the patterns of rest, silence and reflection that are necessary for healthy human development.*

These thoughtful words are at the heart of what caregivers, teachers, and those seeking a reflective life often consider.

Don't Let Electronics Shrink Your World

The extensive use of electronics is often the path of least resistance. Instead of having outlets for our senses and creative abilities, we narrow our being into a smaller, less sensory world. It becomes easier to sit passively at a screen than engage with friends, reach deep inside to stretch our abilities at sports, or to play a musical instrument—all of which expand our senses and thus our capacity to enjoy creation.

We need to keep these questions in mind when it comes to technology: How can we use it wisely? What is its role in developing healthy children with nonviolent values? How do we keep the circle of head, heart, and spirit in balance?

Nothing Can Replace Close Relationships

There will never be a substitute for arms to hold you when you cry, someone to cheer for you when you shine, or hear the excitement in a parent's voice when you talk about a new discovery. A face-to-face relationship is multidimensional, as opposed to an Internet- or text-based relationship, which lacks voice, sight, sound, and, often, the art of language. Real human interactions are nuanced and include facial expressions, eye contact, touch, laughter, and the felt presence of a person who is deeply listening.

These connections have roots; they go deep and take effort and vulnerability. They are a microcosm of our relationships with our community, the earth, and the world.

Think about the real, heartfelt, authentic relationships in your life. Do you long for deeper connections with others?

Concerns about Technology and Sexting

In a 2008 interview, a high school dean of students told me, "Ten years ago cell phones weren't even mentioned in our handbook for students, and now they are our biggest headache. We confiscated nine hundred of them this past year and that's probably one for every twenty-five a kid was using in school."

He continued, "Recently, the problems with 'sexting' have gotten huge—needing to call the police, kids getting arrested for sending pornography, being charged as pedophiles, refused college admission, young girls becoming sexual targets by sending naked images of themselves that will forever live on the Internet."

Parents need to educate themselves and their children about sexting and give examples of what can happen. It has devastated numerous lives, and the list of casualties is growing.

We don't know all the answers yet.

Questions to Ponder as Parents and in Community:

Just as it took many years for the public to accept that smoking is a cancer risk or that global warming is a threat to our safety, it will take many years to know conclusively the effects of extended use of electronics. In the meantime, parents need to use their common sense to protect their children.

- What's happening to our brain, our central nervous system, our ability to relax? Are we getting revved up and overstimulated so that we can't enjoy small pleasures?
- Are kids using electronics compulsively or addictively, and what patterns are being set in place by this? Instant gratification? Other addictive behaviors?

- How is it all changing the way we interact with each other? Are we being present? Feeling close? Being relaxed?
- Are kids increasingly getting involved with or hooked on pornography? (Twenty-five percent of hits on the Internet are to pornographic sites, which are easy to find, even accidentally.)
- Are we narrowing our capacity for deeply felt emotions and sensations, such as touch, smell, taste, curiosity, and appreciating beauty?
- What is the effect of fewer face-to-face interactions as we text our friends with abbreviations, emoticons, and truncated sentences?
- Are we contributing to accidents and loss of life by not stopping our children from texting or talking on cell phones while driving?
- What is the effect of thousands of children sneaking cell phones into schools and texting during class? Does this teach disrespect? Cause distraction? Encourage cheating?

Possible Consequences

Research is being done concerning relationships between electronic devices and physical and mental health—not only the widely publicized possibility of radiation from cell phones but also screen time of any sort. Some questions being raised center around:

- Learning comprehension, especially in young children
- Language development in very young children
- Capacity for multilevel thinking in all children
- Loss of concentration
- Decreased frustration tolerance
- Diminished attention span

- Risk of heart conditions and high cholesterol as a result of lack of exercise
- Mental health—especially depression, anxiety, symptoms of ADD and ADHD, and suicide
- Sleep problems
- Obesity
- Early-onset type 2 diabetes

We need to also explore which children are most at risk to become hooked on the Internet, violent images, and pornography, and take steps to create resources for them. Repeatedly, strong family ties, self-confidence, and participation in activities are cited as the best barriers to getting lost in or becoming dependent on the cyberworld.

While people debate these issues and scientists conduct further research, parents are well advised to pay careful attention. Historically we have had industries that deny the harmful effects of their products, while researchers and individuals raise questions and struggle to be heard. There are frequently numerous harmful consequences that occur before the research is validated and recognized.

I urge all parents and teachers to read "Fool's Gold: A Critical Look at Computers in Childhood" that can be found on the Web site of the Alliance for Childhood (available in both English and Spanish). It contains an excellent description of childhood development, including information on the brain.

Violent Images and Their Effects on Children

Numerous studies on the effects of playing violent video games suggest that watching violence and playing interactive games where people routinely kill other people heighten aggression in children, especially those who are not old enough to differentiate between reality and screen images, or those who already have hostile feelings.

A deeper concern from a Quaker or Buddhist perspective (and that of many others) is that these games create simpleminded, black-and-white concepts of good people ("us") and bad people ("them," everyone else), whom we dehumanize and kill. This way of thinking is counter to the development of a mentality that sees ourselves as related to all people everywhere.

This is a complex subject because child development includes kids grappling with conflicting inner feelings of kindness and anger—such as portrayed by the Good Witch and the Wicked Witch in *The Wizard of Oz*. For example, the question, "Do I let my kids play with toy guns?" always needs to be put in context. Jerimy, who grew up in a family dedicated to nonviolence, said his parents allowed him a cap gun after much family discussion and debate. "I think it was a good decision because it didn't separate me from the other kids, and our identity as Mennonites was strong.

"I grew up with kids playing cops and robbers. While it's still about good guys and bad guys, the difference from video games is that we weren't watching a realistic screen image while shooting others and seeing gore. We were running around outside, hiding, chasing, making up stories, and being creative. We would often take turns being the good guy and the bad guy."

Even so, many parents do not allow toy guns and if they do, they do not allow children to point them at each other. Some use water pistols, but others use spray bottles for play. This is a personal decision that every family needs to think over in terms of its hopes for its children.

....

We need to ask ourselves: How do we balance technology and wisdom? How do we stay involved with each other and avoid using technology as a babysitter for our kids, a means of escape, or a substitute for genuine connection?

....

A Question About the Cyberworld and Infant Bonding

When I heard a story about a teen who sent more than five thousand text messages in a month, I pondered what would happen if she became a mother. Would she be able to relax deeply and give her baby the complete, heartfelt attention that is crucial to creating a secure bond? Or would she feed her baby in a perfunctory way while texting or talking with a friend on her cell phone? Will she feel awestruck the first time she sees her baby smile or observe it in a detached way? Will she be preoccupied, less attuned to subtle cues, and less able to attach deeply? This is a serious concern related to making peace in the world: the more we dissociate from tenderness, awe, and wonder with our children, the more we dissociate from each other and lose our capacity for empathy, the barrier to violence. How can you nurture a child when your attention is divided?

A Teacher's Experiment

John Whalen, a teacher at the Escola Americana do Rio de Janeiro in Brazil, told me that his school suspended the regular seventh-grade curriculum for one week a year to concentrate exclusively on drug and alcohol awareness. The children knew the week would be devoted to instruction on addiction.

"I decided to try and replicate the feeling of addiction by having my students abstain from the use of TV, video games, and screen time," John told me.

"On Monday, I announced that students could not watch television or spend any time on their computers or video game systems for the entire school week except that which was 'prescribed' by a teacher. I explained that I gave them the assignment to simulate the feelings and symptoms of addiction.

"The students reacted with anger and disbelief. 'You're kidding, right?!' They told me what I was asking was 'impossible.' What were they going to do with themselves?

"On the second day, I asked who had done their homework. Most laughed and admitted that they didn't even try. A few said that they had been able to do it, but that it was hard. I asked the ones who didn't try, 'What does it say to you that you can't give up TV for one day in your life? What is that about?' After a discussion, many more students decided to take part in the exercise. One kid asked, 'How will you know if we do the assignment?' I said, 'I wouldn't know, just as your teachers or parents won't be there when you are offered drugs or alcohol for the first or second time. The purpose is for you to be more aware of yourselves. Just tune in and think about it.'

"Throughout the week, I asked the students who did the assignment how they filled their time. Most said they did their homework. Others said they talked on the phone, played music, did something artistic, read, or called grandparents or friends. Free time, and what to do with it, became the main topic for the rest of the week.

"When I asked the others why it was so hard, they described a fear that sounded like falling into an empty pit. They simply had no resources to draw on, no activities or interests to sustain them. By the end of the week the students who had stuck with it said that it was hard initially, but it had enormous effects. 'It was wonderful,' one student said. 'I felt so much better. I read a whole book—I haven't done that in a long time.' Other student comments were: 'I spent time visiting with a friend.' 'I did better with my homework.' 'I had a nice time going shopping with my mother.' 'I could feel a difference in my mood.' 'I have more energy.'"

We often don't know the harmful effects of a habitual behavior until we stop doing it. This experiment is an excellent way for children to develop their critical capacity to learn about themselves.

This experiment also brought to mind a high school dean of students I interviewed. He told me that very few of the kids who are in after-school activities—playing on teams or in drama or the arts—ever make their way into his office with problems. It's usually the kids with too much free time, too few interests, and not enough parental guidance who are his frequent visitors.

John's experiment with the seventh-graders underscores the need to put statements about use of electronics in context. If a child is upbeat, has good friends, is respectful, open with his parents, participates in family activities, is doing well in school, and takes part in sports or musical activities, he is likely to be okay.

But if a child is lonely, tends to withdraw, is irritable, has trouble in school, is angry, blames others, and increasingly watches violent videos and TV programs or reads books with violent content, that child is more at risk for an addiction to some version of the cyberworld and other addictions. Parents need to become more involved and explore what's going on in that child's life.

Even if a child is getting good grades, if he's showing signs of withdrawal, irritability, and depression, parents are wise to be concerned.

Children Have Different Inclinations Toward the Cyberworld

It's also important to consider the nature of each child. One father said, "My older son likes to play video games occasionally and it's no problem, but my other son is drawn toward video games like a magnet, and I need to watch him very carefully. I can tell from my own history that he is pulled to video games in the same way I was pulled toward drugs. I can see how easy it is for him to get hooked." These two boys are healthy, bright, talented, well-loved children in a solid, cohesive family, and yet they are very different from each other.

In all cases, oversight is important. There is considerable research suggesting that there is a huge gap between what parents *think* their kids are watching and what they are *actually* watching, especially when it comes to sexually explicit material. Parents should also monitor what kind of personal information their children are giving out on the Internet.

Think About What Cybertime Leaves Out

It's not just the risks of the cyberworld that parents need to be concerned about. Think of other things your kids could be doing instead of sitting in front of a screen—activities that contribute to their emotional and physical development, like playing, creating, reading, visiting friends, hiking, or exploring outside. Let your common sense be your guide. It's not all or nothing. It's about engagement, balance, and being attuned to your child's life.

Suggestions for Parenting in a Media World

As always, there is a rhythm and timing to talking with your children. Some of the following suggestions may be relevant, others not. It's up to you to tune into your children so you can reach them.

I encourage every parent to go online if possible and explore for yourself various articles on children and screen time. You can talk about yourself when you discuss things with your kids, such as, "I realize I'm getting hooked on having my cell phone with me at all times; I'm going to start leaving it at home when I don't really need it." It's a balance between trusting the intelligence of your children, keeping them informed, and tuning in to their behavior. You don't want to sound like someone on a soapbox, but you don't want to abdicate your role as parent and guide, either.

1. Talk with your children. Explain your concerns. Educate them about the effects of screen time on their brains, and help them understand the consequences of sexting or sending sexually explicit pictures of others. Tell them about the addictive nature of violence.

2. Set limits and explain your reasons. Talk them over with your children and see if they can understand what you are saying. It's best if the policies make sense to your child, even if you sometimes make exceptions.

3. Teach children about the dangers and the possible consequences of giving out personal information.

4. Teach children to be savvy about advertising.

5. Make it a family experiment occasionally to take a day off from screen time, text-messaging, TV, and cell phones. What could you do to have fun together? Try it in the spirit of scientists doing an experiment on what it's like to take a break from cybertime. Then have everyone check back in on how it was for them.

6. Decide as a family to do a volunteer project as a way of contributing to others. There are projects large and small. Habitat for Humanity is a great place to work together as a family, but there are many other options. One family heard that the local food bank liked having stuffed animals available for kids, so they picked out twenty of them at the Goodwill store and then took them to the food bank, which was an eye-opener for the children. They didn't realize that people in their own town sometimes went without food.

7. As a family, decide on a movie or TV program to watch together. Studies repeatedly urge parents to watch TV with their children.

EXERCISE: QUESTIONS FOR PARENTS

Our kids certainly have minds of their own. But at the same time, they take the lead from their parents. Here are some questions for parents or caretakers to explore for themselves:

1. What is your use of electronics?
2. Does your use of electronics preempt doing other things you'd like to do or that would enhance your life (gardening, talking with friends, reading, catching up on projects, studying a cookbook)?
3. Are there aspects of electronics that feel compulsive, so much so that you'd feel nervous without them (TV, cell phone, texting, constant music or sound, chat rooms, pornography, checking out news stories)?
4. Is there anything you are doing online that you are keeping secret from your spouse or partner? What's that about?
5. Is there anything you would be ashamed to tell your child about your cyber use?
6. Have you had fights or disagreements with your partner over cyber use?
7. Could you have a media-free day and be okay—no TV, Internet, or extensive phone use?
8. Can you tolerate silence for extended periods—a half hour, an hour, or more? What happens when there is silence in the house or in the car?

9. What would it be like to refrain from turning on the TV unless you were planning to watch a particular program? Could you play music instead, avoiding radio stations with loud commercials?

10. What would it be like to pick out fewer than five hours of TV programs to watch during a week and then watch only those? Can you watch a program then turn off the TV?

11. If you didn't watch TV or go online, what would you be doing instead?

12. Are you able to set clear limits on screen time? Can you stand up to your children's protests against the limits that you set?

Play with these questions, and see which ones apply to you. Talk with your partner or with a friend. For some families this will be easy; for others it will be a challenge.

"What Mommy Says, Daddy Says; What Daddy Says, Mommy Says"

Jessie laughed as she used this phrase during an interview. "We are a team—a united front when it comes to setting limits. They can't play us against each other when it comes to decisions we've made about videos and screen time. We can be different in other things, but not this. We talk things over and then make decisions that we think are best for the children's age and development. We don't allow violent videos and games in the house. We know they probably play them occasionally at their friends' homes, but we decided not to make an issue of it."

It helps children when parents send a clear, unambiguous message. It is also a way for parents to create safety for their children.

Whether you are living together as a committed couple or separately, it's crucial to talk over the limits for children and to act as a team. Don't undercut each other. Remember that allowing a child to have endless screen time, or expensive stuff because "he or she likes it so much," abdicates your responsibility to be older, wiser, and protective of your child.

Nonattachment, Habits, Compulsions, Addictions

People often refer to the terms "addiction" and "compulsion" when talking about cyber use. Cyber addiction is a growing concern for younger and younger children.

In a study performed by the Campus Charité of the University of Medicine in Berlin, Germany, researchers found that of 7,069 gamers in their study, 11.9 percent (840 participants) fulfilled diagnostic criteria of addiction concerning their gaming.

We can look at cyber use as existing on a *continuum*, from nonattachment to compulsion to addiction:

The Continuum of Being Hooked

1. From complete freedom to feeling driven to total powerlessness to control our desires, or in Buddhist terms, cravings.
2. From being present and connected, to being preoccupied and tense, to being withdrawn into an addictive trance much of the time.
3. From freedom to chart our lives, to centering our lives around our compulsive needs, to the serious consequences of a life reeling out of control.
4. From ease in controlling or stopping our behavior to discomfort and agitation, to feeling powerless to stop and

experiencing withdrawal symptoms such as jumpiness, anxiety, depression, feeling lost, and having suicidal thoughts.

5. From being honest and straightforward, to making up stories to justify our use, to minimizing, denying, making excuses, or blaming others for our behavior.

6. From a calm state to having our physiology get increasingly activated in anticipation of entering into our addictive screen time trance.

NOTE: With an addiction, it takes more and more of a certain stimulus or a bigger and bigger hit of violence or sex (for example) to get the same physiological reaction. That's why it escalates.

Use this list to reflect on yourself and to be aware of your children. The best thing is always prevention. When someone gets lost in an addiction it's a huge challenge to help them pull out. Keep remembering as parents how important your involvement is to your child's well-being.

....

When we get lost in a cyber trance, we lose the ability to be present, to give our undivided attention to a friend, listen to sounds, and notice shapes, sizes, and colors of the world around. Life shrinks.

....

Returning to Buddhism: The Need for Meditation as a Central Part of Making Peace with Ourselves

Meditation can be a momentary pause for stillness. The body breathes deeply, the nervous system slows down. It can be as simple as savoring a cup of tea—really tasting it, feeling its warmth, or taking a moment to notice the design of a leaf or listen to a birdcall. More and more, adults fill in every moment with cell phones, TV, and background sound rather than seeing, hearing, and observing what is around them. The more we feel compelled to fill in the spaces, the more anxious we become. As a result, silence and stillness—those deep sources of grounding within—disappear from our lives. It's like losing our balance.

Cyber Guidelines for Young Children

There is considerable research on the effects of TV, computers, and video games on children, particularly infants and toddlers. Here are some directives based on current research:

BIRTH TO THREE YEARS OLD

No TV, *no* screen time in the first two years according to the American Academy of Pediatrics (AAP) and a host of other researchers and child specialists. The High Audiovisual Council of France has ruled against any programming for children under *three* years old, stating that it "hurts the development" and "poses a certain number of risks, encouraging passivity, slow language acquisition, overexcitedness, troubles with sleep and concentration as well as dependence on screens."

The first three years of life are the most critical for the development of the brain, language acquisition, and basic trust. If a child has lags in this period, part of his development is lost or compromised, and it will take great effort to make it up later. It's like laying an uneven foundation for a house, because each stage always builds on the one that came before it.

You don't have to be an expert. All you really have to do is watch the faces of babies or toddlers when a TV set goes on. It instantly grabs their attention, their eyes lock onto the screen, and they go into a passive trance. Conversely, notice how they look when you sing to them, play with them, bounce them on your leg, or rock them and recite a nursery rhyme. Notice their faces when they play on their own.

WHAT ABOUT BABY EINSTEIN AND LEARNING VIDEOS?

Baby Albert Einstein didn't watch videos. He played. *Learning is interactive, sensory, and real.* Videos of any kind at an early age—whether or not they are labeled "learning"—are harmful because they are two-dimensional and lead to passivity. There will be time for videos later. There is absolutely no need for such "learning" videos. Children can get everything they need from your words, attention, kindness, songs, stories, creative play, and friendly interactions. It is far more instructive for a child to pick up an apple, touch it, smell it, and taste it, than to look at a picture of one on a TV screen. The best messages you can send are free—your loving presence!

STORIES FOR CHILDREN WHILE PARENTS TAKE A BREAK:
A HEALTHY, FREE BABY SITTER

Parents and grandparents have been telling stories to their children for thousands of years. Children snuggle up to their parents and listen to their voices. One part of the brain hears the words, and then another creates images, thus integrating different parts of the brain and strengthening neural connections.

You can buy CDs of children's stories, or make tapes of yourself and others reading stories so that your child can listen to them when you need a moment to relax. (Although many recorders now are digital, it's still possible to get a little tape recorder and make cassette tapes that are easy to record and easy for a young child to play.)

I made a collection of tapes for my daughter with friends and grandparents reading stories to her when she was three. I also collected stories on records and tapes. When she listened she stayed alert and wide awake. I also had tapes of songs with which she sang along, and later, she and her friends danced to them. If children get in the habit of listening to stories as opposed to watching TV, they will be content with them. Like all paths of least resistance, if they get hooked on TV, stories may not seem so appealing.

THREE TO SIX YEARS OLD

There is no need to start children watching TV or looking at any kind of screen, but if you do, it's a good time for public television, because in most children's programming the images move slower, the stories are about kids learning to get along or deal with their feelings, the voices are quieter, and there are no commercials. The general recommendation is to limit viewing to an hour a day. Videos of animals and nature are beloved by children at this age. Don't watch violent cartoons with people or animals slamming into trees or being run over and squashed. They can be deeply disturbing. Remember, your child is vulnerable and his brain and nervous system are forming.

If you see that your child is getting disturbed or upset, or starts having bad dreams, you might want to take a break altogether. Television should be a side event, not central to their lives. This is a precious time in a child's life for learning that is interactive and real. The more a child becomes attuned to the natural world, is able to play on her own or with friends, and is creative, the better. Keep the TV turned off in communal areas when your child is present.

What the Parents Say

Kaye and Brad: "We had TV, but it was a very small part of life. We monitored what the children watched—mostly nature and family movies, and we watched with them. It was not the center of our leisure time together. Mostly, we were active as a family—we rode bikes, had picnics, the kids all did sports and played musical instruments, so TV wasn't a big deal."

Jeanine: "We had a policy of no TV or computers in the bedrooms. Bedrooms are for sleeping. We had a family computer and we had to sign up for times on it. They sometimes used it for writing papers for school and I can see the benefits, but I sure see the downside—they turn into zombies when they play those computer games."

Carleton: "I took a perfectly good TV set to the Goodwill. We were having arguments over the TV with my two boys, who were eight and twelve. I didn't like the conflict, or that dazed look they got when they watched it. I was afraid they'd be really mad, but it was amazing: the afternoon the TV disappeared, they got on their bikes and went to a local park and never complained. They grew up without any TV and did perfectly well in life."

Jeanne: "We put the computer in a central space near the kitchen where it could be seen by anyone in the house. Later, when the kids were teens, they could have a computer in the bedroom because it was clear they weren't using it excessively. They were all engaged in sports."

Jerimy: "We allowed no more than two hours of screen time a day by the time they were juniors in high school. That included everything. We stayed pretty connected as a family—ate together, talked, took vacations, did activities, and the kids went for a month in the summer to a

Mennonite camp where they did community service. We also talked about the content of video games, the idea that the good guys think they have a right to kill the bad guys—just like governments do when they want to justify going to war. We didn't try to stop them so much as help them think about what they were being shown, and the underlying message . . . or propaganda."

Martin: "Our daughter wasn't getting to sleep because of constant text-messaging at night. It was as if she went off to her room—her cave—to go into a texting trance. We finally had to take the cell phone away by eight P.M. so she could get to sleep. Something about texting makes it hard to sleep for several hours after. It had become an issue all through the day—she'd bring her cell phone to the table and text friends during dinner. It's a constant source of concern and conflict in the family."

Adam: "My parents were determined not to let me and my brother play video games. We were determined to have them. My mother hated violent videos, and she screened everything that came into the house. No shooting people. No violence. Together, we came up with a system: We'd do physical exercise—run a mile, do community service—and had other options to earn screen time. We banked up hours. Then we wanted a Nintendo console. We had a lot of discussion about it—a lot of heated discussion, I should say. We finally got one, but use was limited."

I asked Adam—he's now twenty-two—what he thought about his parents' policy. He said, "It was probably a good thing. I've seen how video games have really messed up some of my friends. They get so hooked they don't want to go out or do anything else. Some computer games are very addictive."

As you can see, managing your family's cyberworld is not always easy, but these parents consistently set limits. By the late teen years, children can have a fairly good capacity for critical thinking, or at least recognizing some of the propaganda they've been taught.

Don't expect your child to instantly get the message. It's a process. When my daughter watched MTV, I noted as to the positioning of the males how women were portrayed as victims or seemed to enjoy being dominated. Mostly I didn't watch it with her; I told her I didn't like the message. One day she came to me quite excited and said, "Come watch this one with me. It's okay. It's a good one." And sure enough, it was. My voice had crept into her consciousness and she was developing a capacity for observation and critical thinking.

To help children develop the inner strength to sort through the cyberworld, help them be aware, observe, think, then come to their own conclusions. While you may create some restrictions, avoid handing down authoritarian rules that the child must swallow without understanding. Plant seeds, model the behavior you want to see, and let your child know your values while respecting their differences and questions.

Now, to Leave the Cyberworld

Let's take a trip to a starry night in the desert. Byron Katie, founder of TheWork.com, writes of spending time alone in the desert in *A Thousand Names for Joy*. To make the transition from our talk about the cyberworld, take a deep breath, think of a warm starry night, relax your belly, and exhale.

"To be in the desert ... no sound—just mile after mile of sameness. ... And at night, in the moonless world, amid the smells and the silence, you lie down ... look up at the stars, and receive the ground, the coolness of the sand.... Nothing of life imagined can compete with the beauty of nothingness, the vastness of it, the unfathomable darkness."

Notice how your body feels as you take in these images. The media world is here to stay, but remember the wonder of the natural world around you—a profound source of wonder and peace.

17 The Circle of Money, Energy, and Time

*To you the earth yields her fruit, and you shall not want if
you but know how to fill your hands.*

*It is in exchanging the gifts of the earth that you shall find
abundance and be satisfied.*

*Yet unless the exchange be in love and kindly justice, it will
but lead some to greed and others to hunger.*

  —KAHLIL GIBRAN, *THE PROPHET*

The Web of Money and Living in Peace

"Live simply so others can simply live."

  —MOHANDAS GANDHI

We are all in a circular relationship with money, the earth,
energy, and time.

In Buddhism, everything is understood as being woven together
in a matrix of all life. To make peace in the world is to trade in mate-
rialistic values for human values like kindness, justice, equality, and
sustainability. This is no easy task, but there are many families who
impart these values to their children every day, making a difference

even in the smallest ways. Just as buying has its thrill, so does getting rid of excess stuff, living in simplicity, and joining with others in community projects. We can impart these values to our children to help them be naturally mindful of money. It's not necessarily the amount of money one has that is problematic; rather it's one's relationship to it. Someone who earns a great deal of money without exploiting others and supports projects to help the less advantaged can be in balance and at peace with money. Likewise, a person who is compulsively tight with money because they are driven by fear and insecurity can live a very simple lifestyle yet constantly be stressed and withholding.

In its basic form, money is energy, totally intertwined with the energy of our bodies, the earth and the well-being of everyone. Ideally, we develop a balance between working, spending, and helping others so that we are able to live peacefully within our means and in harmony with others.

For some people, money is associated with success, power, self-worth, and status—an attitude that can take on an addictive, desperate quality—and there can never be enough to permanently sustain the feeling of being worthwhile or lovable or ease the panic of falling into emptiness.

From a Buddhist perspective, money becomes a problem when it takes us away from our core values of mindfulness, loving-kindness, generosity, and living in balance with our neighbors and the earth.

....

In the absence of love and belonging, people often fall into grasping and hoarding. When this takes over, everything goes out of balance at a personal level and in the energy system of the earth. This can lead to the exploitation of people and the contamination of all that sustains life: clean air, water, forests, and the earth itself.

....

On a personal level, our desire for more money than we need is related to how content and secure we feel within ourselves. Our generosity with money comes out of a sense of inner abundance and belonging and sometimes by the example set by our parents. Our skill in handling money is a result of what we have learned about planning, working, and resisting impulses. What we choose to buy and acquire is tempered by our awareness of living in balance with others and the earth.

....

Teaching kids about money isn't just teaching them about dollars and cents. It's also teaching them to set goals, plan ahead, delay immediate gratification, enjoy free time, and share what they have with others.

....

Gain a Global Perspective with Money

Love is "like a magic penny / Hold it tight and you won't have any."
—FOLK SINGER MALVINA REYNOLDS

Anything that widens the chasm between the haves and the have-nots plants the seeds of violence in society in the form of despair, anger, and resentment. Quakers talk about needing to address the "occasion for war" as the way to peace.

From a planetary perspective, it is no longer an issue of survival of the fittest, it is survival of those who can cooperate and work together for the good of all. Thus, teaching children about money also means teaching them to recycle, to buy only what they need, to avoid excessive plastic packaging, to use money to help those who are less fortunate, and to be willing to accept help when they need it.

In other words, we need to spread it around, like the magic penny: "lend it, spend it and you'll have so many." This is the opposite of the trend we've seen in this country over the past twenty or thirty years, where greed and indifference to others have created an ever-widening gap between the rich, the poor, and those who are in between.

A Picture of a Family with Balanced Money Values

> *Wise parents provide economy class accommodations and then charge tolls in time and effort when children ask for more.*
> —H. STEPHEN GLENN, JANE NELSEN, *RAISING SELF-RELIANT CHILDREN IN A SELF-INDULGENT WORLD*

I spoke with Adam, age twenty-two, who was brought up in a Quaker family. "I'm not a consumer, I don't want much, I never have," he said. In our lengthy talk he told me that his mom shopped at thrift stores and that his parents reshingled the roof themselves to save money for a trip. When the kids were little, his father was a stay-at-home dad. This allowed them more time together as a family and lowered the stress of having two full-time working parents. It also meant economizing. But that was fine with everyone, because it was a core value in the family to use it up, wear it out, and pass it on. Being frugal didn't mean a lack of fun. When the kids were adolescents the family hiked, went camping, and even took a three-hundred-mile bike trip together.

We impart values about money to our children in hundreds of ways, many of which are expressed in Adam's description of his family. The way of peace is to raise children to believe that they have to put in time and effort for what they get rather than to develop a sense of entitlement, meaning that they realize that the world doesn't owe them a living.

A secure family bond, open conversations, awareness of values, hard work, and a wide array of interests all help to create a barrier against children mistaking money and possessions for love.

Teaching Skills, Imparting Values of Work

My book group read *Nickel and Dimed* by Barbara Ehrenreich, which led to all of us talking about our jobs as children and young adults, in high school and through our twenties. Those early experiences, many of which were summer jobs—babysitting, waiting tables, working in a nursing home, working in a fishery in Alaska, firefighting—were recalled with a lot of laughter and warm feelings. I talked about my first job at five years old digging dandelions for our next door neighbor at a penny a plant.

Having a wide variety of jobs while growing up broadens a child's life immeasurably and teaches her that it feels good to earn your way in the world by making an effort to get what you want.

Learning to accept hard work and being frugal also helps us reach for larger goals. When my father was in graduate school, he and my mother played violin and the clarinet at Sunday night church gatherings, so they could eat for free. I still have their immaculate budget book in which they wrote down every expense. Even though they barely had enough money for food, my mother said they didn't feel the least bit deprived because they were working together toward a goal.

Teach Financial Planning

When we are mindful about money—resist impulse buying, buy quality goods, make things, repair them, reuse them, recycle them, and buy from yard sales, eBay, and thrift stores—children are likely to follow our lead. Frugal doesn't have to mean cheap; it means being mindful of sustainability. It doesn't mean we can't occasionally splurge a little—yet as people become aware of their relationship with the earth and other people, they tend to be happier when they are careful of their impact on landfills and pollution.

No matter what we teach them, children will vary in their relationships to money: one may start hiding money in the drawer at an early age, while another may spend it immediately on pretty things, toys, candy, or maybe even on friends. One will become a little entrepreneur; another won't think about making money at all.

To help children live within a budget, start by letting them know the plan before a trip to the store, restaurant, or carnival. Tell children how many rides they can go on at the fair, how much you can afford to spend on fall clothes, how much you are willing to contribute to a particular purchase (a lot of people have a fifty percent policy). If a child knows in advance he gets five rides at the fair, for example, he can look around and decide on the ones he wants. This will help him learn to consider his choices and live within certain means. Every now and then, if you can afford it, you might say "tonight you can have as many rides as you want" or "buy anything you want to eat."

If you are taking a family vacation, you might encourage your kids to bring some of their savings, or you can give them a specific amount to spend while you're away. Once you remind them to think through their choices, let them decide how to spend it. If they run out on the second day, resist all lectures and let the natural consequences do the teaching. *"I know it's hard to be flat broke."*

Separate Objects from Love

Money is not love. Objects are not love. A thoughtful present can be a token of love or care, but it should not become the emotional currency between parents and children. It sometimes takes exploring one's motivation to realize that money is being used to curry favor, assuage guilt, or as a quid pro quo: "If I give you this, then I expect that."

Parents need to reflect on what they are actually "saying" to their children when they buy things or give them money. *"I will pay you to be a certain way. You can get things by pleasing me."* This is an all too common example of conditional love—a behavior that tends to create a false persona in our children. Using money to control children takes away from their having an intrinsic sense of belonging. Think about the ramifications for their future relationships when children are conditioned to believe, *Love equals people buying me things.* This will never help them feel truly loved.

> If the need for love is fulfilled, children are less likely to develop a driving hunger for money and objects. They will enjoy what they have and possessions won't be mistaken as proof of being special or being loved.

What About Having an Allowance?

This subject raised fascinating conversations among the people I interviewed for this book: Should kids get an allowance at all? At what age? Should they be expected to do chores around the house? Should they be expected to tithe, or donate some of the money to charity? At what point should children start a savings account, and should some of their allowance go into it?

There were few absolutes about allowance and chores, except that all the families I interviewed believed that it's a natural part of family life for children to participate in the household without always being paid. Some kids earned money by doing specific chores, others had an allowance, and some had a bit of both—an allowance and the option to earn extra money with bigger tasks.

In one family, there were no allowances: the parents gave their children what they needed (not everything they wanted) and the children were always reasonable. They knew their parents did their best given a shifting financial situation. The mother told me her son said to her, "I know things are tight right now, but is there any way we can get me new sneakers? These don't really fit me anymore." This child was mindful of his parents' situation, didn't want to overburden them, but was also secure enough to let them know his needs. As his mother said, "When you get a request like that, how can you say no?" She was also amazingly generous. For example, she saved up money from cleaning houses and surprised the whole family with a cruise.

It was true across the board that parents who were successful in teaching their children about money were open about the subject and explained why they set certain policies regarding money. The kids had a voice in allowances and the financing of school supplies such as band uniforms, sports equipment, and high school trips. The parents were generous when it came to supporting activities, studies, lessons, trips, and sports, because they saw the value in them for their children, both in happiness and in developing their potential.

EXERCISE: REFLECT ON YOUR HABITS WITH MONEY

"You do with your money how you do with your love."

—Ken Keyes

The parallel between love and money was the theme of an afternoon workshop I attended at Ken Keyes's Cornucopia Center in Kentucky in 1980. The insights were startling. Some of the questions that arose were: *Do you hoard it, give it away without a thought, or make plans? Are you consistent, chaotic, or impulsive?* You might use these questions for reflection.

1. Do you give so much to others that there isn't enough for you or your family?

2. Do you give conditionally? Expect something in return? Do you keep score or feel hurt if others don't give back?

3. Do you give presents or pay for others so they will like you?

4. Talk about guilt and money. Did you or do you still get money from your parents by using guilt or manipulating them? Do your parents use money to control you? Describe what they do, any conflicting feelings you might have, and your role in the dance.

5. Do you exhaust yourself earning money?

6. Does money seem to slip through your fingers?

7. Do you hoard money, worry about every dime you spend, and have a hard time letting loose or being generous?

8. Have you ever lived on a budget?

9. Do you notice prices? Look for good value? For example, do you know what fruits and vegetables cost in season as opposed to out of season?

10. Do you buy things to make up for hurting someone or to keep them from leaving you?

11. Are you able to save up for something special, or sometimes let loose and not worry about what something costs?

12. Are you able to go without things you would like in order to live within your means?

13. Can you live frugally and not feel deprived?

Successful Approaches to Money and Responsibility

Families I spoke to told me how they've taught their children about money. (I often heard from the children, too.)

1. They were open with their children about money. They might show them the bills and credit card statements, or talk about how they plan to use money. *It will take us two more years to save up for a car and we'll get a used one because it's a better value.* They explained savings accounts, the cost of credit card interest, and their long-term goals as soon as their children were old enough to understand. By the time I was a teenager, my father had explained to me that buying a house was usually the best hedge against inflation. I used his arguments to get my husband to buy a house shortly after we got married—he would have waited— and it turned out to be an excellent investment.

2. They can live on limited means with dignity and creativity. They neither complained to their children nor led them to feel anxious about money. One single woman with three children and limited means spoke of making up songs together, telling stories, buying children's books at thrift stores, going to the library, pitching a tent in the backyard, using crepe paper to make Christmas ornaments, saving up to buy chocolate chips then making cookies. She succeeded in raising children who felt secure and not deprived.

3. Those with considerable wealth often lived modestly, imparted values of working to earn money, and did not overindulge their children. They were active in community service and deeply involved with their family.

4. The parents taught that their money belongs to the whole family—it isn't the parents' to have and the kids' to receive. One

man said, "If the kid dinged the car, it wasn't that he dinged his father's car, it was that he damaged the family's car. It all belonged to all of us. It got repaired with family money."

5. They let their children know when their financial situation was tight and enlisted the children's contribution to being careful with money. They didn't say, "You need to stop wanting so much." Instead they said, "We have extra expenses with Grandma," or "I'm going to school part-time, so we're going to have to be careful and creative with money and cut back on spending. We'll need your help."

6. Some parents create a beautiful or artistic home, but not for the purpose of impressing the neighbors. They love to express their creativity, have fun, and enjoy the pleasure of bringing beauty to their home. Some people do this on a low budget, using second-hand furniture, or by their own effort, such as by refinishing furniture or going to estate sales. This gives an important model to the children: *We can find ways to live well and be happy on a limited income.*

7. The parents didn't feel guilty setting limits about spending on luxury items. They followed the philosophy of going economy class and having their children work if they wanted extras.

8. If the children blew their allowance the parents did not bail them out.

9. They put a strong value on education; it was often their highest priority. They saved specifically so their kids could have music lessons, go to summer camp, and eventually go to college.

Teach Children to Appreciate What Parents Provide

Both of my parents expressed great appreciation of their own parents, who worked hard simply to put food on the table and to help them go to college. It was a family effort and everyone pitched in. My dad jumped trains in the summers when he was in high school to bail hay for ranchers and send the money home. Mother learned to sew her own clothes at an early age.

Parents I talked with often commented on the sense of entitlement common to the younger generation and spoke of their efforts to teach their children to appreciate the parent's efforts and the value of work.

Carla told me, "When I was driving my son Jess to soccer, he mentioned that the neighbors paid their kid fifty cents a room to vacuum." Without batting an eye, Carla responded, with a smile, "Okay, I'll pay you fifty cents to vacuum and you pay me fifty cents to drive you to soccer."

A teenage boy told me that in his family, if the kids didn't help or got lippy, the mom would simply say, "No, I'm busy," when he asked her to drive him to a friend's house. The implication was clear to him, and he liked the fact that there were no lectures or yelling.

Steve told me, "We'd use the family dynamics to teach the kids about fairness. We'd pay for extra jobs, but not for cutting or stacking wood, because we all need the heat. The payoff was that they got to drive the car on a date or to a game. The family needs heat, the family needs to get places. It's all part of working together; we all matter to each other."

He commented that at one point, his kids still seemed to think that money grew on trees. They asked him for a computer as if it were a minor expense. To bring his point across, Steve brought home his whole paycheck in ten-, twenty- and fifty-dollar bills and dealt them out to the four kids as they sat around the dining table. He then put all the bills on the table—mortgage, utilities, insurance, and so forth. He also had a list of automatic deductions, and the contribution to the slush fund they kept for one-time expenses like new tires or house repairs. He said, "At first the kids' eyes were popping at the sight of all that money. But as they had to pay out money for the bills, they were surprised. They had no idea how much it cost to run our household."

Affluence, Happiness, and Sustainability: What Is Our Legacy to Our Children?

> *Having more and more does not really leave us feeling fuller or more fulfilled. The less we get out of what we have, the more we seem to want.*
>
> —PAUL L. WACHTEL, THE POVERTY OF AFFLUENCE: A PSYCHOLOGICAL PORTRAIT OF THE AMERICAN WAY OF LIFE

If we bring up children to experience that true affluence comes from a sense of belonging, developing one's talents, and caring for others, we will stem the tide of consumerism that is unsustainable in the long run (more and more automobiles, electronic gizmos, extraction of petroleum, manufacture of plastics, etc.). It's a conflict because we are urged to acquire more and more stuff as part of "helping the economy." This means we are bombarded with advertisements to create cravings, which is totally antithetical to the principles of Buddhism and Quakerism.

In accordance with Gandhi's teaching to "Live simply so others can simply live," we need to think of simplicity not as deprivation but rather as coming back to our center, our peace of mind, and our sense of being global citizens.

In *The Poverty of Affluence*, Paul L. Wachtel points out that Americans doubled energy consumption between 1960 and 1990. He asks, "but did we become twice as happy?" The American form of capitalism and the sustainability of the earth are essentially incompatible. We are in a terrible spiral. The economy is based on consumerism, which is based on people feeling insecure, lonely, and unhappy, and often leads people to be stressed out, working long hours and being over their heads in debt. I believe at some level we all know this, and we will have greater peace of mind when we wake up from a kind of trance about the unsustainability of our lifestyles.

When the Buddha said, "May all people be happy," I don't think he meant may all people have "tons of stuff" to be happy. He didn't say, have a big house to be happy. His teachings centered around *the middle way*: just enough to be comfortable coupled with truth, kindness, compassion, and inner peace.

True affluence is measured by living in community with simplicity, generosity, and love.

18 The Circle of Food, Health, and Pleasure

Loving Foods That Love You Back

Our connection with food is one of the deepest, most powerful relationships we have in our lives. It encompasses nurture, nature, pleasure, satisfaction, health, concentration, feeling good, and our relationships with other people. Helping children develop a positive and healthy relationship with food is one of the greatest gifts we can give them. Ideally, our relationship with food starts while nursing or being fed, curled up in our mothers' arms. It gradually evolves to feeding ourselves with our fingers, then lifting a spoon to our mouths. It can evolve into shopping, growing vegetables, tending animals, cooking, and understanding where food comes from—a knowledge that is deeply imprinted on human history. Our relationship to food can also be deeply entwined with our spiritual journey, reflecting our loving-kindness and our connection to our bodies, the animals, and the earth.

What we eat, how we eat, when we eat are all part of the rhythm and ritual of our bodies and our days.

Food is medicine. Food affects every cell in the body. It is related to the health of our teeth, heart, liver, digestive process, fingernails, muscles, energy, and mood. As we become tuned in to our food habits, we notice the connections between our energy levels and sense of well-being and the foods we've been eating. *Why am I so tired this morning? Maybe it's all that ice cream I ate last night. Why is the baby so jumpy? Maybe it's because I've been nursing after drinking caffeine.*

Food is ritual. Part of using food as good medicine is eating in a relaxed, friendly setting with other people—the social ritual of breaking bread together, having an enjoyable time, and talking about your day, a good book you're reading, or a fun adventure with a friend.

Food is also a part of celebrations, holidays, and religious and spiritual rituals: Halloween and pumpkins, Fridays and fish, Thanksgiving and turkey. Some pairings of food with religious observances have long-forgotten roots. For example, the tradition of having chocolate bunnies and colored eggs at Easter stems from the pagan fertility symbols of the equinox that Christianity tried to displace by scheduling Easter near that time. Some of our customs are more folklore than history. For example, at the original Thanksgiving in Plymouth Colony they probably ate venison and eel, not turkey. Our food rituals can feel comforting and pleasant to anticipate, or they can become rigid. It's important to notice the difference.

The Family Blessing

Many families start dinner with a blessing. This is a way to slow down, remember our connection to the earth and the animals and vegetables that contributed to our meal, and express appreciation. The Quaker way is to hold hands, sink into stillness, and invite anyone to speak out of the silence if so led. It could be to offer an appreciation, give thanks, or welcome a guest to the home. Some people send a blessing to the world. If no one speaks, we squeeze each other's hands, and take that as a blessing. Or, you could say a version of the Buddhist blessing: *May all people be happy. May all people have food.*

Yum Yum: Pea Soup and Salad

It's my birthday, and I'm sitting in a lovely restaurant with a few friends. Kerri, the mother of two young girls in brightly colored clothes, reads the menu with excitement. "Oh, pea soup and salad! Would you like that?" My eyes pop even wider as Miriam, Kerri's six-year-old, says, "Yes." On another occasion, at an informal dinner recently, I watch the two young sons of my friends Margaret and John go back for seconds of brown rice, fish, and salad.

At the other end of the spectrum, seven-year-old Jill has probably not had a vegetable or fruit since she stopped eating baby food out of a jar. Her diet is primarily Chicken McNuggets, french fries, white bread, cookies, Jell-O, and ice cream, and she rarely brushes her teeth. Instead of water, she has learned to go to the fridge for a swig or two of Mountain Dew when she is thirsty. She is often jumpy and restless, has a hard time concentrating on a simple puzzle or game, and gets irritable and agitated if they run out of soda. It's like watching someone in withdrawal: life has become a cycle of eating, a drop in energy, having cravings and going for more stimulating food or drink. At the tender age of seven Jill has already had most of her teeth extracted because they were full of cavities and her gums were inflamed.

All of these parents love their children and want the best for them. The difference is that Jill's parents are not aware of the connection between food, health, and the ability to concentrate and learn.

Many parents who love their children need education about nutrition, eating habits, and health, and this knowledge needs to become
mainstream.

The Habits of a Health-Conscious Family

Kerri told me how she and her husband raised their children to be
healthy eaters. "First of all, I nursed them for a long time and made
sure it was a relaxed and close time. Then Mark and I made most of
the baby food so it was free of sugar and additives. Then the kids
started eating the same food we ate—lots of soups, lentils, fruits,
vegetables, fish. We've never had chips, soda pop, or junk food in the
house."

I asked her about snacks and treats. "We started early with fruit
and whole-grain crackers and we limit how much they can have. We
use mostly whole grains and maple syrup (instead of sugar) when we
bake." A treat is definitely that—a treat.

If their children visit other kids, Kerri doesn't worry about it.
"I know they might eat some junk food there, but I don't want to
make a great big issue of it or have them feel weird." She laughed.
"They already think we're weird enough having a vegetable garden in
the front yard, riding bikes most of the time, and driving an old car."

I asked Margaret about her boys, the ones I observed going for
seconds of brown rice, fish, and salad. Other than using commercial
baby food, her story was similar to Kerri's. In nursery school and
preschool her children were given healthy food and did not have
sweets or even fruit juice, which has a high concentration of sugar.

"After they were off baby food, I never made separate food for
them." she said. "They always ate what we ate. I'd fix it in ways they
liked, like grilling vegetables with a little butter." She told me that
she'd been told to feed infants vegetables before anything sweet, like

fruit, so that they wouldn't expect that sweet taste, a method she has used for thirteen years. She laughed. "Carrots don't taste so good after apple sauce." They also keep sugar and junk food out of the house for the most part. Chips or soft drinks are an occasional treat, maybe once every few weeks. Margaret recently started teaching the boys portion control with snacks. "They put crackers or nuts in a small dish when they watch TV instead of eating mindlessly out of a bag."

Growing and Preparing Food Is Good for a Child's Brain

Help children participate in their relationship with food. In a fascinating article in *Scientific American Mind*, one of my favorite magazines, Kelly Lambert, a neuroscientist, writes about the positive mental and emotional effects of effort-driven rewards, especially when they involve using your hands in a way that directly relates to your survival. They "activate the problem-solving prefrontal cortex plus the movement-controlling striatum and the reward/motivation center known as the accumbens, leaving you with a fuller brain experience that prepares you for life's next challenge." In other words, taking part in the cycle of growing food, preparing it, and eating it is a powerful way to stimulate different parts of the brain.

The more children are involved with preparing food, the more they become connected to their own survival. Even if you don't have a place or time for a garden, you can visit a friend's garden, take them to a market, or go to a farm. You can help children learn to name and buy vegetables, grains, and forms of protein. They can participate in meal planning, washing and chopping vegetables, cooking, setting the table, cleaning up.

Eventually a child will learn that a pork chop doesn't grow under cellophane—it's part of a pig—vegetables come from the earth, and most of the milk you buy comes from a cow and is likely to have hormones in it.

Children may get curious by watching you read labels. If they show an interest, you can explain the choices you make regarding antibiotics, corn syrup, and other additives. (To learn more, search the Internet for "super foods," "food additives," "antibiotics in food," "high-fructose corn syrup," "artificial sweeteners," and "acid and alkaline diets," to name a few of the things it's good to be aware of.)

My eighteen-month-old nephew Noah can already mumble "crot" (carrot) and "ornge" (orange) when he shops with his mother—she uses vegetables and fruits to teach him colors—and he is also learning to identify things in nature. Whether you are married or single, male or female, young or old, making the effort to buy or grow, prepare, and eat healthy food brings you into the circle of nature and is a lovely way to care for yourself and others.

Breaking Bread Together: The Positive Effects of Family Mealtime

If we remember that healthy attachments are an ongoing, lifelong process, it makes sense that regular mealtimes can provide a steady way for families to stay engaged and involved with each other. When we link nurture, food, pleasure, and listening to one another, we contribute to the positive circle of our relationships.

For some people, "regular meals" means every night; for others "regular" means a few times a week. There is a lot of data on the emotional health of families who eat together, as well as the negative effects on children who don't. These studies can be summarized as follows: Maintaining good connections with your child on a daily basis has many positive effects, and a great way to do it is at mealtime. This contributes to everyone in the family staying connected and keeping up a running dialogue. One of the young adults I talked to spoke fondly of family dinners: "That was a really good part of growing up. I'll do that with my children one day."

Dinner doesn't need to be complicated or fancy. Even if it's take-out, heating something out of a box, or the same food you prepared yesterday, slowing down, sitting down, and being together are what matter most. And remember, mealtime is not a time for criticism or lectures. It's about everyone checking in or having a good discussion and just being together.

What About Wine and Alcohol?

The eightfold path, or "right" living, includes responsible use of all substances, and includes no proscription on the use of alcohol, although I know many Buddhists who drink occasionally. The deeper message in Buddhism is to follow the middle way and be responsible in every aspect of life—and that includes alcohol and other drugs. It can take some deep introspection and honesty with oneself to bypass the denial and minimization of their use.

For some families, a glass of wine is customary with dinner. However, daily or heavy alcohol consumption can be detrimental in two ways. First, it models the use of daily alcohol use, and puts children at higher risk for problem drinking. Second, at some level it pulls the parents away from being fully present to their children. I suspect a lot of people would argue with this, but having worked with addiction for thirty years, I've seen again and again that families who always associate drinking with eating or being together are often less emotionally transparent and engaged with one another.

One child described family conversations while drinking as pleasant but empty. Another spoke of daily dinners at which wine was always offered to her after she turned seventeen. "It was almost as if they were pushing me to drink, to join them. When I started having blackouts at twenty, I was scared to tell my family about it, because drinking was so much a part of their daily ritual." If you encourage children to drink, either in subtle or overt ways, ask yourself why.

Try experimenting with not drinking several days a week, having less, or taking a break. Notice if it's difficult, or if you get irritable or if alcohol is often on your mind. Notice any signs of withdrawal, such as feeling tired or having cravings, or escalating your use of sugar and salt. Some people find that they feel better and more in control of their lives when they lower their alcohol consumption.

Anyone who has had blackouts, or loses his temper when drinking, or feels she can't relax without a drink would be wise to talk with an addiction counselor. You could also ask someone you trust to tell you if they think you might have a drinking problem, starting with your partner and close family or friends.

Relax, There's No "Right" Way to Eat

Okay, so organic is good. Natural fresh fruits and vegetables are very good. Whole grains are good for many. However, getting compulsive about eating can be negative. It's helpful to think about *good enough* eating. You don't have to be perfect. At the same time, you can combine eating with developing your consciousness about health and sustainability.

There are many theories about food: some say to eat a big breakfast, eat fruit until lunch, eat only raw food, don't combine starch and protein, eat local foods in season, and so on.

Every body has its own rhythm and flow, and children are often different from their parents. The tasks for parents are helping children learn to listen to their bodies and, at the same time, introducing healthy foods so that they develop a taste for them. Parents would do well to also focus on listening to their own bodies.

It is important to notice when a child truly doesn't like a food or may even have a sensitivity to it, and not assume the child is just being obstinate. As a teenager I had daily fights about food—I should say breakfast fights—with my father in the breakfast nook. The idea of drinking milk the first thing in the morning was about as appealing to me as cold Brussels sprouts for dessert. It curdled my stomach. I didn't have much appetite for anything in the morning other than fruit, or possibly an egg, and if I did eat too much it made me sleepy.

My father, however, was convinced that a big breakfast was the only way to go. While everyone else dutifully ate, I resisted. What he didn't realize was that I wasn't rebelling against him, I was just trying to feel good. Later, when I learned about food combining, eating right for your blood type, and other aspects of diet and nutrition, my early preferences were validated. I had intuitively tuned into myself. How much better a pleasant conversation would have been than those repeated fights and the stress that invaded our household because of my father's need to control my eating and his certainty that he knew what was best for me.

Parents walk a fine line between respecting their children's tastes and tuning into the messages from the children. Kids go through phases where their tastes differ dramatically. Try to step back, keep the junk out of the house, not get intense, and remember, this too shall pass. One day your child will probably eat all kinds of foods.

Don't Use Food as a Reward, Punishment, or Bribe

Because food—what we put in our bodies—is personal, parents need to be careful about making food feel like an invasion—a forced march toward better nutrition.

Too often mealtimes are turned into an ordeal. The parents, determined to have their child "eat right," sit with their eyes glued on the child, praising and coaxing him to eat six peas and drink *all* his milk (and they probably don't taste or enjoy their own food). The child rebels and secretly takes pleasure in his power over his parents. *Wow! I can get all their attention by not eating, or picking at my food!*

Parents need to take an active role in presenting kids with healthy food, but they also need to step back and not over-monitor a child's eating, or make it about punishment, reward, or gaining their approval. Bribery, while tempting, especially with a picky eater, usually leads to more difficulties, because eating becomes a battle of wills. Nutrition is important, but it's not worth stressing out over the optimal levels of proteins and carbohydrates with a resistant kid.

Down with the Clean Plate Club

May we forever put the Clean Plate Club to rest, along with the phrases, "Children are starving in _____" (I grew up with Armenia), and "Good girl" or "Good boy" for eating something. Raising children to be at peace with themselves means helping them learn to attune to themselves.

I've also heard hundreds of descriptions of another age-old power struggle: "Sit at the table until you eat that!" One woman told me of her childhood memory of being found asleep at the dining table in the morning, ten hours after her aunt had pronounced, "You're not to leave the table until you eat those peas." Her aunt was mortified when she saw her niece asleep with her head resting on the plate as light was dawning in the house.

Don't make children go hungry because you want them to be thin, or because *you* are trying to be thin. I've heard many stories in therapy of kids not being allowed snacks and frequently suffering hunger pangs before they were allotted a meal at a prescribed time. One child was so hungry she'd sneak to the kitchen in the night for a few crackers, which her mother had put on a top shelf so the child couldn't reach them. The story has a sadistic quality to it.

I've also heard stories of scolding, of kids being sent to their room for not dutifully eating what they were given or being handed a plate of food and being timed, of kids storming off from the table, and even of a father throwing the Thanksgiving turkey against the wall in a drunken rage. In one heart-wrenching story, the daughter would hide the distasteful food in her cheek, then sneak to the kitchen to spit it out, only to be caught and beaten by her screaming mother: "You will eat everything I cook!" Food became associated with force, lying, anxiety, violence, and dread—not a good recipe for digestion or a positive relationship with food.

> If you want your children to have a healthy relationship with food, encourage them to develop a "feel" for when they're truly hungry (not just bored) and when they've had enough. It's also good to let them develop their tastes and a "vocabulary of the palate": sweet, sour, tart, bitter, tangy, etc.

Don't equate a child's food behavior with your self-esteem. Parents may inadvertently send the message, *If you eat what I cook and clean your plate, you are good. If you don't, you are bad.* When I spoke with Daniel Hughes, author of *Building the Bonds of Attachment,* about reward and punishment in relationship to eating, he said, "There is something wrong with thinking you have to reward and punish a child when it comes to eating. Micromanaging a child's eating really hurts the child's awareness of his body and how he feels. It also really messes up the parents' relationship with the child. Instead of eating together being an intrinsically good thing—a reciprocal, enjoyable activity—it becomes about power and control: I have to entice you to do what is natural."

Food Basics for Kids

- Start with small servings and allow for seconds if your child is still hungry.

- Help your child explore the questions: "How do you know when you're full or when you've had enough?" "Can you feel it?" "You just kind of know it?"

- You can help children learn that some foods may start to taste better after they have tried it several times—some foods are an "acquired taste"—but it's okay not to like it.

- Help children learn to focus on the taste of what they eat so they are conscious of the sensations and pleasure it gives them. (On what part of the tongue do they sense the taste? On the tip, or the back, or the sides?) "Is that yummy?" "Ooo. That must be sour." Or, "You don't like that so much, do you?"

- Children can also learn to be polite, as in saying, "No, thank you" for salad, or "I don't care for that" as opposed to "Yuk."

- Help children become conscious of chewing their food. Ask them how it feels when they chew. Which teeth do the chewing? How do their teeth compare with those of other animals? A tiger's? A dog's or a cat's? Explain that the point of chewing is to break down the food into small pieces so they don't choke when swallowing, and also so that big chunks of food don't go crashing down into the stomach, which freaks out and has to work really hard to break down the food for digestion.

- Always allow children healthy snacks if they are hungry and do not make them go hungry. Take the food off the table when it appears that everyone is full. You can sit around afterward with water, tea, coffee, or a little treat. This helps prevent having just one more bite—those bites that may add up to twenty pounds over the years.

- Teach children to ask, "May I be excused?" or "Is it okay to go now?" instead of jumping up and leaving the table. Rituals need a conscious beginning and end.
- A child's healthy relationship with food includes her feeling that she has a right to monitor what she puts into her body, and that she doesn't have to hurt herself to please others. If Aunt Martha looks wounded when your child doesn't want a slice of her banana bread—well, that's what Aunt Martha does, and we can love her anyway. Parents can help a child be respectful without compromising themselves. It's okay to say, "No thanks. I'm full."

What About Picky Eaters?

Tastes for food are developmental and change over time.

Some parents who attempt to feed their children in a healthy way have children who are very picky about food. This can arise from a number of factors—some are physiological, others indicate an underlying power struggle with the parents. This behavior usually appears as children enter the toddler stage, and is likely to ease up around age four or five.

The first steps for parents to take with a picky eater are to calm down and not turn eating into a battleground, to avoid bribery, and not to get caught up feeling like a lousy parent. The next thing to do is to be creative. For example, a child might like whole-grain cereal, so let them eat it for dinner. Offer a wide variety of food; the more children are exposed to various foods, the more likely they are to try and like them.

Again, avoid saying "Good boy" or "Good girl" when a child eats a particular food or cleans her plate. Eating is not about being a good kid; it's about a relationship with food. It can take effort to be patient and present more choices, but in the long run it will help your child develop good habits for life. With picky eaters, it can help to take a deep breath and remember the phrase, "This too shall pass."

A lot of good practical advice is available online; you can find articles on sneaking healthy food into the diet, recipes for picky eaters, and the like. The Mayo Clinic offers a number of useful tips at www.mayoclinic.com. The University of Michigan has an article ("Turning 'Yuck' into 'Yum' for Picky Eaters") that ends with two important points to remember:

• Bribery isn't the answer. Enticing your child with sweet treats as a reward for eating vegetables and fruits may actually cause them to dislike healthier foods.
• Accept defeat. This is a normal stage in your child's life, and if he or she is healthy and thriving, it may be time to give up trying to change your picky eater's food habits. [This doesn't have to mean a steady diet of junk food, but it can mean a lot of pasta, whole wheat toast, and potatoes, if that's what the child really wants.]

Be Consistent: Understand the Principle of Intermittent Reinforcement

If you have created policies—for example, no buying junk food in the grocery store—stick to no. I recently watched a child begging and whining for junk food in the grocery store. Initially, the mother said, "Honey, this isn't good for you, I really don't want to buy it." More fussing. Mom explained again. The child escalated to whining. The mother paused, then said, "Well, just this once." This mother is now in for at least twenty more tries, since she has just reinforced begging and whining.

Remember, the best way to encourage a behavior is to reward it, either every time or occasionally.

An alternative approach is to tell the child, "I'm not willing to buy that, but you can pick out some fruit or whole grain crackers and jam." You can also try to preempt the child having cravings in the grocery store by letting her have a snack while you shop. Or let her bring a plastic baggie of tasty apple or orange slices.

You may need to say a permanent *no* to candy if it is a persistent problem. Some stores—mostly natural foods stores—have candy-free checkout lines. If gum ball machines or candy at checkout lanes don't get on a child's radar because you never use them, it's less likely to become a problem.

Help Prevent Obesity

Much has been said about the growing rate of obesity, which has contributed to an immense increase in health problems and health care costs in the United States. It has been predicted that the present generation of young children will have a shorter life span than their parents as a result of obesity-related illnesses. With all the junk food luring us—from checkout lanes to schools—it takes more education, commitment, and effort for parents to create healthy eating habits in children than it may have taken in the past.

You may need a major overhaul in your household. Get the chips, soda, and highly processed sugary foods out of the house. They are designed to create cravings. Keep a food journal and write down everything you eat. Watch much less TV, get the kids involved in sports, music, and other activities (with an emphasis on "active"), and get to work on cooking real foods.

Changing your taste toward savoring and loving healthy foods is a process that may take some time, but you'll learn to love that apple. Eventually your mind makes a connection between feeling good and what you eat. Add exercise to your family's rituals. Read up on healthy foods and start to be aware of food values: an apple has as many calories as a piece of chocolate. Then explore the psychological factors underlying the overeating for both parent and child, and other underlying factors in the family relationships.

It's good to be reasonable and let your kids have an occasional treat, but remember that a lot of what goes into junk food—from white flour to high-fructose corn syrup to any number of additives—is calculated to create cravings and food brand loyalty. Try being loyal to nature instead.

Red Flag Ingredients

There's a lot to think about when moving toward healthy food habits. A simple guide is to eat fresh foods as close to the source as possible. Another guideline is to read labels and avoid foods that are not really foods, or have little food value. Additives and chemicals are not foods.

Some guidelines:

1. Avoid processed grains (white flour) and most cold cereals.
2. Look for the word "enriched." It means the manufacturer has taken out all the natural goodness and put back one tiny little bit of it.
3. Notice "made with hydrogenated or trans fats" (unsaturated fatty acids, linked to an increase in blood cholesterol). The body does not recognize these fats as a food (they are in most margarines) and has no way to break them down or to assimilate or process them. They are high-stress on the body and have been linked to an increase in blood cholesterol.
4. Don't buy foods that have high-fructose corn syrup. There is a huge amount of research on the harm caused by

high-fructose corn syrup. *Sugar is preferable.* Also be aware of other sweeteners: dextrose, corn sweetener, corn syrup, fructose, glucose, malt syrup, maltose, and sucrose, to name a few. The sugar alcohols sorbitol (also known as glucitol) and mannitol can lead to abdominal gas and diarrhea, as they are not absorbed by the body.

5. Read labels and be aware of the types of sugars or sweeteners that are added to soup, bread, jam, canned vegetables, and other foods you eat regularly. Compare. The brand just to the left or right may have less (or fewer) sugars or sweeteners.

6. Avoid foods with dozens of ingredients.

Lighten up. Doing pretty well is to do very well. Do the best you can, try to improve your habits, and then enjoy. Don't become the food police. The body wants to be healthy and works hard to manage what you put into it. Different people have different constitutions for handling food. Some can mix anything together and be okay, but others don't do well mixing starch and protein and they have a lot of food sensitivities. Notice your reactions to foods and experiment.

Sometimes let your children have exactly what they want and don't worry about it. Don't make a religion out of eating perfectly. It's much more important to have friendly, peaceful feelings around food rather than to be rigid or controlling.

Think of food and the body as an ecological system with many additional interrelated factors. From drinking enough water to exercising, having love in our lives, along with healthy food, joy, purpose, friends, sleep, and intimacy, we contribute to keeping the body and spirit in balance.

A positive image to have about natural foods is this: The sun, rain, soil, and air are all contained in an apple, orange, carrot, green bean, or leaf of lettuce.

The living elements of the universe go into living foods that enter your living body. This puts you in greater harmony with the earth and all that sustains life.

A Healing Story Around Food

Earlier in the chapter I spoke of Karen, who would hide distasteful food in her cheek and sneak away to spit it out, only to get discovered and punished. Eating with other people became fraught with anxiety for her, until she became close friends with a woman who often had informal dinner gatherings. At first, Karen's stomach would knot up and the familiar anxious feelings would roll in. But, as she was repeatedly with people who were friendly, relaxed, uncritical, and enjoyed being sociable around food, her anxieties started to ease. In her words, "Everyone was so nice. No one got annoyed or noticed what you ate. No one got upset when someone spilled something—which would have made my mother furious. It was a whole new world of eating and being with people."

Whatever your history with food—your struggles, sense of balance or imbalance, cravings or ease—you bring to your parenting a long history of relating to food, starting at birth.

Your relationship to food may also become more complex as other factors enter the scene: allergies, food sensitivities, hormones, yeast infections, thyroid abnormalities, menstrual cycles, and many other conditions. It can often take an experienced naturopath, psychologist, or doctor to help unravel the complex mosaic that has resulted from one's relationship to food.

No matter what your situation, remember loving-kindness and learn to love food that loves you back.

Sustainability: An Afterword

> *Use it up, wear it out, make it do, or do without.*
> —NEW ENGLAND PROVERB

Part of a commitment to raising children to make peace in the world is helping them understand the concept of sustainability. It's about learning that everything has a life of its own—it comes from somewhere and has to go somewhere. Throwing it in the trash isn't the end of it. Rather, it goes into landfills, waterways, recycling centers, incinerators, or even on ships to other countries—often creating toxins that leak into the air and water.

This kind of consciousness is crucial to our relationship to one another, the earth, and the generations to come. Sustainability starts with parents' awareness of their own relationships to food and possessions, and filters down to their children through their actions and words.

SUSTAINABILITY IS NOT JUST ABOUT WHAT WE RECYCLE OR THROW AWAY

Just as the wings of a butterfly send a vibration around the earth, we can teach children that their smallest actions are linked to the well-being of the planet. We can let our child know that we carry canvas bags to the grocery store because we don't want to use plastic, and we avoid packaging that can't be recycled. As much as possible we buy fresh food that has been grown without using chemicals, and we wash the last bits of dog food out of the can so it can be recycled. Casually explaining these things to our children, especially when they ask us, will help them develop holistic thinking about the world of food and packaging.

....

We can start by teaching children that food, packaging, and other stuff comes from somewhere, goes somewhere, and affects the complete ecosystem.

....

Teach through your example. When children grow up seeing their parents routinely living simply and recycling newspapers, cans, plastic, and bottles, they will think it's a normal part of life. One family put a list on the fridge of the time it takes for various substances to decompose in a landfill—more than eighty years for plastic!

At the same time, don't become the environmental police or endlessly lecture your children. Raise your own consciousness and act accordingly. With awareness comes the natural desire to make choices that do no harm. Three videos you could watch with your child online are "The Story of Stuff," "The Story of Electronics," and "The Story of Weather," by Annie Leonard. The easiest way to find them is under the author's name.

BECOME AN ACTIVE VOICE IN SCHOOLS AND IN YOUR COMMUNITY

Parents need community support to improve children's relationship with food, especially in schools. Encouraging the administrations, teachers, and PTA to work together to create healthy food choices will help your children realize that mindfulness about food doesn't just come from a couple of food-obsessed parents.

The University of Montana took on a project to raise the consciousness of students and faculty about food, plastic bottles, and waste. In the School of Music, there are signs over the water fountains reminding you that if you refill a plastic water bottle it costs nothing, compared to $1 a day for a new bottle, five days a week,

22 days a month—which comes to $22/month, $264 per year, and $2,640 for ten years. The Food Zoo dining hall on campus did away with trays so that people carry only one plate. This simple act cut back immensely on food waste as well as on washing trays. When you take your plate to be washed, you pass a series of signs: *In the United States we waste twenty-five percent of all our food—that's ninety-six billion pounds; It costs one billion dollars a year to dispose of food waste; The methane released as food rots in a landfill is twenty-one times more toxic than carbon dioxide, and a major contributor to global warming.* These repeated reminders at home and in the community can help keep us mindful that everything matters and that we can be part of the solution.

Think of five or ten small steps you can take at home to leave a lighter footprint in the world.

> *When they had all had enough to eat, he said to his disciples, "Gather the pieces that are left over. Let nothing be wasted."*
>
> —JOHN 6:12, NEW INTERNATIONAL VERSION OF THE BIBLE

19 "My Parents Rock"

What Successful Parents Seem to Know

> We have not come here to take prisoners
> But to surrender ever more deeply
> To freedom and joy. . . .
> For we have not come here to take prisoners
> Or to confine our wondrous spirits,
> But to experience ever and ever more deeply
> Our divine courage, freedom, and Light!
>
> —HAFIZ, "WE HAVE NOT COME TO TAKE PRISONERS,"
> FROM *THE GIFT* TRANSLATED BY DANIEL LANDINSKY

Our gift to our children is to love and let go, not to confine our children's wondrous spirits with endless rigid rules, fears, and scripts. Instead, we should support their divine, wondrous spirits.

This chapter includes stories from children of all ages talking about parents in ways that illustrate many of the positive traits we've explored.

Here are their stories.

At a recent ice cream social with international students and members of the community, I saw my friend Ruth and her daughter

Angela, a college junior. I fondly remembered attending Angela's bat mitzvah, when her mother had looked at her with tender, glistening eyes and said, "We're so glad you're our daughter. We completely trust you because you have never given us any reason not to."

I approached Angela at the gathering and asked if we could arrange an interview. She responded with a big smile. "My parents rock! I really like them." I saw tears well up in her mother's eyes as she overheard her daughter. Earlier, when I had asked Ruth for her perspective on parenting, she said, "I don't know if we can be helpful. We've never had any trouble." I smiled. "That's exactly what I want to hear about. Maybe you can help a lot of other parents." "I don't know," she said. "I think we're really lucky."

Lucky. That was a comment I frequently heard from parents who had had smooth sailing with their children or were unaware of the skills they brought to parenting. They often gave the credit to their children. While there is some justification for this, the deeper truth is that these were committed, wise parents.

There are families where there has not been a lot of contention, fighting, or major problems, even during adolescence. The parents liked their kids and the kids liked their parents. The children had been responsible, and generally the parents had given them a lot of freedom and trust. It created a positive upward spiral.

The most effective parents were the first to say they weren't perfect: *We argue sometimes. I've gotten mad. I don't always know what to do*. It was this very humility that made them approachable parents. Several suggested I talk with their kids: they were curious about what they might say.

I interviewed a wide range of families for this chapter—Jewish, gentile, Buddhist, Muslim, married, single, divorced, rich, middle-class, and low-income. The families were lesbian and heterosexual, African-American, Native American, and Caucasian. It was a great pleasure to hear children tell stories about the positive traits of their parents. I interviewed the families separately or together, depending on what people wanted. A consistent trait in the children was that they engaged naturally with me, made eye contact, and appeared relaxed, as if they trusted adults as people.

Qualities of "Parents Who Rock"

"MY PARENTS DON'T FREAK OUT."

This was the number one positive trait that children expressed in myriad ways. The sons and daughters said things like: *My parents stay calm, don't fly off the handle, don't get sarcastic, are fair, can apologize, or will respond to reason. They might get upset, but they don't act irrational or make everything a big deal or flip out or ground us for life, like some of my friends' parents.*

When children or teens are learning to manage their emotions, it helps enormously if the parents can modulate and manage their own. Many of the children expressed great relief that their parents didn't yell or go nuts the way other kids' parents did.

Adam, who is in his early twenties, said, "I can't ever remember my parents being violent. They've had occasional shouting matches. It was rare, very rare—maybe once every five years—for someone to call someone a name. As far as abusive language or abusive feelings toward each other, those things have never been present in my life. That's something that I appreciate."

"I CAN TALK TO THEM AND THEY LISTEN."

The second message was, in the words of one teen: "My parents really listen and talk things over . . . so it's easy to go to them."

Angela, college age, said: "When I'm in trouble, they are the first people I think of to call. When I got in a pretty big mess I didn't want to tell them, but I knew I could talk to them and there wouldn't be big repercussions. In general their advice is always very logical and usually helpful. I can take what they say and apply it in my own way."

A similar thing happened with me when I was young. When I was in an accident while driving with my father in the car, the first thing that he did when I pulled over to the side of the road was to put his hand on my arm and ask, "Are you okay?" I felt so bad about myself, but he never got mad and was completely caring.

Mark, a teenage boy with two moms, told me: "I trust my parents completely. They do listen well. They are smart enough to see when a rule isn't working, and they back off. So it doesn't end up in a power struggle. Actually, we don't really do 'rules.' It's more like we ask, what's a good idea?" I asked Mark to tell me more about what he meant by trust. He said, "I don't know the alternative very well. They are not people I'm forced to inconveniently live with. They are great parents. We can talk with each other."

Even when there had been alcohol abuse, divorce, and hard times in some families, if the child had the safety net of one consistent parent who would respectfully engage and listen, the child experienced a core sense of safety. It was like a rope to grab on to when life got tough, even after leaving home.

PARENTS HAVE A SENSE OF HUMOR

There is nothing like a smile, a twinkle of the eye, a knowing look or a lighthearted comment to create a relaxed environment.

One time when I was getting up on my high horse with my seven-year-old daughter, my housemate, also a mother, jokingly said in her crisp English accent, "Yes, Ginelle. And you'll never get to have any cookies again." We all cracked up laughing.

Yolanda told this story of an exchange of text messages with her nineteen-year-old daughter that reflects the safety of their relationship. The daughter had recently graduated from high school and lived in her own apartment. She had dated her boyfriend for three years.

Daughter to Mother:	"Do you think it would help regulate my period if I went on birth control pills?"
Mother:	"Do you think I just got off the banana boat?"
Daughter:	"Well, no."
Mother:	"Do you know where Planned Parenthood is?"
Daughter:	"Sort of."
Mother:	"Would you like me to go with you?"
Daughter:	"Yes."

"I CAN GET UPSET AND THEY TAKE ME SERIOUSLY."
Children said they appreciated being able to have their own feelings—sometimes very strong ones.

Eleven-year-old Izzy told this story:

> *One time I got really mad at my mom: I was about four and I had a stroller. I loved to play with it. She took it to the dump. I screamed at her for three hours, told her I hated her. [She then told me] Tell the parents in your book to make sure a kid is done with something before they throw it away!*

I asked Izzy what her mother did when she got really mad. She replied, "She'd say, 'Izzy, calm down.' But then she would listen to me and try to help."

Most of all, Izzy's mother allowed the child to play out her anger and sadness over the next few days. She apologized several times and said she had made a big mistake. Izzy said, "I knew she was really sorry, but I was still upset." She paused, "I don't scream like that anymore." Izzy's mom owned up to her mistake instead of trying to squelch Izzy's strong feelings with common parental injunctions such as: *Ssshhh. It's not that big a deal. Don't make such a big fuss. You're being a baby. Think of how lucky you are.* As a result, Izzy was able to get past her anger and sadness and talk about it openly eight years later. Some people might disagree with allowing such strong feelings, but, by staying calm in the presence of Izzy's feelings, the mother helped Izzy to integrate them. Her mother's strength was in not being afraid of strong feelings.

"THEY HELP ME FIGURE THINGS OUT FOR MYSELF."

One teenager told me, "I can talk things over with them—kind of like a friend, but not quite, because I know they are my parents. They might have some ideas, but mostly they help me try to figure it out. If my father makes suggestions he always says, 'But it's up to you to decide.' And it really is. I know what he'd like, but he won't get mad or upset if I do something different."

PARENTS KNOW HOW TO BE ENGAGED AND INVOLVED BUT NOT INTRUSIVE

These parents were engaged. They'd listen, ask useful questions, set limits, and were clear about expectations. For the most part, they'd talk *with* their children, not *at* them. They also respected their children's privacy, sensibilities, and taste—such as having their bedrooms the way they wanted them, which often included being messy, or the freedom to close their doors or talk with friends without anyone listening in.

They didn't try to pry information out of an upset child. Instead, they were comforting, made room for a conversation, and seemed to have a good sense of timing in making a response. They seemed to know that growing up includes sudden changes in friends, interests, and moods.

PARENTS WERE ABLE TO BE CLOSE YET ALLOW
THE CHILDREN FREEDOM

The underlying message that the children conveyed was that they were seen as separate people, and their parents loved them, but did not live through them. They weren't their parents' sole identity. While kids naturally wanted attention for themselves, they also admired the skills and interests of their parents.

Children spoke about their parents as people who had talents, interests, jobs and friends. They take part in community events, or have their own struggles. For instance, one said, "I like knowing that my parents have friends and go out and have fun."

For my part, when I was growing up I loved seeing my mother play the violin. She was usually this cookie-baking mommy, and it was magical when she turned into a special person who could make beautiful music. Part of my passion for learning piano was wanting to grow up and play music with her.

LEARNING IS AN EVERYDAY EXPERIENCE

It didn't matter if the parent was teaching a child how to use a fly rod, ski, stack wood, fry an egg, put up a tent, cook, fix a bike, or write a term paper. It was usually a positive experience with the parent attuned to the child's capacity for learning. One eight-year-old boy I interviewed said, "Tell people it's good when parents help you. My dad is going to help me build a model airplane." He was obviously looking forward to the event.

Cooking with my mom was always fun—a kind of mother-daughter ritual we both loved. She was always relaxed and never got mad when I put too much milk in the powdered sugar icing, spattered the whipped cream around the room by using too shallow a dish, or made a mess trying to create striped cupcakes. To this day I love cooking and never worry if I make a mistake.

My father taught us how to play poker—any self-respecting

Montana kid of his had to learn—and we had to play for pennies so we'd be serious about it. I also fondly remember my dad showing me how he could accurately estimate the height of a tree—a competition he always won at the forestry picnics.

The parents I spoke with generally take time to determine if the child's interest has depth to it, or "staying power." They don't immediately buy the best equipment for a new sport or enroll the child in a class when a child shows a passing interest in something. At the same time, they encourage their talents.

Steven Hesla, a piano professor, fondly recalled his first piano lesson in rural North Dakota. His family had very little money, yet when he was five, his father, aware of Steven's talent, asked, "Would you like to drive to town when I deliver hay, and visit Mrs. Robson?" Steven laughed as he recalled the huge hay truck seeming terribly out of place as it lumbered down a small side street to take him to meet his piano teacher.

PARENTS GIVE CHILDREN RESPONSIBILITY FOR HOMEWORK . . . MOST OF THE TIME

I asked children if their parents reminded them to do homework. "Occasionally," "sometimes," and "almost never" were the answers I got. One mom said that early on she needed to remind her son on a daily basis, but now he comes home and does it without prompting. In several families there is a no TV rule until homework is done or on weeknights, but many of the parents don't check up on their kids to make sure they have done their homework.

Izzy commented indignantly, "No, my parents don't *tell* me to do my homework. It's up to me!"

The children seemed to take pride in being responsible for themselves. Parents didn't turn school work into a power struggle—they were more interested in children finding their strengths and taking pleasure in learning. Some would occasionally help with homework. If kids asked for help or wanted ideas for a project, the parents readily helped, but didn't take it on as their project. Generally the parents didn't push kids to do well or get good grades; the notion of doing well seemed to be picked up by osmosis. It was the norm of the family. Some parents also allowed their children to learn the consequences of lackluster effort through their grades or school reports.

PARENTS DON'T USE PUNISHMENT TO
CONTROL THEIR CHILDREN

Many of the children I interviewed said they had never had a time-out or been grounded or punished. One said he was occasionally grounded for being out long past curfew, but he referred to it as "legitimate and not a big deal." When asked if she had ever been grounded, Izzy, the eleven-year-old girl introduced above, said, "No. I never did anything to get grounded," as if it were an insulting question. Izzy commented that while her family didn't have time-outs, her mother would sit with her in the great big overstuffed chair to help her quiet down when she was little. She might be told it was time to read or take a break.

Alan, a teenager, said, "I had so much freedom, there was nothing to rebel against. I got good grades, did my homework, took part in after-school sports and music, and had a lot of fun with friends. My parents got me into the right school, where I fit in. There were a lot of nerds like me. It was okay to get good grades and be smart. I have all A's." I laughed at his comment about being a nerd and asked, "Do you consider yourself a nerd?" "Yes, definitely," he answered with ease.

Alan had two moms, and I asked him what that was like. He said it was great: he didn't have to live up to some male image and his mothers were really great people. He also added that in their liberal community it was accepted and he wouldn't have time for people who had a problem with it.

There was virtually no form of punishment in these homes. There might be a time when a child was grounded, or got a couple swats on the behind, but for the most part spanking, hitting, threatening, or taking away things a child loved was rare to nonexistent. Parents readily apologized when they got angry or were unfair.

One mother said, "I've lost it a couple times with my daughter and spanked her or yelled at her, but I came back and apologized and said it wasn't right. I said that I had taught her not to hit, and that I shouldn't hit."

One parent said, "The idea of hitting a child feels so awful. They are little, vulnerable, and that violence stays in them."

....

There is a Quaker teaching that working for peace means to prevent the occasion for war—poverty, injustice, and prejudice. Likewise, as parents, our task is to do our best to prevent the occasion for fighting, hitting, screaming, and threatening children.
....
....
In all cases where parents moved in the direction of nonviolent parenting, it was because they learned better ways to interact: diplomacy, respect, kindness, and the amazing power of listening.
....

These families were a testament to the power of nonviolence in raising children.

PARENTS REMEMBER WHEN THEY WERE YOUNG

Parents remembered their past and could laugh about themselves—the mistakes, achievements, wild times, and major errors in judgment.

- I was much wilder than my daughter.
- I felt as if my mother didn't really like children, so I thought a lot about that and waited until I wanted a child before I got pregnant.

- I've never liked anyone telling me what to do, so it's not something I wanted to do to my daughter. I didn't want to be bossy.
- My mother was hysterical and shouted a lot. I've had a lot of therapy so I wouldn't do the same thing.
- We weren't close as children in my family. I always felt sad about that and wanted my kids to be close. (They are!)
- My father was never there, so I made it a point to be the dad I dreamed of having.
- I saw my brothers being afraid to call a girl for a date, so I can really appreciate how scary it is for my boys.
- We had very little money, but we all pitched in and everyone did well. I wanted to foster that spirit in my children as well.
- I'm really sympathetic to feeling left out because I felt that way a lot. I was happy when one of my kids made friends easily, but I could also be understanding of the other one, who was very sensitive to feeling left out.
- I didn't like all the drinking and fighting, so I've made it a point never to drink. I also know that there is residual anger in me from my childhood and I made a vow never to hit my children.

If I start to get triggered and angry, I ask my wife to take over. We help each other recognize when we are not able to handle a situation.

Not only did these parents remember the past, but they also made a concerted effort to be different from the negative aspects of their parents in order not to hurt their own children.

....

When parents had not had a happy childhood, it was their ability to reflect, learn, and change that made the difference.

....

Many parents were living examples of the belief that people do not have to pass on the painful legacy of their childhood—a powerful belief to pass on to their children.

PARENTS GIVE CHILDREN A VOICE IN DECISION MAKING

These parents wanted their children to find their own voice in the world. They started by giving them a voice in the family. Since many of the parents had themselves stood against the tide of popular opinion in their commitment to peace or justice, they also modeled these behaviors for their children.

> Giving children a voice in the family helps create a two-way sense of respect because the children know they have power in the relationship. This helps avoid the growth of resentment and rebellion.

Many of the families had family meetings or times when they could talk over what was bothering them. The kids could lobby for changes in the family guidelines, such as allowance, chores, curfew, or how they keep their bedrooms. Izzy said, "My family used to have family meetings. It was just nice to sit and talk together and it makes it easier to say what's on your mind—kind of like that's what's expected."

What these families label "speaking up" might be regarded as "talking back" or being disrespectful in more authoritarian families. Bruce fondly called his daughter, Angela, the little lawyer:

Starting very young, she would present her case for why she should get to do something, and we would listen. It felt important that she would win some. There was a time when she was in high school when we tried to get her to wake up earlier on the weekends. One day she handed us a bunch of articles on why teens need lots of sleep and would do much

*better if they didn't have to go to school so early. We read the articles
and backed off. She eventually did more research on sleep for her senior
project and presented it to the school board.*

By responding to Angela's "research" on teens and sleep, the parents validated her intelligence, which led to the girl's eventually talking with the school board. Think of all the messages they instilled: *My opinions count. I'm intelligent. They respect me. I can talk to them.* And think of all the adolescent energy that did not turn into resentment or rebellion.

....
When children have a voice and can respectfully discuss, protest, or debate with their parents, it validates their intelligence and gives them confidence.
....

This doesn't mean that children are allowed to be disrespectful and nag or that the parents don't sometimes say, "No, it's nonnegotiable." As one father said, "We are still a limited democracy. Actually a parentocracy." *When the response from parents is mostly a respectful yes to their children's lives, the children are more likely to accept an occasional and necessary no.*

PARENTS TEACH THEIR CHILDREN—ESPECIALLY GIRLS—THAT THEY HAVE THE RIGHT TO SAY NO

Having the ability to say no underlies our self-respect and sense of power. "I don't have to do something that is not right for me." This is central to standing strong in the world.

Katie has three biological daughters and a foster daughter, all now young adults and doing well. She told me a story of her efforts to teach them that they have the right to say no—and that this lesson must start with a girl's parents.

There was a time when I was feeling the need to say an honest "no" to my husband more often—about time, sex, and money. He reacted by pouting and getting down in the dumps. I said to him, "It's not about you, it's about me being honest. I have to be able to say no so I can really say yes." He didn't get it.

Then I said, "It's important for your daughters to know a woman can speak up for herself. They need to see me saying no, and see you accepting it." He still didn't get it. Then I said, "Okay, do you want your daughters to say yes to sex with some guy at sixteen because they don't feel they have the right to say no?" He got it! (She laughed.)

All children need clear permission to say a respectful no to either parent about touching, tickling, kisses, hugs, or going against their values. This is crucial "preparation" for being able to say no to others.

PARENTS ARE HONEST AND OPEN ABOUT THEIR OWN LIVES IN APPROPRIATE WAYS

These successful parents didn't shield their kids from life events, including sickness, death, loss, emotional distress, or hard times. Parents who are honest about their core feelings are teaching their children not to be ashamed of their feelings and their lives.

Many of the children I spoke with struggled to find words to express what it was they liked about their parents. "Real" was a favorite word: "They didn't hide their feelings, they weren't emotionally removed, and they didn't hide the times when they had difficulties."

"I liked that they told me when they weren't getting along with one of their friends. I felt as if they trusted me, that I was included."

"They were interested in me," was another expression I often heard. The parents weren't just authorities who told you what to do. Also, the word "friendly" often came up.

CHILDREN LIKED KNOWING ABOUT THEIR
PARENTS' YOUNG LIVES

While the timing needs to be right, when parents tell stories about their own young lives it gives the children a rich narrative about the history of their family, and it can actually help the younger generation sympathize with their parents as individuals. What was their childhood like? Did they get in trouble? Were they good students? How did they meet each other.

This may include stories that often were taboo, such as the forced internment of Japanese-American families in the western states during World War II, or the violence and alcoholism on Native American reservations, or tales of ancestors who didn't want to be seen as immigrants and didn't teach their native language to their children. The parents' shame was often passed on to the children by their silence. Yet children want to know their history.

One Native American friend, Denise, said, "I've told my children about all of it. I told them the proud history of our ancestors and traditions, and how losing their heritage and access to their homeland, and children being taken away to Catholic boarding schools, [these things] really harmed our people. I also told them that there was a lot of alcoholism and violence and families torn apart. They are proud that I sobered up and I took them to the sober New Year's Eve party for Native Americans in our city. They've seen me go to college and get a degree at forty to become a chemical dependency counselor. I want them to feel proud of who they are."

As an aside, I urge all parents to write down or record stories from their childhood. It can be simple—it doesn't have to be a huge, ambitious genealogy project—but even if children don't show an interest at present, they are likely to be fascinated by these accounts later on, and they will be grateful. I treasure the stories my parents wrote down, the letters they kept, starting with their courtship days. My father, who loved books, often told us of his favorites from childhood. It touches me to read them now and think of him. My Aunt Margaret made a tape called, "What It's Like to Be Starving," that told of her family's experience being interned in the Philippines for three years during World War II.

As a family, keep a journal of trips you take together. Write down where you stayed, whom you visited, what you saw, family squabbles, funny events. Let all the kids make entries and ask them what they want it to say. It will be a treasure later on.

Similarly, encourage children to keep journals. My teenage journals used to be embarrassing to me. I wrote about a boy who kissed me, and how I hoped he'd kiss me again because it felt so good. I mentioned loving to play a Chopin scherzo, and in the next breath wrote about getting all excited over a really cute guy. I then switched to being mad at my parents, then to a really fun overnight with girlfriends, then to my happiness at getting three first ratings for accompanying people on the piano in state competitions. It was a wild ride, with moods that could swing in a second. These journals helped me immensely later on as I struggled to feel more kindly toward myself.

PARENTS LET THEIR KIDS FIND THEIR WAY

Some children know exactly what they want to do after high school, while others flounder. Yolanda's daughter Lindsay had just graduated from high school and didn't have a clear interest in academics. She decided not to start college, even though she got excellent grades and the teachers at school were all asking, "Where are you going to college?" Yolanda's response to her daughter, "Honey, it's okay. Don't do it if you don't want to. Sometimes it takes a while," was one she repeated several times in the coming year. There was the time when they were sitting together at the health sciences orientation before medical technology classes started when Lindsay turned to her mother and whispered, "Mom, I don't want to do this." There was the afternoon when Yolanda found her daughter sitting at the dining room table in tears, looking at the blank application for beauty school. "I don't want to be a loser," she sobbed, "but I don't want to do this." Again, Yolanda comforted her. "Honey you don't have to, it's okay."

Lindsay later took up her dad's offer to help him by working in his local business. While she had previously helped out with only modest interest, something clicked and she got excited about working in the business. She was good at talking with customers, answering phones, and learning how to place orders. Within a few months, her father was teaching her how to do estimates. The gift from her parents was being relaxed and not trying to make her life "smooth" by boxing her into a career she didn't really want.

THE WISE FATHER WHO STAYED CALM

I'll close with a story that combines many elements of the parents who rock. Indeed, it was told in separate interviews with Angela, and her father, Bruce. It was Angela who inspired this chapter with her exuberant remark, "My parents rock."

As a senior in high school, Angela had flexible curfews. It was okay for her to call home if she was having a good time, and arrange to stay out a bit later. Because of this she wasn't worried when, one night, she and some girlfriends decided to drive to a party at a cabin on a lake about fifty miles from home. She figured she'd be home on time. Even though the area was familiar to them, they got lost on a back road, got upset, then rammed into a stump and wrecked the radiator. After finding that their cell phones didn't get reception, they started to panic. One of the girls said, *O my God, what if there are rapists in the woods*, and they all started to get extremely agitated. Within a half hour, they had walked to a place where they could call home.

"I was kind of dreading calling my parents, but I knew it would be okay," Angela said. "The first thing my father did was to help me calm down. He slowly asked, Was I okay? Where was I? What was the situation? How were the other girls?"

One of the other girls' parents drove out to pick them up. In the meantime, Angela's father called the parents of one of the other girls in the hope they wouldn't blow up at their daughter. He chatted with them and talked about how lucky they were to have such good kids: they got good grades, weren't into drugs, and were respectful. He also said that, at their age, he thought it was natural that they would venture out, and he wanted the kids to learn how to think clearly in difficult situations.

When Angela arrived home, her parents gave her a hug and said how glad they were that she was safe. Then Bruce said, "I want to talk with you in the morning about some errors in judgment I think you made." "But we weren't out past curfew," Angela objected. "I know," he said calmly, "but there are some things I want you to think about."

The next morning Bruce said, "I want you to use this experience to learn, so in the future you think more carefully in an accident or stressful situation.

"First, when you go far away like that you should let us know, just as when someone hikes alone they let people know so they can be found if they have an accident or get lost. People have died because they didn't do that.

"The second error was driving off on a side road in an area where it was dark. You didn't know the way and you didn't have a map. Another one was getting panicked and banging into the stump and damaging the radiator. That panic stopped you from thinking clearly, which is the most important thing when something goes wrong. It also fed into stirring up fear about rapists in the woods, which was highly unlikely."

He paused. "It's all part of learning and growing up. I just want you to think about it."

Angela nodded. Bruce gave her a hug and they both went about their day.

As a therapist who has listened to countless stories of parents screaming, shaming, humiliating, lecturing, punishing, and hitting kids when they mess up, I find this a breathtaking example of great parenting. Bruce stayed steady and never broke his caring bond with her. He respectfully used the phrase "errors in judgment" rather than any derogatory phrases or words. At one level Angela learned from this example about letting people know where you are when put yourself in harm's way, being prepared (think twice before going to an unfamiliar, secluded place at night, and take a map), paying attention, and staying calm. At an emotional level she internalized that her parents were beside her all the way, from helping her calm down during the first phone conversation, to being supportive of her friends, to welcoming her home with a hug, to a calm and lucid conversation the next morning about what they hoped she would learn from the experience. No yelling, no losing it, no grounding her. Just connection, wisdom, teaching, and love.

20 "Us Thinking"

How to Bring Up a Generation of Peacemakers

There is no way to peace. Peace is the way.
—ANONYMOUS

*I*f there is one idea I hope you will take from this book, it is that "there is no way to peace, peace *is* the way." In Buddhist thought, peace is found in the details of our days: in your warmth, smile, honesty, tone of voice, the way you breathe, move, listen, take care of yourself, and in the way you are fully present to others. Peace is about stepping beyond your conditioned mind, seeing into the hearts of others, being able to apologize, accepting change, and realizing that we are all created from one life energy, no matter our race, religion, or culture. Peace is being clear with others, being straightforward in our speech, being able to calm ourselves down and not react in anger. It's seeing the many sides to a story, a theory, or political discourse and developing a capacity for critical thinking, which helps us recognize a would-be deceiver, someone who would exploit us, as well as one who genuinely cares.

Peace is active and alive, and it has a strong voice that combines kindness and understanding with being real, courageous, and respectful. The desire to raise children with values of cooperation, respect, hard work, and care for others is not bounded by or limited to any single religion, culture, or class.

We bring peacefulness to our lives and to those of our children when we learn to see below the surface. What's beneath the anger, the hurt, the pouting, or the fear that fuels indifference. In peacefulness, we see through the surface behavior of others, knowing that we've all been conditioned to see the world in a certain way. Ken Keyes (introduced in Chapter 17) teaches us to imagine ourselves standing in a circle, even when we feel judgmental of another person or bewildered by their behavior, then to say to ourselves, "*One of us* is crying." "*One of us* is being difficult." "*One of us* is grieving a lost child." It doesn't matter so much which one of us it is—a stranger or a friend—the important thing is that we realize that we ourselves could be having the same feelings at any given time. This creates an "us" mentality that puts us all in the circle together. Or, to put it another way, this mind-set allows us to see the connections we already have.

Teaching Peace

I spoke with Daniel Hughes, a master at his craft of working with deeply disturbed children. I have had the good fortune to attend his workshops and see him work with children; he is always kind, humorous, relaxed, and engaged. Here is something he said to me that I think is very wise.

If you want to bring children up on a fast track toward peace, the most important factor is that they feel safe inside themselves. This is often called *attachment security.* Children feel safe and at ease walking in the door of their home because they know they will be seen, known, understood, and cared for.

Safety means that children can express who they are to their parents. They can say if they feel hurt, sad, angry, confused, or unhappy, and know their parents will listen. The caregivers won't judge, dismiss, dispute, get upset, or minimize what children say. This sounds easy, but for many parents, their own anxiety or difficulty in handling feelings blocks their ability to listen and respond appropriately. They quell their own anxiety by giving unwanted advice, trying to fix the situation, minimizing the child's feelings, or placating the child. Most of this behavior has nothing to do with helping the child; often it is solely to help the parent stop feeling anxious. Many parents jump immediately from hearing their child is having difficulty to feeling that they, the parents, are at fault or that it is a reflection on themselves: *I'm not a good parent. What will people think of me?"*

....
Stresses and strains are normal in life, and our job as parents is to help children deal with them and not go off on a private guilt trip because we interpret their difficulties as a reflection of ourselves.
....

Parents will say, "I don't want my child to hurt." But as Buddhism teaches us, hurts and losses are normal in life. It's part of the deal. Yes, we can kiss a skinned knee or an "owie," but hurts such as getting left out, not making the team, or being called names by a bully are practice for life. We can't get rid of bullies or prevent rejection, but we can kindly help our children handle tough situations and learn to manage their emotions, and not take things personally.

Quoting Dan Hughes again, "We also need to recognize the special, unique qualities of our children. Parents get tied up in feeling they have to tinker with their children's inner lives, but this will take care of itself when we model for our children the right values and expose them to lots of creative, respectful people. Being comfortable with diversity in the world starts with showing respect for the diversity of our children's inner life. They don't have to think what you think or feel what you feel. We don't have to have the same religion or political beliefs. We can be different and still enjoy each other. This is so important to bringing up peaceful children. *I want you to be you.* We don't need to say this in words, but we need to show it."

Peacefulness in our lives begins with kindness and self-acceptance. It brings depth to our thinking, warmth to our responses, and mercy to ourselves and others. It's about being present against the backdrop of an expansive consciousness that allows us to smile at human foibles, enjoy the great big messy show of life, and realize how rich and surprising life can be. Peace includes the altruism and selflessness that emerge as we live from our deepest truths, grounded in the awareness that we are part of the whole.

If we accept that peace is the way, then we have a daily guide to follow. *What is the most respectful, caring way to handle this particular situation? How can I correct a child or set limits in a way that is fair and teaches in a positive way?* If peace is the way, we don't coerce or use guilt or fear to control our children. Instead, we cooperate, talk situations over, and encourage children to have a voice. Parents dignify little people by realizing he or she has deep feelings and original ideas, and then treating them with the respect they deserve.

Peace values evolve as children learn to live from the inside out. *What feels clear for me to do? What am I ready, willing, or able to do?* We must take time to help them listen for *their* answers. There is the story of the Navajo mother who said in response to her daughter's request for advice, "Put it in your holy middle and sleep on it." Living out of these questions is the genesis of helping children live with the perennial question, *Who am I?* The answer to this will eventually lead to the next big question, *How can I be of service in the world?*

21 Pass It On

Family Stories of Teaching Peace

> A single word or expression ... can have four
> different meanings corresponding to the four levels
> of interpretation, known as the four modes of understanding,
> which are:
> (i) the literal meaning;
> (ii) the general meaning;
> (iii) the hidden meaning; and
> (iv) the ultimate meaning.
>
> —THE DALAI LAMA, THE PATH TO TRANQUILITY

Parenting that teaches nonviolence is many-faceted. We etch memories into our child's mind of a positive way to be in the world. Generosity, kindness, fairness, and empathy are the values we teach them to hold above all else. These values live on as guides to loving actions—a mind-set about our place in the world.

The stories in this chapter come from seemingly small or insignificant acts on the part of parents, or in one or two cases, a teacher. I offer them as a means to reflect on your own life and to help you realize how much your behavior lives on through your children. It is often the heartfelt nature of a parent's or a relative's generosity or courage that has a positive, life-changing impact on a child.

Accepting and Welcoming Friends

My dad felt a bit like the poor boy from the country who made good and never forgot what it meant to be left out or alone. On Thanksgiving, Christmas, and Easter, he invited international students home for dinner. He wanted them to have a good experience in the United States and to share with them his pride in his home and family. I met people from all over the world and learned about differences in culture and race.

As another example, when I was in high school I could always count on my father to reach out his hand and welcome any friend I brought to our home—black, white, Jewish, gay, straight, rich, poor, or just . . . weird. (I was part of the arts and theater crowd in high school.) He would gladly sit down and talk with them with sincere interest. More than one friend over the years has commented to me how much it meant to be welcomed into our home with such kindness and respect.

Don told me about his Buddhist father, a first generation Japanese immigrant. "I remember my father as a very gentle man. He worked long hours in the fish store that was attached to our house. The store also sold fishing gear. One time we were in the store, a guy came in with a reel to have a new line put on it. It was a very light spinning reel and I made a comment about the poor quality of the line he had. It wasn't as good as ours. My father gave me this look that said, 'You shouldn't have said that.' After the man left, he took me aside and kindly explained to me that we should be happy that this man had brought the reel in. He had come to us for help and we should be grateful. He added that not everyone could afford a better line and we shouldn't make anyone feel bad because of that.

"He also explained it in the context of running a business: that I should always be respectful of the customer." Don drifted into a reflective tone. "This incident had a great effect on me and has always stayed with me, because my father was willing to explain and did it so gently." Tears welled up in his eyes. "He didn't embarrass me in front of the man, and he clearly wanted to help me understand why it's important to be thoughtful toward others. Throughout my life this memory comes to mind and I'm thankful for the kindness of my father."

Seeing Parents as Political Activists

Jerimy, brought up in the Mennonite tradition and now the father of two grown boys, said this about his childhood: "There were lots of family stories that made an imprint on my mind. Mother told of her father, a bishop who was saving money for a greatcoat—his was tattered and worn out. When he saw that some children nearby didn't have shoes, he gave the money he was saving for a new coat to help buy their shoes. I saw my father participate in antiwar demonstrations, and I remember when he was arrested for protesting at the Pentagon. He called from a pay phone to tell [Mother] he was all right. I was in high school at the time. It was important for me to know that my dad was taking that kind of risk.

Jerimy continued. "There was another, more recent time that stays with me. We were living with my brother and sister-in-law in the inner city when my children were little. We were out on the porch when we saw a young black man run up the street and head toward the back of our house. We watched the police officers capture this man in front of our house and start to beat him. My uncle—an imposing presence—came out and made it very clear he was watching them and they stopped. Uncle Ed had been a nonviolent witness. These and many other experiences all contributed to my identity as a Mennonite, which means nonviolence and being there for others."

I've given several negative examples—some not-so-happy memories—of my own mother earlier in the book. Here is a positive one that had a profound effect. It took place when I was about fourteen. When we heard that a Catholic friend with small children had gotten sick and couldn't shop to fill the children's Easter baskets, my mom immediately said to me, "Let's take our candy to Naomi's kids. It means so much to them." I agreed that we didn't really need it; we were teens. With no hesitation, she swooped up the candy we had and we dropped by a store to get some bunnies. I remember her total, heartfelt response: her friend was sick, Easter was important to them, and my mom was out the door. It's hard to describe the immense love I felt for her in that moment. It was as if her openheartedness spilled into me.

The memory of my mother took root within me and expressed itself much later in life, quite by surprise. I had called some friends to invite them over for Christmas Eve and hadn't heard back, so I called again right before the holiday. They weren't home, but I found myself talking to a woman who had recently arrived from France and had rented the couple's house while they were away. We chatted for a few moments, and I learned that she had two children near the age of my daughter. As if I became my mother, I spontaneously invited them over for Christmas Eve. She was taken aback for a moment and asked me a few more questions before accepting. I had the sense that she was trying to figure out if I were a crazy person. A few minutes after their tentative entrance into our house, we were all festive and feeling the Christmas spirit—laughing, getting food together, playing games. We had some fascinating conversations about the differences between France and the United States, and we ended up getting together the following day.

The heartfelt apology. In a surprising burst of anger, Ron verbally lashed out at his wife in front of their son, Paul, something he had never done before. Later that day, feeling greatly disturbed by his behavior, he went to his son's school and asked to see him outside of class. He said to the boy: "Paul, it was wrong of me to speak to your mother like that. That was no way to speak to anyone and I want you to know how sorry I am. Your mother didn't deserve that, and I want you to know that. I don't want you to think it's ever okay to talk like that." It took considerable courage for the father to own up to his wrong behavior, especially to his young son.

After arriving home from his corporate consulting job in the South in the 1950s, my father told me the following story. He was at an elegant dinner gathering when the conversation drifted to civil rights and the status of blacks and whites in the South. In front of an African-American man who was serving dinner, the host said, "Oh, everyone is fine with the way it is here." He then turned to the man waiting on them and said, "Isn't that true you like it the way it is?" The man lowered his eyes and nodded in the affirmative. My father then said to me, "Wasn't that a terrible thing to do to that man? What could he have said?"

Somewhere deep inside of me I wish my father had spoken up, but I can also understand how daunting that would have been. His repeated comments on unfairness and prejudice did, however, sink deeply into me, helping to create an internal radar for oppression in all its forms . . . well, he didn't always get it about women.

Kevin is a dedicated teacher who helps in an after-school program. "There was an eight-year-old boy in the program who spent all his free time aiming anything and everything at others or watching violent videos. It was always about good guys and bad guys. Whenever there wasn't a structured activity, violence was his automatic default behavior. Instead of coloring, or playing with other kids, or using blocks, he was shooting something. In a friendly moment, Kevin struck up a conversation.

Kevin: Why do you need to fight?

Jake: I'm killing a bad guy.

Kevin: What makes him bad?

Jake: He's not like me.

Kevin: What does he do that's bad?

Jake, pausing, less sure of himself: "Well, he's bad."

[Kevin told me that there were a lot of "just because" answers.]

Kevin: Well, how are your actions any different than his?

Jake: I'm a good guy. I only go after people like him, that are hurting people.

Kevin: But you're hurting him, too. If you hurt him, how does that make you different from him?

Jake, after a long pause: Well, it's like war.

Kevin: What's war about?

Jake: Because they are bad.

Kevin: How do you think he sees you? Are you a bad guy to him?

Jake squirms, apparently searching for an answer: Well, he might think that, but, I'm not a bad guy.

Kevin: Maybe you're both just guys.

Jake is silent.

Kevin: Do you think he has a mom and dad, or a sister maybe?

Jake looks startled.

Kevin: Why do you think that he's hurting other people? [Kevin pauses again while Jake thinks.] Do you think he's unhappy? Maybe someone hurt him?

Jake: Yeah, maybe. [He taps his finger, eager to get away.]

Kevin, closing the conversation on a positive note: What do you enjoy doing, beside videos. What's fun for you?

This conversation aimed at teaching peace will probably not stop Jake from playing his video games, but some other voice might creep into his head. *If you hurt him, how does that make you different from him? Why do you think he's hurting other people?* Somewhere, deep in his unconscious, this voice is also asking, "Why do *you* want to hurt someone?"

Our peace stories are often small daily events, but if they become our way of life, they have a powerful impact on other people in many ways.

No Thanks for Now, but the Seed Is Planted

A parent's efforts are not always appreciated or noticed in the moment. Some teachings or examples plant a seed that will take a while to grow. As a case in point, I once went to the neighborhood supermarket in South Minneapolis with my twelve-year-old daughter to return a bag of grapefruit. I was told to take them through the swinging doors to the employee room in back. I was immediately stunned by two pictures on the wall. One was a picture of a cow with sections marked off with dotted lines labeled rump, ribs, hind end, and so on. The other large picture was a virtually naked woman divided up the same way: breast, hip, ribs, and so on.

I could feel the burn rising, took a breath, and, attempting to sound relaxed, said to the grocer, "It feels really upsetting to have my daughter see a picture of a woman compared to a cow here in our neighborhood grocery store." The man responded that it was just a joke. I persisted. "But it's still disrespectful to women. You don't have a picture of a man looking like that." After a few more exchanges, he jumped up on the counter top and ripped it off the wall. I took a breath and responded, "Thank you."

As we walked out of the room, I imagined my daughter thinking of me as a Susan B. Anthony–type hero. Instead, she said, "Mom, I was *soooo* embarrassed." But years later, I was glad to see her growing awareness of pictures or images that were disrespectful of women . . . and men.

Our actions as parents help our children build awareness of sexism, racism, and prejudice, as well as kindness, compassion, responsibility, and a willingness to stand up for justice. As these become your family stories and memories, your children will internalize a sense of fairness and decency to others.

....

As we come to feel more openhearted and connected with others, nonviolence becomes the natural way of things because we experience deep within us the knowledge that to harm another is to harm ourselves. Likewise, to show kindness and compassion for others is to be kind and compassionate to ourselves.

....

KINDNESS THAT LASTED A LIFETIME—A CARING TEACHER

In *Delivered from Distraction*, by Edward M. Hallowell and John J. Ratey, an excellent book on ADD and ADHD, one of the coauthors tells about his experience in the reading circle with his first-grade teacher, Mrs. Eldredge, who never ridiculed or embarrassed anyone. When it was his turn to read, "Mrs. Eldredge would pull up a little chair and sit down next to him, putting her arm around him. . . . As he would stammer and stutter, unable to produce the right sounds . . . none of the other children would laugh at his clumsy reading because he had the enforcer sitting next to him." He later goes on to say, "Her arm took fear out of my learning to read. Her arm made it so I felt no shame in having the kind of brain I have." It eventually got him through Harvard and medical school.

EXERCISE

Think of the peace stories in your life that were inspired by a friend, teacher, parent, neighbor, or someone you have never met. What has touched you and made an impression? This could make for an ongoing conversation in your family. What acts of kindness or courage did you see in school today?

The Christmas Truce

One of my favorite accounts of people making peace—which also illustrates the terrible and senseless nature of war—is the famous Christmas truce of 1914 between the English, German, Belgian, and French soldiers during World War I. An estimated one hundred thousand soldiers along the dreaded Western Front took part in this brief break in violence to connect with each other.

It was a cold clear night with frost on the ground. Albert Moren, a British soldier in the 2nd Queens Regiment, wrote in his journal that he could see little lights coming from the German side. They turned out to be candles on Christmas trees. Then they heard the soldiers singing a Christmas carol, "Stille Nacht." The British soldiers responded by singing the English-language version of the song, "Silent Night," and the exchange of songs continued. He wrote that this night was one of the highlights of his life.

Slowly, at different places along the front, men held up signs that said truce. Some even agreed on a time. Eventually the Germans climbed out of their trenches. Many English feared it might be a trick, but as time went on they, too, came out of their trenches.

The erstwhile (and future) enemies talked, showed pictures of their families, and exchanged presents of cigarettes, buttons, cookies, and food. They also helped each other bury their dead. Some attended an impromptu Christmas morning church service together, and there are many accounts of makeshift soccer games along the front, as well as of soldiers questioning each other about the fierce and negative propaganda they had heard about the other side.

Kurt Zehmisch, a German soldier in the 134th Saxons, recorded in his diary, "How marvelously wonderful, yet how strange it was. The English officers felt the same way about it. Thus Christmas, the celebration of Love, managed to bring mortal enemies together as friends for a time." The truce lasted all of Christmas Day and for a day or two after.

Captain J. C. Dunn, a British medical officer, wrote in his journal:

> At 8:30 I fired three shots in the air and put up a flag with "Merry Christmas" on it, and I climbed on the parapet. He [a German] put up a sheet with "Thank you" on it and the German captain appeared on the parapet. We both bowed and saluted and got down into our respective trenches, and he fired two shots in the air, and the War was on again.

What if we took this event as a glimpse into what's possible. What if we come out of our trenches of belief about violence and war and put our energy into talking with each other, becoming fascinated with our differences, seeing through the media propaganda, and discovering that we are inextricably tied together?

It's hard to imagine what took place in the men's minds as they shifted out of a war mentality to talk with each other, share meals and drinks, and then switched back and retreated to their cold, wet trenches to resume killing and being killed as part of a war that eventually resulted in more than fourteen million deaths. What if we realize there is no freedom to be gained by killing another? There's no such thing as "winning" a war when thousands (or millions) of people die.

It's daunting to grasp the socialization process by which a

newborn eventually becomes conditioned to hate, fear, to go numb, and be willing to kill or be maimed or lose his life, usually in a conflict he didn't create.

What if we question this process of indoctrination? What if we examine the ways we civilians contribute to the capacity for young men and women to shut off their natural humanity? What if we decide that it's inhumane to ask any person to make that switch inside—a switch that often leaves them fragmented, traumatized, and unable to ever make peace within themselves? We need to focus on the trauma of harming others as much as the fear of being harmed.

What if we helped children learn that military conflicts are often born of financial interests disguised by demonizing others and glorifying war with words such as "patriotism" and "service"?

When the U.S. soldiers arrived to help after the earthquake in Haiti in January 2010, they carried no guns so they would not be perceived as taking over or attacking. It was inspiring to watch them working hard, helping people, distributing food, proudly wearing their uniforms.

What if we change the concept of "hero" and "patriot" to a person who is dedicated to service—to building schools, digging wells, creating medical clinics, and protecting others?

My image, my hopeful vision, is that the military might gradually be transformed to a service organization where men and women can work their way out of poverty, get an education, learn skills, and serve their country through being of service both within the United States and abroad.

In *Silent Night*, Stanley Weintraub's account of the Christmas Truce of 1914, he closes with a chapter called "What If?" What if the soldiers' Christmas truce had been able to stop the war? He suggests there would have been no Russian Revolution, no Communism, no Lenin, no Stalin, no Hitler, no Nazism, and no World War II.

We need to believe that together we can move toward a tipping point where there is a global shift in consciousness about the use of violence and aggression. Instead of fighting let us embrace the concept of *ahimsa* (Sanskrit for "not harming"), as Gandhi describes in his autobiography: "It is quite proper to resist and attack a system, but to resist and attack its author is tantamount to resisting and attacking oneself. For we are all tarred with the same brush, and are children of one and the same Creator ... to slight a single human being is to ... harm not only that being but with him the whole world."

What if we focus on the deeply human longing for connection that helped the soldiers edge out of their trenches in order to spend those precious few hours in friendship and peace? What if we raise our children to believe that war is obsolete, and that a true "preemptive strike" takes the form of education, schools, a healthy environment, medical help, respect, diplomacy, and learning about others? What if we truly believe that through the collective small steps of many, inspired by the full-time dedication of others, we might come together to believe that connection, understanding, and love are the natural way of things?

Peace and joy in abundance to you and your loved ones.

May all people be free of suffering.

May all people know peace.

Afterword

$\mathcal{A}$s I reflect on nearly four years of writing and rewriting this book, I imagine the wheel within a wheel, way up in the middle of the air. The wheel is a beautiful mosaic, moving timelessly in space on its own schedule, throughout the events of the past few years. In my personal life, its many pieces symbolize reflection, memories, regret, gratitude, family gatherings, funerals, births, heart surgery, and friendships, including the companionship of my new dog.

It's been more than five years since my daughter died. The first year I was incredibly lonely and sometimes felt as if my heart would stop. But life exists at many levels. During this same time, I laughed with friends, was grateful for my morning walks up Blue Mountain, listening to the meadowlarks and the wind in the pines. I felt energized and lucky. Nearly two years ago, my initial plan to write a book about raising kids in a cyberworld morphed into this book about raising children to create a more peaceful world.

I don't know if writing this book was my way to deal with grief, but I can't say that it wasn't. As I mentioned in the prologue, it's what came to me to do, like a current that carries you downstream. It's a mystery just like life and death.

In the summer of 2009, I went to the memorial and burial of my first cousin, Jane, who was only six weeks older than me. When we were kids, I thought of her as one of the four red-headed Shopes of Helena, Montana—my mother's side of the family—who often visited with our family, the blond-haired Davises of Missoula. We were all close in age and had magical times at holidays, in lake cabins, sleeping in the tepee in their backyard, and putting on a circus with the help of their horses and costumes made by their mother.

Jane had been my ally when I tried to swim the length of Lindbergh Lake at age 11. I fancied I was swimming the English Channel as Jane and my sister rowed the little boat beside me while I drifted into a deeply pleasurable trance for close to two hours. The roar of a motorboat stopping close by interrupted my reverie. "You have to stop before you get too tired," came the parental words from a woman who did physical therapy with children with polio. "She can do it," cousin Jane protested. "She's okay," my sister Lenore chimed in as well. But parental wisdom or fear prevailed and my quest was cut short.

Last summer, some fifty years later, I started swimming laps in a pool to get in shape for a sprint triathlon I'd be doing at Seeley Lake, where our extended family had once been the only people in the five-site campground. I felt winded. My right shoulder ached momentarily as I pulled it through the water. What did I expect after avoiding lap swimming for so long? Lap two, lap three ... lap six, it seemed endless as I flipped over on my back, making it easier to breathe. Then, a few weeks later, I biked the route for the race and as I swam in the designated area on the Seeley Lake beach, my mind drifted back to that day at Lindbergh Lake. The blurry image of the rowboat beside me came to mind, and the feeling of ease came back. My breathing relaxed and the water felt completely soothing, and my legs and arms started moving together—no aches, no struggle.

I think about aging and how our childhood experiences and our parents' voices continue to live within us. Hopefully the strengths are now in the forefront. When I signed up for the sprint triathlon,

I remembered my dad asking my mother to time him as he ran up the Washington Monument. I saw him riding his no-gear bike to his office at the university—"Look, ma, no hands"—and taking us on winter hikes and snow picnics. His idea of a good time was to go winter camping in upper Michigan with a fellow faculty member where they'd build a shelter out of pine boughs.

I think of my mother when happiness pervades my day as I prepare a benefit or holiday dinner with music playing while I arrange a centerpiece, smell the food cooking, and place the beautiful china around the table. (That my mother gave nearly all of her china to my sister now brings more of a wistful smile than a sharp pain. It was a crummy thing to do, but it doesn't seem to matter anymore.)

Then I drift back to my daughter, Ginelle—a child who, amid her problems, had grown up around a lot of strong women. I hear her voice when she was on a weekend visit home from a group home. "Can you believe this," she said, incredulously. "Jetta's boyfriend walked in and just handed his coat to her as if she were a servant—and she just took it and hung it up for him!" "What would you have done?" I asked, smiling to myself. "I would have told him to say please, or to hang it up himself." That's my girl, I thought. Even with all the difficulties that permeated our fragile bond, Ginelle called me when she had a gambling relapse, when she had trouble with a roommate, or to talk about her imminent death. We had many treasured moments among the difficulties.

The role of parent never goes away—it changes, transforms, and recedes. One permanent gift we give to our children is to be growing, stretching people who can change, take good care of ourselves, and leave our children free from worry or guilt.

As a therapist, I have witnessed several mothers over the years who brought their adult children in for therapy to apologize for whatever mistakes they had made, and to make peace. I have often seen tears of relief as voices softened and there was a shift grounded in a new understanding. When a parent could say, "I was afraid," or "I didn't know what to do," it could replace a child's long-held belief such as, "I thought you didn't care." I remember such a moment when my mother observed an assertiveness group I led at Ohio University through a one-way glass. Afterward she said in a deeply reflective way, "I sure could have used a class like that. I so often didn't know what to say." What a sweet revelation.

The rifts and hurts between us begin to heal when we learn the basic Buddhist principle of seeing everyone clearly in reality. Everyone is simply doing the only thing they know how to do in any given moment. That includes our parents, ourselves, and our children. To know this fully is to have complete freedom and opens us to loving-kindness.

This doesn't mean we were always wise, skillful, or helpful, but as parents we all need to forgive ourselves again and again for doing the only thing we knew how to do in any given moment. In doing so, we teach forgiveness and humanness to our children. We also open the way to changing ourselves because transformation starts with acceptance.

Helping with the Last Good-bye

Our last challenge as a parent is saying good-bye as we face our death, or, for some of us, a child who dies before us. We give a priceless gift to our children when we invite them to clear the air as we apologize for our mistakes, and give them our blessing for happiness and a good life. We also help the relationships among our children when we are completely fair in how we pass on our belongings, money, and sentimental possessions. When a parent favors one child over the others, it can leave a painful legacy.

Remembering the Moments of Joy

Two months after Ginelle died, I had a memorial service here in Missoula primarily for friends who had never met her. To bring them into my life with her I showed lots photos with the use of Power-Point, told stories of her life, and put out mementos—the multitude of latch hooks she did to keep herself busy, the pink dotted Swiss dress and the high white shoes she wore the day we met, and the little music box that played "The song of love is a sad song." I also laid out notebooks full of recipes she carefully typed for hours as a way of staying ahead of her goblins.

I ended the memorial gathering by showing two special pictures. The first was of Ginelle's favorite cat Stripey nestled against the front door of the trailer nursing a litter of tiny kittens. This tender scene had greeted me when I arrived back to the trailer after Ginelle's funeral and swept away my feelings of exhaustion. The cat had been missing for a few days, and we had wondered, *where has Stripey gone?* The welcome sight of these innocent creatures nursing brought a smile deep inside and the peaceful awareness of the vastness of our life cycles.

The second picture was of a birthday card Ginelle had given me when she was in her mid-twenties. On the front it said, "Wow, You're Really Looking Good." On the inside it read, "Anyone who brought me up should look like hell by now."

There is so much redemption in parenting, so much forgiveness, humor, and love.

With many blessings to you all,
Your sister,
Charlotte Sophia
Lolo, Montana

Acknowledgments

To you, the reader, thanks for picking up this book. I send my heartfelt wishes that you find wonder, pleasure, patience, delight, and courage in your relationships with children.

A bouquet of roses and a thousand thanks to my longtime agent Edite Kroll for reading and rereading the manuscript, encouragement, faith, understanding, and humor. I still remember our phone conversation when you were considering whether or not to take my first book. After asking a lot of questions followed by an intense pause, you said, "Okay, I'll take it." Along with my elation and surprise, up popped the thought, *you must be hard up for authors.* That was twenty-five years and nine books ago.

Thanks to my editor Alexis Washam for dedication and hard work on this book, especially when I changed focus and rewrote the book, making it a year later than expected. Also to my former editor Janet Goldstein—bright spirit and friend—I will always appreciate our literary journey together through six books including your acceptance of my proposal, "Dating by Spiritual Rules," which morphed into *If the Buddha Dated*, the first of four *If the Buddha* books. Your faith in me lives on. Thanks also to Rebecca Hunt who stepped in for Alexis Washam to help the book go into production, and to Amy Hetzler who took over as office assistant when I suddenly needed help. Your competence, friendliness, and goodwill were blessings to me and spared me a lot of stress and chaos.

To all the people I interviewed for this book: children, parents, teachers, and experts in the field. Many of you spoke about your experience of being both a child and a parent. You are the heartbeat and spirit of this book. I loved our interviews, from sitting at a dining room table with a couple or whole family to having dinner at a deli with student teachers to a group of dedicated teachers at the Lolo Middle School to individual interviews on the phone with people near and far to talking with international students at the university. Your generosity with your time, stories, wisdom, and humor will be appreciated by many. I also treasured hearing you talk about what challenged you—the ways you made an effort to be good parents, what you learned, what you'd do differently, and how you handled tough situations.

Here you are: Lizzie Juda, Kesa, Kaia, and Steven Nelson; Jeanine Walker; Nick Salmon; Bob Lucas; Marmot Snetsinger and Nancy Siegel; Margaret, John, Andrew, and Matthew Baldridge; Adair, Kanter, Bruce, and Ariel Barrett; Greg and Dorothy Patent; Ray and Susie Risho; Carla and Steve Smith; Laura, Lizzie, and Eli Davis; Kevin Cashman; Eric Sedlacek; Owen and Walt Javins; Tobin and Cheryl Miller Shearer; Augusta (Gussie) Kappner; Shohina Toureyeva; Max and Sonja Grimmsman; John Whalen; Alissa, Rick, and Larry Davis; Ron Wakimoto; Colleen Windell; Julianna Engh Peters; Jean Belangie-Nye; Judy Lange; John O'Bannon; David Hansen; and Jennifer Christensen. In addition to these interviews, there were many informal conversations that made their way into this book, along with my own reflections on growing up that filled many journals throughout my teenage years.

Special thanks to Daniel A. Hughes, author of *Building the Bonds of Attachment* and other fine books, for two lengthy interviews; Augusta Kappner, former president of the Bank Street College of

Education, for an interview on curriculum and progressive schools; and Alfie Kohn for his in-depth explorations in his books *Punished by Rewards* and *The Brighter Side of Human Nature*, which constantly challenge conventional thinking about testing, rewards, gender stereotypes, and our relationships with children—and also for our e-mail exchange. Heartfelt thanks to Debra Wesselman, attachment therapist and author of *The Whole Parent: How to Become a Terrific Parent, Even If You Didn't Have One*, for reading and giving feedback on the attachment chapter.

Thanks also to the dedicated clients I've known over the years. Your stories often reflect the difficulties and pain that result from unskilled, negative, stressed, negligent, abusive, or narcissistic parenting. Your efforts to learn, grow, take classes, and read books in order to become good parents can shine like a beacon for others from troubled families bringing the assurance that they, too, can become positive parents.

Once again, I thank Ken Keyes, whose *Handbook to Higher Consciousness* and amazing training program at Cornucopia started my life-changing journey of Buddhism in 1980. Finally, my continuing gratitude to the Quaker community—the Society of Friends—near and far, with its dedication to inclusiveness, simplicity, service, generosity, community, and children's programs that are dedicated to social awareness and nonviolence. The Quaker philosophy of valuing each individual while maintaining the unity of the whole was reflected repeatedly in the families I interviewed, where each child was seen as an individual, yet embraced within the shelter of a cohesive family. Over the past thirty years I've loved watching many children—both Quaker and from other faiths—grow up and take the values of nonviolence and service into the world echoing the Quaker saying, "Walk cheerfully over the world, answering that of God in every one."

My abiding gratitude to special friends and family: Jeanine Walker, Pat Dewees, Rebecca and Jim Sparks, Alexandra Botello,

Diane Shope, Starshine, Henny Ravestein, Traci Reynolds, Steve McArthur, Jack Rowan of the Quaker meeting, Traci Reynolds, Barb Dotson, the Healing Hearts Moms' Group and all those who helped me in many ways through my recent heart surgery and the five years since the loss of my daughter. You were there when I needed you and for the good times as well. Bright blessings and many thanks.

Recommended Reading

While some of the books included here are out of print, they are available used on Abebooks.com, Amazon.com, Alibris.com, and other used book Web sites.

Books for Children

There are many books available that teach about peace, tolerance, racism, and self-esteem through stories of children and biographies of peacemakers.

You can find many lists by searching the Internet for "children's books peace" or "children's books tolerance/racism" or "children's books prejudice" or "children's books multicultural."

You can also go to a library and ask for help finding books on these topics.

SEVERAL LISTS OF NOTE

The Jane Addams Children's Book Awards. These books promote an awareness of social justice, peace, and equality among all people. They are selected on the basis of excellence for children's books.

Logan Library: Children's Books About Peace.

Logan Library: Children's Books About Self-esteem.

Bank Street book list. The Children's Book Committee at the Bank Street College of Education have been compiling books that are "captivating and transforming" and help kids to love literature and reading. It includes an annual review of the best children's books each year for kids' ages infant to fourteen years old. They have been doing this for one hundred years. The Web site is www.bankstreet .edu/bookcom/index.html.

Books on Parenting

I have included many books on child rearing that I like with descriptive comments under some favorites. There are many other excellent books available in this field.

Aldort, Naomi. *Raising Our Children, Raising Ourselves: Transforming Parent–Child Relationships from Reaction and Struggle to Freedom, Power and Joy.*

Beardslee, William R., M.D. *Out of the Darkened Room: When a Parent Is Depressed—Protecting the Children and Strengthening the Family.*

Bettelheim, Bruno. *Dialogues with Mothers.*

Biddulph, Steve. *The Secret of Happy Children: Why Children Behave the Way They Do—and What You Can Do to Help Them to Be Optimistic, Loving, Capable and Happy.* Clear, concise, and accessible with good illustrations.

Blades, Joan, and Kristin Rowe-Finkbeiner. *The Motherhood Manifesto: What America's Moms Want—and What to Do About It.*

Block, Jennifer. *Pushed: The Painful Truth About Childbirth and Modern Maternity Care.*

Bowlby, John. *Loss: Sadness and Depression.* Volume II of the author's classic Attachment and Loss trilogy explores the effects of a death in the family on children and adults.

——. *The Making and Breaking of Affectional Bonds.* Spans twenty years of Bowlby's exploration of forming and leaving relationships.

——. *A Secure Base: Parent–Child Attachment and Healthy Human Development.* Clear, concise, and accessible to parents.

——. *Separation: Anxiety and Anger.* Volume II of author's classic Attachment and Loss trilogy.

Bragdon, Allen D., and David Gamon, Ph.D. *Brains That Work a Little Bit Differently: Recent Discoveries About Common Brain Diversities.*

Caplan, Frank, and Theresa Caplan. *The Power of Play.*

Clarke, Jean Illsley. *Time-In: When Time-Out Doesn't Work.* An important book that questions the impact of "time out" and suggests alternatives that promote security and attachment between parent and child.

Cline, Foster, M.D., and Jim Fay. *Parenting with Love and Logic: Teaching Children Responsibility.*

——. *Parenting Teens with Love and Logic: Preparing Adolescents for Responsible Adulthood.*

Both books are wonderful resources with specifics for how to deal with challenging behavior and many good tips for prevention. Advice to help parents stay calm and handle situations without nagging, yelling, or giving up.

Clinton, Hillary Rodham. *It Takes a Village: And Other Lessons Children Teach Us.*

Croyle, John, with Ken Abraham. *Bringing out the Winner in Your Child: The Building Blocks of Successful Parenting.*

Davis, Laura, and Janis Keyser. *Becoming the Parent You Want to Be: A Sourcebook of Strategies for the First Five Years.* A flexible approach to child rearing that helps parents think about the impact that their choices have on their children.

Doidge, Norman, M.D. *The Brain That Changes Itself: Stories of Personal Triumph from the Frontiers of Brain Science.* Clearly written with numerous fascinating stories, this book underscores the wonders of the brain from the cradle to the grave. It can be an inspiration for adults and help them realize the vast impact they have on their children's development.

Dreikurs, Rudolf, M.D., and Pearl Cassel. *Discipline Without Tears: What to Do with Children Who Misbehave.*

Dreikurs, Rudolf, M.D., with Vicki Soltz, R.N. *Children: The Challenge.* An excellent book with many stories about how to use logical and natural consequences in parenting. An oldie but goodie.

Evans, Dr. Simon. *Brain Fitness: A Recipe for Feeding Your Child's Dreams and Unlocking Their Maximum Brain Power.* An excellent, clear guide to helping your child develop on all levels. Includes suggestions for nutrition and exercise.

Faber, Adele, and Elaine Mazlish. *Liberated Parents, Liberated Children: Your Guide to a Happier Family.* A classic on how to talk with children.

Foster, Celia. *Big Steps for Little People: Parenting Your Adopted Child.*

Fox, Matthew. *The A.W.E. Project: Reinventing Education, Reinventing the Human.*

——. *Original Blessing: A Primer in Creation Spirituality Presented in Four Paths, Twenty-Six Themes, and Two Questions.*

Ginott, Dr. Haim G. *Between Parent and Child: New Solutions to Old Problems.* Used copies of this original book can be found at bookstores on the Internet. The following newer edition is also available: Dr. Haim G. Ginott. *Between Parent and Child: The Bestselling Classic That Revolutionized Parent–Child Communication.* Revised and updated by Dr. Alice Ginott and Dr. H. Wallace Goddard.

——. *Between Parent and Teenager.*

Both books were mentioned by several parents with adult children as their basic parenting books. They promote excellent understanding of the importance of attachment, staying calm, and being clear.

Gladwell, Malcolm. *Outliers: The Story of Success.* A helpful book for parents to question their beliefs about excellence and success. Note: it's primarily about opportunity and hard work!

Glenn, H. Stephen, Ph.D., and Jane Nelsen, Ed.D. *Raising Self-Reliant Children in a Self-Indulgent World: Seven Building Blocks for Developing Capable Young People.*

Hughes, Daniel A. *Attachment-Focused Parenting: Effective Strategies to Care for Children.*

——. *Building the Bonds of Attachment: Awakening Love in Deeply Troubled Children.*

Kaplan, Louise J., Ph.D. *Oneness and Separateness: From Infant to Individual.*

Karr-Morse, Robin, and Meredith S. Wiley. *Ghosts from the Nursery: Tracing the Roots of Violence.* An excellent in-depth look at the roots of violence, often stemming from early attachment deficits and trauma in childhood.

Kindlon, Dan, Ph.D. *Too Much of a Good Thing: Raising Children of Character in an Indulgent Age.*

Kindlon, Dan, Ph.D, and Michael Thompson, Ph.D. *Raising Cain: Protecting the Emotional Life of Boys.*

Kohn, Alfie. *Punished by Rewards: The Trouble with Gold Stars, Incentive Plans, A's, Praise, and Other Bribes.* This is a great book to help parents, teachers, and social workers get away from a reward and punishment system that relies on a "do this and you'll get that" approach. It includes numerous studies showing that feeling intrinsic pleasure in what one is doing is the best motivator and the most empowering for children.

———. *Schools Our Children Deserve: Moving Beyond Traditional Classrooms and "Tougher Standards."* Questions deeply held assumptions about education and supports the author's assertions with research and excellent examples.

———. *Unconditional Parenting: Moving from Rewards and Punishments to Love and Reason.* An excellent in-depth book that is profoundly nonviolent at all levels of parenting and interesting to read.

Kurcinka, Mary Sheedy. *Raising Your Spirited Child: A Guide for Parents Whose Child Is More Intense, Sensitive, Perceptive, Persistent, and Energetic.* This excellent book helps parents accept "spirited" behavior in a child as within a normal range of behavior, rather than pathologizing it.

———. *Sleepless in America: Is Your Child Misbehaving or Missing Sleep?* A very important book to help children get enough sleep so they are able to function optimally.

Lewis, Steven. *Zen and the Art of Fatherhood: Lessons from a Master Dad.*

Lovejoy, Sharon. *Sunflower Houses: Inspiration from the Garden—A Book for Children and Their Grown-Ups.*

Magid, Dr. Ken, and Carole A. McKelvey. *High Risk: Children Without a Conscience.*

McCracken, Anne, and Mary Semel. *A Broken Heart Still Beats: After Your Child Dies.*

Mogel, Wendy, Ph.D. *The Blessings of a Skinned Knee: Using Jewish Teachings to Raise Self-Reliant Children.*

Nelsen, Jane, Ed.D. *Positive Discipline: The Classic Guide to Helping Children Develop Self-Discipline, Responsibility, Cooperation, and Problem-Solving Skills.* A warm, practical, step-by-step sourcebook for parents and teachers.

Nelsen, Jane, Ed.D., and Cheryl Erwin, M.A. *Parents Who Love Too Much: How Good Parents Can Learn to Love More Wisely and Develop Children of Character.*

Northwest Earth Institute. *Discussion Course on Healthy Children–Healthy Planet.*

Pearce, Joseph Chilton. *Magical Child: Rediscovering Nature's Plan for Our Children.*

——. *Magical Child Matures.*

Postman, Neil. *The Disappearance of Childhood.*

Reuben, Carolyn. *The Healthy Baby Book: A Parent's Guide to Preventing Birth Defects and Other Long-Term Medical Problems Before, During, and After Pregnancy.*

Ricci, Isolina, Ph.D. *Mom's House, Dad's House: A Complete Guide for Parents Who Are Separated, Divorced, or Remarried.*

Satir, Virginia. *Peoplemaking.*

Seligman, Martin E. P., Ph.D. *Learned Optimism: How to Change Your Mind and Your Life.*

———. *The Optimistic Child. A Proven Program to Safeguard Children Against Depression and Build Lifelong Resilience.* Stresses mastery in helping children develop confidence and resilience.

Siegel, Daniel J., M.D., and Mary Hartzell, M.Ed. *Parenting from the Inside Out: How a Deeper Self-Understanding Can Help You Raise Children Who Thrive.* An in-depth parenting book that reinforces the importance of early attachment and helping a child develop a secure core within.

Sills, Judith, Ph.D. *The Comfort Trap, or, What If You're Riding a Dead Horse?*

Spock, Benjamin Ph.D. *Dr. Spock's Baby and Child Care.* Updated and revised by Robert Needlman, M.D. The classic parenting book that fostered massive change in our approach to child rearing.

Sroufe, L. Alan, Byron Egeland, Elizabeth A. Carlson, and W. Andrew Collins. *The Development of the Person: The Minnesota Study of Risk and Adaptation from Birth to Adulthood.*

Thomas, Nancy. *Healing Trust: Rebuilding the Broken Bond for the Child with Reactive Attachment Disorder* (audiobook). The author is a master at staying calm and adult with deeply troubled children along with being nurturing and understanding. If you need help setting boundaries for children and maintaining a sense of humor, listen to this audiobook. Good for all parents.

Tracy, Louise Felton, M.S. *Grounded for Life?! Stop Blowing Your Fuse and Start Communicating with Your Teenager.* Includes good advice on getting out of entrenched negative patterns.

Vannoy, Steven W. *The 10 Greatest Gifts I Give My Children: Parenting from the Heart.*

Warner, Penny. *Baby Play and Learn: 160 Games and Learning Activities for the First Three Years.*

Weinhaus, Evonne, and Karen Freidman. *Stop Struggling with Your Child: Quick-Tip Parenting Solutions That Will Work for You—and Your Kids.*

Wesselmann, Debra. *The Whole Parent: How to Become a Terrific Parent Even If You Didn't Have One.* An encouraging, detailed book for people who feel adrift as parents due to lack of healthy models or a traumatic childhood. It includes an excellent section on early attachment.

West, Melissa Gayle. *If Only I Were a Better Mother: Using the Anger, Fear, Despair, and Guilt That Every Mother Feels at Some Time as a Pathway to Emotional Balance and Spiritual Growth.*

Books on Buddhism, Sufism, Quakers, and Related Topics

Arden, John B. *Rewire your Brain.*

Barks, Coleman, and A. J. Arberry, translators. *Like This: Rumi.* A Sufi poet.

Barks, Coleman, with John Moyne, translators. *The Essential Rumi.*

Bly, Robert, translator. *The Kabir Book: Forty-four of the Ecstatic Poems of Kabir.* A Sufi poet.

Boorstein, Sylvia. *It's Easier Than You Think: The Buddhist Way to Happiness.*

Bunson, Matthew E. *The Wisdom Teachings of the Dalai Lama.*

Chödrön, Pema. *Start Where You Are: A Guide to Compassionate Living.*

——. *When Things Fall Apart: Heart Advice for Difficult Times.*

——. *The Wisdom of No Escape: And the Path of Loving-Kindness*.

Das, Lama Surya. *Awakening the Buddha Within: Tibetan Wisdom for the Western World*. This is a clear, easy to understand, basic book on Buddhism.

Fromm, Erich. *The Art of Loving*.

Gibran, Kahlil. *The Prophet*.

Hanh, Thich Nhat. *The Diamond That Cuts Through Illusion: Commentaries on the Prajñaparamita Diamond Sutra*.

——. *The Heart of Understanding: Commentaries on the Prajñaparamita Heart Sutra*.

——. *Peace Is Every Step: The Path of Mindfulness in Everyday Life*.

Johnson, Susan M. *Emotionally Focused Couple Therapy with Trauma Survivors: Strengthening Attachment Bonds*. This approach is based on attachment theory and has clearly delineated steps for therapists in working with couples.

——. *Hold Me Tight: Seven Conversations for a Lifetime of Love*. A wonderful book for couples to read together. Wise understanding of what helps couples feel close.

Kasl, Charlotte Sophia, Ph.D. *Finding Joy: 101 Ways to Free Your Spirit and Dance with Life*.

——. *A Home for the Heart: Creating Intimacy and Community with Loved Ones, Neighbors, and Friends*.

——. *If the Buddha Dated: A Handbook for Finding Love on a Spiritual Path*.

——. *If the Buddha Married: Creating Enduring Relationships on a Spiritual Path*.

——. *Many Roads, One Journey: Moving Beyond the Twelve Steps.*

——. *Women, Sex, and Addiction: A Search for Love and Power.*

——. *Yes, You Can!: Healing from Trauma and Addiction with Love, Strength, and Power.* (Available via my Web site, www.charlottekasl.com, or by writing to Many Roads, One Journey, Box 1302, Lolo, MT 59847.)

Ladinsky, Daniel, translator. *The Gift: Poems by Hafiz.* A Sufi poet.

Linssen, Robert. *Living Zen.*

Rahula, Walpola. *What the Buddha Taught.*

Suzuki, Shunryu. *Zen Mind, Beginner's Mind.*

Tagore, Rabindranath. *Gitanjali.*

Weintraub, Stanley. *Silent Night: The Story of the World War I Christmas Truce.* An amazing account of the Christmas truce that brought soldiers from several countries out of their opposing trenches for a time of peaceful connections.

Resources

Intensive Psychotherapy for Individuals and Couples

For more detailed information, see my Web site at www. charlottekasl.com. I am available for intensive psychotherapy sessions for individuals and couples in my office near Missoula, Montana. Sessions are generally twelve to sixteen hours spent over a three- or four-day period with individuals and couples in these intensive sessions. I have worked with trauma, addictions, and couples for more than thirty years as well as with depression, anxiety, and other emotional difficulties. I approach therapy with a holistic perspective and use a number of approaches. I also do phone consultations. My office phone number is 406-273-6080.

I have a Ph.D. in counseling from Ohio University, and I am a licensed clinical professional counselor (LCPC) in the state of Montana. Prior to this, I was a licensed consulting psychologist in the state of Minnesota. I am also a certified addiction specialist in the areas of chemical dependency and sexuality and received a lifetime achievement award based on my book, *Women, Sex, and Addiction: A Search for Love and Power.*

I have trained extensively in traditional approaches such as cognitive therapy, psychodynamic therapy, EMDR (eye movement desensitization reprocessing), quantum psychology, ego-state therapy, and emotionally focused couple therapy as described in *Hold Me Tight*, by Dr. Sue Johnson.

Therapy Referrals

Please note: I do *not* have referrals for therapists around the country to give out personally.

To find a therapist, it is best to get personal referrals from people who have had a positive experience and talk with a prospective therapist to check her or him out for yourself. Most therapists will have a short conversation with you by phone if you ask for one.

You can look up therapists trained in EMDR at the EMDR International Association (www.emdria.org). This site includes a listing of EMDR certified therapists, but there are also many excellent EMDR therapists who are not certified.

I also recommend sensorimotor psychotherapy and body-centered therapy. For sensorimotor psychotherapy, contact Pat Ogden, Ph.D., 303-447-3290, or search the Internet for "Foundation for Human Enrichment—healing trauma."

For couples I recommend someone trained in emotionally focused couple therapy. Call the Ottawa Couple and Family Institute, 613-722-5122, or visit www.iceeft.com.

For people with sexual concerns, you can go to the Society for the Advancement of Sexual Health (SASH), www.sash.net, which has information about sexual compulsivity and addiction. Again, there are many excellent therapists who deal with sexuality and sex addiction who are not listed on this Web site.

Other Resources

Brain Gym® International. Brain Gym includes simple sequences of exercises and movements to help a person calm down, focus, increase energy, concentrate, and create a positive mood. I have taken classes in Brain Gym and found it extremely helpful in lessening an overwhelmed feeling, enabling one to focus on one step at a time and gain confidence, whether it's cleaning out the basement or writing a book. It is simple and fun, and parents can participate with children. Check community education programs for local classes or visit www.braingym.org.

Emotional Freedom Technique (EFT). On the Internet, search for "EFT Home—World Center" to get information by Gary Craig, the creator of EFT. Books by Gary Craig are available from online booksellers. Another excellent manual is by James Mercola—search for "EFT manual" on www.mercola.com. Mercola's manual is accessible, easy to use, and alters the tapping technique to make it incorporate aspects of EMDR. I do not endorse the more recent claims for using EFT to create abundance and have perfect health and happiness, which go beyond the basic intention of EFT.

This is a self-help technique that uses tapping on a series of acupuncture points while saying an affirmation to help change negative beliefs to self-acceptance. An example of an affirmation could be: "Even though I got angry at my daughter, I completely and deeply accept myself." This approach fits with Buddhism in that it operates on the belief that transformation starts with acceptance in the moment. The basic aspect of EFT that I have seen to be helpful is using an affirmation while going through the acupuncture points.

There are numerous citations and claims about EFT that have emerged, but I am only talking about the basic teachings of Gary

Craig and the manual by James Mercola. Craig also has a list of translations. There are many YouTube videos you can watch on the Internet.

There is also training available for therapists to learn to use EFT as part of counseling or psychotherapy.

AVAILABLE FROM PENGUIN

BY CHARLOTTE KASL, Ph.D.

If the Buddha Got Stuck:
A Handbook for Change on a Spiritual Path

ISBN 978-0-14-219628-1

If the Buddha Married:
Creating Enduring Relationships on a Spiritual Path

ISBN 978-0-14-019622-1

If the Buddha Dated:
A Handbook for Finding Love on a Spiritual Path

ISBN 978-0-14-019583-5

PENGUIN BOOKS